The Reimagined Lawyer

The Reimagined Lawyer

Bruce J. Winick

with contributions by
Sean Bettinger-Lopez

CAROLINA ACADEMIC PRESS
Durham, North Carolina

Library of Congress Cataloging-in-Publication Data

Names: Winick, Bruce J., author.
Title: The reimagined lawyer / by Bruce J. Winick.
Description: Durham, North Carolina : Carolina Academic Press, LLC, [2019] |
    Includes bibliographical references and index.
Identifiers: LCCN 2018059087 | ISBN 9781531013363 (alk. paper)
Subjects: LCSH: Practice of law--Psychological aspects. |
    Lawyers--Psychological aspects. | Attorney and client--Psychological
    aspects. | Legal ethics.
Classification: LCC K120 .W56 2019 | DDC 340.023--dc23
LC record available at https://lccn.loc.gov/2018059087

eISBN 978-1-5310-1337-0

CAROLINA ACADEMIC PRESS
700 Kent Street
Durham, North Carolina 27701
Telephone (919) 489-7486
Fax (919) 493-5668
www.cap-press.com

Printed in the United States of America

Contents

Introduction

Sean Bettinger-Lopez

Swan Song: A Final Work from an Extraordinary Life

This book is the final work of Bruce J. Winick, a great lawyer, scholar, and humanitarian. Bruce possessed that rare combination of a warm heart and brilliant mind that brought him great success in achieving his life's passion: helping others. Bruce expresses that passion here by reimagining the role of the lawyer to challenge certain harmful values and practices of the modern legal profession. His vision expands the definition of a lawyer's work to include attention to non-legal issues, psychological and emotional context, and therapeutic goals and values. It seeks a more humane experience for those who make contact with the legal system; a muting of the law's great power to harm. If ever there was an example of a man who embodied the same values he espoused professionally, it was Bruce. In litigation, in scholarship, and in life, Bruce consistently championed those who were most vulnerable when pitted against the Goliath of the State.

Looking back at Bruce's career as an impact litigator, we see a man passionately defending those whose lives were at risk of being crushed in some way by a legal system that could be callous, insensitive, and blatantly unfair. In the 1970s, Bruce argued a landmark case that ended the death penalty in New York.[1] He represented hundreds of selective service registrants in the Vietnam War era and helped litigate groundbreaking selective service law cases.[2] He drafted and spearheaded a successful effort to pass the 1977 Dade County Human Rights Ordinance prohibiting discrimination based on sexual preference.[3] And he successfully argued a case establishing the right of openly gay attorneys to practice law in Florida.[4]

In the 1970s, Bruce began what turned out to be an exceptionally prolific academic career. Yet, even while maintaining his regular duties as a law professor for the next four decades, he continued to participate in high profile impact advocacy. For example, Bruce championed the cause of Haitians fleeing an oppressive dictatorship by serving as co-counsel in a suit seeking to prevent forcible repatriation of Haitians intercepted at sea.[5] He championed the liberty interests of those facing involuntary civil commitment by contributing to amicus briefs before the U.S. Supreme Court,[6] and by successfully advocating for procedural protections for Florida youth in foster care.[7] He also participated in efforts to abolish the longstanding practice in Florida and other States of indiscriminately shackling youth in juvenile court proceedings.[8]

Bruce's career as an impact litigator was exceptional, and showed a man inspired by law's power to help others, even in the face of law's power to cause tremendous harm. It is no wonder, then, that as an academic in the 1980s he co-founded and developed a field of inquiry known as "therapeutic jurisprudence" (or "TJ," to some) to focus scholarship and law reform on the ways that law can impact mental health, for better or for worse.[9] Therapeutic jurisprudence has since become an international movement influencing the work of scholars, lawyers, and judges worldwide.[10] Literature from the field has been translated into several languages, and it continues to influence scholarship and legal reform efforts across the globe, especially in Australia, New Zealand, and Europe.[11] In addition to therapeutic jurisprudence, Bruce helped develop the burgeoning field of mental health law in the 1990s and 2000s by dealing comprehensively with subjects ranging from civil commitment to the right to refuse medical treatment.[12] Indeed, it was ultimately Bruce's scholarship, not his litigation feats, that brought him international recognition.[13]

When Bruce passed away in August of 2010, testimonials from around the world flooded into the University of Miami School of Law where he taught for 36 years.[14] The testimonials celebrated his generosity of spirit, concern for the welfare of others, and the impact he made on individual and collective lives. Bruce was an exceptionally kind and generous person, cherished both for his personal compassion and for his vigorous defense of humanistic values. Bruce was a rarity: someone who practiced what he preached. Perhaps the most remarkable thing about Bruce was his ability to achieve so much—professionally and personally—in spite of slowly losing his eyesight since the age of 32 to a rare genetic disorder called *retinitis pigmentosa*. He was legally blind while writing this book. Bruce overcame this formidable obstacle by utilizing cutting-edge technology[15] to read and write, by walking with his guide-dog, "Bruno" (remembered fondly by many), and by maintaining an attitude of optimism and gratitude. Many remembered Bruce as much for his courage and perseverance in the face of adversity—his own, or others'—as they did for his impressive professional accomplishments.

I experienced Bruce's warmth and graciousness in late 2010 when I came to the University of Miami to do research in law and psychology and to help Bruce develop his Therapeutic Jurisprudence Center, which he had founded the year prior. My excitement was tempered by learning that Bruce had taken ill with an aggressive cancer, and that despite the experimental treatments he was pursuing to beat back the disease, the amount of time he had left to live was uncertain. Bruce and I had the opportunity to discuss a book he had been working on called *The Reimagined Lawyer* and what it meant to him. The draft contained six substantially completed chapters and notes indicating further contemplated chapters. He was writing it to summarize for lawyers and non-lawyers his career-long thinking about lawyering in a humane and therapeutic mode. In his final months, Bruce worked on this book at an astonishing pace; one that most healthy people would find impossible to sustain. When not dealing with medical treatment or his duties to family, friends, and colleagues, Bruce absorbed himself with writing the manuscript. He viewed this endeavor as his swan song, a final statement on a topic dear to his heart. All too aware that his time to complete the project could end abruptly, he said the writing of it flowed like never before.

The task of editing this manuscript and preparing it for publication fell to me. Fortunately, most of the editing was superficial. I can think of one or two occasions where I had to make educated guesses at Bruce's intent, and even here getting it wrong would have minimal impact. I can therefore faithfully say that this is entirely the book Bruce wanted you to read, notwithstanding those revisions and inclusions he might have made had he more time with it. This introduction is my own. I am writing it with an awareness that not everyone reading this book will have been familiar with Bruce's work. He wrote the book with a more colloquial feel than his usual academic writing because he wanted it to reach a wider audience. I have tried here to further that appeal by offering some background about the man behind the ideas, mentioning some of the criticism that his ideas provoked, and suggesting new questions not directly addressed in the book, all of which may catalyze further interest and engagement with the book's mission. It would be a most fitting tribute to Bruce should this final work become a platform for further thinking, research, and engagement with his ideas.

A Problem and Its Solution:
A Brief Synopsis of *The Reimagined Lawyer*

Bruce's title, *The Reimagined Lawyer,* at once suggests a problem and a so-lution. The problem, discussed in chapter 1, is the legal profession, which has been indicted for fostering a culture of self-serving, aggressive, and unethical lawyers. The negative values cultivated and rewarded by the legal culture lead to anti-therapeutic behaviors and outcomes for all: clients, third-parties, and the lawyers themselves. The good news is that the solution to this malaise also lies with the legal culture and the ability of lawyers to rethink who they are, what they do, and why they do it. Lawyers can learn to practice law in ways that are psychologically helpful, rather than harmful, to others. Recapitulated in this single book are decades of Bruce's scholarship and thinking about lawyering in a therapeutic mode, including applications to more recent devel-opments like the economic downturn of 2008 and corporate banking scandals. Written primarily for practicing lawyers and law students, this book was meant to inspire and guide those most at risk of losing themselves in the quicksand of the legal profession. Bruce wanted to point the way toward a meaningful, ethical, and fulfilling practice of law.

Chapter 1 begins with an exposition of lawyers' dissatisfaction with the pro-fession and their personal lives. We learn how increasing workloads, substance abuse, depression, and other psychic distress, along with decreasing job security, moral accountability, and professionalism, has plagued the profession for decades. Lawyers untrained in healthy coping mechanisms turn to patho-logical ones to survive this bleary landscape, making things worse. This vicious cycle begins in law schools, where students traditionally have been indoctrinated into an adversarial view of lawyering. Extrinsic values like pro-fessional recognition and wealth prevail over intrinsic ones like helping clients solve problems. The Socratic method and analysis of appellate cases prevails over teaching actual lawyering skills. The formal logic of legal precedent is what matters—not extraneous details such as emotion, context, or justice. If lawyer-ing skills are taught at all, they are usually litigation and trial skills, sending the message that first-class lawyering means being adept at legal combat. Skills in counseling, problem-solving, and prevention are accorded second-class status. By the end of the third year, law students have absorbed the role of gladiator, ready to do battle in a zero-sum game where the winner takes all, and the loser takes nothing.

This is not what many law students thought they were signing up for. Some may not have realized the impact that law school would have on the personal values they held before entering law school. Chapter 1 lays out this incongruence between personal values and professional training and sets the stage for what follows. The remainder of the book explains how law students and lawyers can embrace an alternative model of lawyering to the one presented by law schools and the reigning legal culture. It is a model enabling lawyers to decrease their distress, increase their satisfaction, and become the kind of professionals they aspired to be when they first chose a career in the law.

Chapter 2 outlines the contours of this alternative model of lawyering and names it: the therapeutic jurisprudence/preventive law model of lawyering (or "TJ/preventive" model, hereinafter). Admittedly unwieldy, this label derives from the academic literature produced by Bruce and others seeking to integrate therapeutic jurisprudence with preventive law, another body of literature advocating the avoidance of litigation in most circumstances. The model is premised on the idea that lawyers are unavoidably therapeutic agents whose actions impact their clients' psychological and emotional well-being. Once this insight is absorbed, it is hoped, lawyers will strive to avoid imposing psychologically damaging effects on their clients. They will consider clients' emotional well-being when analyzing a solution to a client's legal problem. They will promote not only their clients' legal rights and economic interests, but also their clients' best interests more broadly defined. The book offers normative prescriptions for ensuring that a lawyer's therapeutic impact is a positive one. The prescriptions include everything from law office procedures and client interviewing and counseling approaches, to a call for lawyers to consider insights drawn from the behavioral sciences.

Chapters 1 and 2 present the problem and its solution. The remaining chapters (3 through 6) flesh out the TJ/preventive model in the context of various practice areas. These chapters progress through the life-cycle of an attorney/client relationship, starting with the initial client interview in chapter 3. In that chapter, we learn how to signal confidence, trust, and a new kind of attorney/client relationship to our clients. In chapter 4, preventive law concepts such as "legal check-ups" are introduced with examples from elder law, business planning, and the work of in-house counsel. Chapter 5 discusses settlement and alternatives to litigation such as negotiation, mediation, and collaborative law. Potential harms of litigation are explained and techniques to recognize and overcome clients' psychological barriers to settlement are explored. Chapter 6 deepens the model in the context of criminal law. Lawyers are encouraged to recognize and deal with the emotional fallout of clients' legal situations, to seize opportunities to address the root causes of clients' legal problems, and to help set them on a course of rehabilitation.

A Closer Look

What follows is a discussion of the general approaches and specific techniques presented in chapters 3–6, with commentary on how these suggestions might be, or have been, received. Therapeutic jurisprudence has been criticized as an intellectual paradigm lacking a clear identity,[16] and as a well-intentioned but misguided legal reform movement that seeks sweeping reforms in various contexts, especially court reform.[17] Although therapeutic jurisprudence has been applied to many areas,[18] this book is concerned with one of them: lawyering. Many of the lawyering proposals found in this book—which have appeared in Bruce's earlier writings or the writings of other TJ or preventive law scholars—have received robust reactions and responses.[19] For example, the TJ-minded suggestion that criminal defense clients might consider apologizing for a crime, as a first step toward rehabilitation, for some appears to undermine the presumption of innocence.[20] Critics worry more generally that the adoption of TJ-inspired lawyering will lead lawyers to abandon due process protections altogether in the service of therapeutic ideals, thereby eviscerating the ideal of zealous client advocacy that has been a pillar of professional ethics.[21] Having a pre-set agenda of transforming clients who may or may not need transforming, or may not have the resources to succeed at it, for some suggests a paternalistic approach that may weaken the lawyer-client relationship.[22]

Such critiques must be reckoned with in any serious consideration of the approach outlined here. I offer, however, that the most fruitful way to read the book is not as a collection of narrow normative prescriptions that must be followed to transform the legal culture. Rather, it should be taken as a broad challenge to consider, discover, and refine the most effective techniques for fostering the kind of change envisioned by it. Whatever one might think of therapeutic jurisprudence generally or of the merits of specific lawyering proposals, there is a strain of truth in this narrative that even Bruce's most ardent critics will recognize. Who, for example, will reject Bruce's call to change the orientation of lawyering toward something more intentional, aware, and humane? Who would reject the idea that we should make it our business to be sensitive to the emotional impacts and unintended consequences law can have? Does it not behoove every lawyer to consider the way his or her practice might cause harm, and to imagine how that could be different? This book puts us in a mindset for asking just those kinds of questions. It points us toward discussions we should be having about fostering change in the legal culture—change many see as long overdue.[23]

The Initial Client Interview

In chapter 3, Bruce describes the initial client interview as critical to laying the foundation for a relationship of trust and concern, itself a prerequisite for practicing in a TJ/preventive mode. He suggests a variety of office practices and behaviors, even down to the placement of office furniture and the attorney's body language, that are likely to facilitate such a relationship. Drawing lessons from the literature on "procedural justice," he suggests the importance of giving "validation" and "voice" to client narratives, and of treating clients with dignity and respect.[24] Simple techniques such as avoiding interruptions, asking open-ended questions, and active listening are some of the tools discussed. Making clients comfortable, showing empathy, and encouraging clients to open up are all part of the effort to establish rapport. A poorly conducted interview and failure to establish rapport risks not only client dissatisfaction, but also the potential loss of valuable information to the case, and a client less likely to comply with the attorney's advice. Many of these insights were drawn from medical literature surveying the effectiveness on outcomes of initial doctor/patient interactions.[25] Indeed, Bruce often turned to the medical profession for guidance on developing a therapeutic role for lawyers. While attention to "bedside manner" has been a part of medicine for millennia, only relatively recently has clinical training focused on such things as empathy, listening skills, or recognition of non-verbal cues.[26] As medical schools and even insurance companies come to recognize the importance of these skills, a cultural shift seems underway.[27] Law schools, then, might take a lesson from the arc of medical education and attempt to teach a "deskside" manner that may ultimately lead to better client outcomes.[28]

Reaching Out: A Radical Step for Expanding the Traditional Lawyer's Role

Chapter 4 presents fine examples of what I believe to be the defining feature of the TJ/preventive model: the approach gives the lawyer permission to consider and further the non-legal interests of the client. For example, Bruce explains how an attorney initially presented with an estate planning issue winds up counseling his client about the client's vision problem noticed in the first office visit. Rather than ignoring a major issue in the client's overall well-being—one that may have implications for the legal issue at hand—the lawyer encourages the client to discuss the emotional and practical consequences of not dealing with the vision problem head on. Traditionally trained lawyers would reflexively shrink from engaging a client on such a sensitive issue with attenuated relevance to the specific legal issue at hand. In another scenario, the lawyer talks to a client whose mother had Alzheimers about the risk of Alzheimers, even though the client does not present symptoms or a diagnosis of Alzheimers. These can be awkward or off-putting topics to be raised by an attorney. But raising the issues has the potential to generate life-changing discussions that people should be having with experienced, trusted, neutral advisers. Bruce is suggesting we stop closing off the possibility that attorneys should be a part of these broader conversations. Lawyers can do more good in the world if we allow them space within their professional role to practice the art of helping. That message is at the heart of this model. Perhaps with a proper foundation laid at the initial client interview, and the development of a relationship of trust and concern, such questions as "How is your vision?" or "Can we talk about Alzheimers?" would not seem strange or off-putting. In a world where law students were trained to ask open-ended questions, to listen with sensitivity, and to consider non-legal issues, such questions could not only be appropriate but life-altering for a client.

Taking the Risk

Interesting questions arise in chapter 5 concerning the implications of representing oneself as a TJ/preventive lawyer. The book does not comment on whether adoption of the model is to be primarily internal—a subjective reconfiguration of one's values and approach to the world—or an external representation to the public that the lawyer is in fact working from the model. Are pioneering practitioners of this model going to hang a shingle that reads: "A TJ/preventive practice"? Or will they simply incorporate the values and approaches of the model into their practice without any explicit representations as to their guiding principles? Unless and until the model becomes mainstream, representing oneself as a TJ/preventive lawyer may carry certain professional risks. There may be perceptions, however erroneous, that TJ/preventive lawyers will not be as aggressive or zealous as traditional ones. There may be concerns that such lawyers will shrink from litigation, even where litigation might be the best option. In a legal marketplace that rewards power, pooled resources, and aggressive tactics, it will not always be easy to carve out a professional identity as a lawyer seeking peace, reconciliation, compromise, and psychological well-being.

Although Bruce does not address what TJ/preventive lawyers should write on their business cards, he does offer suggestions for winning over clients already sitting in your office. Bruce was mindful of the misunderstandings that might occur between new clients and lawyers attempting to practice the model. The key to minimizing such misunderstandings, he suggests, is to focus on developing trust and confidence with the client. If trust and confidence are established at the outset, awkward or sensitive conversations become possible as the lawyer-client relationship develops. If my clients truly trust me, for example, I might be able to open a conversation about the merits of taking responsibility or even apologizing for harm done to an adversary. If they trust me, they are more likely to work with me to redirect the goals they had when they entered my office to ones more compatible with their long term well-being.

A final consideration is that the TJ/preventive model will certainly require more resources from the attorney in a world where attorney resources are increasingly stretched thin. Conscientiously training oneself to adopt this model will surely take additional time, energy, and money. Some lawyers will be better at it than others. Is it reasonable to ask every lawyer to be more than just a traditional lawyer, but a problem solver, peacemaker, social worker, and healer? Bruce would say lawyers are already asked to be all these things all the time—we just need to help them be better at it.

Keeping the Model Client-Centered

An important check on the TJ/preventive approach—and one that Bruce wholeheartedly endorsed—is ensuring that the attorney/client dialogue remains "client-centered" at all times. The meaning of "client-centered" enjoys a rich literature and has been subject to various modifications and perspectives.[29] For Bruce, "client-centered" usually meant the lawyer diligently ensured that client decision-making remained at the forefront of the lawyer's actions. His concern was to avoid the excesses of "paternalism" by respecting client "autonomy."[30] Where there is disagreement about a potential course of action, lawyers might "persuade" so long as they do not "coerce" the client to adopt the attorney's advice. Notably, this is a voluntary or self-imposed check on the aspiring TJ/preventive lawyer. It is fundamental to the model, but ultimately relies on the attorney's diligence in exercising its constraints, as well as the attorney's acumen in understanding the point at which persuasion becomes coercion.[31] With no standards or professional guidance (other than this book and related academic literature) to steer those who want to adopt this model, there is some risk these techniques could be misused or misunderstood. How can we be sure our actions and advice are in fact "client-centered" rather than a projection of our own needs, desires, or beliefs? What if after extensive counseling in a TJ/preventive vein the client still wants to go to trial, or does not want to apologize? At what point exactly would the lawyer accept these as the true wishes of the client and proceed accordingly? Does the lawyer keep working to chip away at what is perceived as the client's intransigent "denial"? If so, will the client begin to feel manipulated or feel the lawyer is practicing unlicensed psychology? These are not easy questions. Nor are they reasons to eschew the model. In fact, these questions raise a plethora of issues that can be explored in law school courses and lawyer training programs that seek to incubate more mindful, ethical lawyers who are eager to engage in the project of figuring out what "client-centered" means to them.[32]

Many of Bruce's proposals here are not controversial and in fact compliment the more traditional models of lawyering. He recommends that lawyers be trained to develop skills such as "active listening," and to work to enhance their aptitude for "emotional intelligence" and "empathy."[33] He advises lawyers to follow the precepts of "procedural justice" by treating clients with "dignity and respect" and by finding opportunities to provide "voice" and "validation" for the client.[34] None of these techniques have been particularly objectionable, and in fact may be hallmarks of the most successful lawyers.[35]

Some of his other suggested techniques, however, seem to draw more deeply from the therapy manuals and might raise concerns about overstepping professional lines. Attempting to identify psychological defense mechanisms such as "denial" and "transference" in the client, for example, however useful this might be to understand what might underlie a client's intransigence, becomes problematic should the lawyer slip into the role of treating the denial or transference.[36] Even techniques such as "motivational interviewing," in which the lawyer uses questioning techniques to steer a client toward what the lawyer believes to be the best course of action, has the potential to slip into paternalism or to overstep disciplinary boundaries.[37]

One can also see where the suggestion that a lawyer should help the client find a catharsis might raise eyebrows. Should it be a lawyer's role to "help the client let go of anger or other negative emotions that otherwise would diminish the quality of his life"?[38] Bruce suggests that while lawyers should not take the place of psychologists or psychiatrists, they should also not ignore clients' emotional experience altogether. He suggests there is a middle ground—a rich space between playing therapist and simply acknowledging and responding in helpful ways to the emotional issues that attend the legal issues presented in a law office. Lawyers need to recognize this space and learn to navigate it with finesse.

Criminal Justice:
Therapeutic Alternatives and the Role of Prosecutors

In chapter 6, Bruce applies the TJ/preventive model to the practice of criminal law. This chapter primarily concerns itself with a particular type of lawyer—the criminal defense attorney—and a particular type of client—one suffering from a mental health or substance abuse issue. In this context, the work of the TJ/preventive criminal defense lawyer becomes one of steering appropriate clients into the various modes of rehabilitative sentencing and diversion that have sprung up in the last few decades. There is, for example, "deferred sentencing" in the federal system, which Bruce promotes as a singularly promising example. With this tool, defense attorneys seek deferment of their clients' sentencing hearing to allow time for the client to obtain treatment and the possibility of a reduced sentence should treatment prove successful.[39] Then there are drug courts, mental health courts, and other "problem-solving courts" that favor treatment over incarceration. These are perhaps the most well-known, and controversial, of the new diversion options. Concerns over paternalism, coercion, and lack of due process have featured prominently in debates surrounding the problem solving courts.[40]

One need not embrace problem-solving courts as a panacea, however, to agree that criminal defense attorneys should be trained to tailor their clients' individual needs to the most favorable and least harmful outcomes. Defense counsel might know of a particularly "good" drug court in the jurisdiction for which the aforementioned concerns are at a minimum, and feel more comfortable recommending this option to the client. Or perhaps, in consultation with the client and the client's doctors, counsel may believe the drug or mental health issue is manageable and the evidence in the case portends a favorable outcome for the client, such that a recommendation for trial or traditional court process might be made. It is no small fact that for many clients, the prospect of receiving treatment instead of any amount of prison time can make a monumental difference to their outcome. Concerns over paternalism or coercion are legitimate, but perhaps no more so than under the status quo, where attorneys and judges wield tremendous power over their clients and cases. At least in theory, TJ/preventive lawyering will orient criminal defense attorneys toward an understanding of these and other potentially therapeutic opportunities. Attorneys already have a duty to explain the risks and potential outcomes of significant legal choices, such as a plea-bargain, to their clients.[41] A TJ/preventively-trained lawyer would be well-positioned to fulfill this duty and even exceed it by helping clients with substance-abuse or mental health issues to understand and select the most appropriate course of action for their individual needs.

While primarily concerned with criminal defense lawyers, Bruce suggests prosecutors can also modify their practice along TJ/preventive lines. Using the context of domestic violence cases, he suggests that prosecutors can do more than simply prosecute batterers. He suggests they can actually help victims heal or break the cycle of violence by using key steps in the criminal process itself—arrest, deposition, trial, victim impact statement—to afford victims opportunities for catharsis, healing, and empowerment. By encouraging victims to "open up," particularly in writing, prosecutors are seen as therapeutic agents who can help victims overcome patterns of isolation and secrecy, learned helplessness, and post-traumatic stress.[42] To those concerned about lawyers overstepping into the domain of therapists,[43] and to those acutely aware of the potential harms that often befall victims who seek help from the criminal justice system,[44] these suggestions may be greeted with alarm. Indeed, unlike with defense attorneys, it will be difficult if not impossible for prosecutors to maintain relationships of trust or loyalty with victims, particularly where prosecutors are inclined or mandated to override victims' desires not to participate in a prosecution.[45]

In comparison, Bruce's other suggestions for domestic violence prosecutors appear far more benign. Bruce exhorts prosecutors to listen, empathize, give voice and validation to victims, and attempt to work with them in a manner that causes the least psychological distress. With respect to the decision to prosecute a case, prosecutors should "always take account of the likely impact on the victim, including the children of the victim...."[46] As in the civil context, where we have seen the same maxims applied, these appear unobjectionable and perhaps even a salve to the tensions that exist between prosecutors and victims. Yet the approach to merely "take account" of victim impacts does little to resolve deep and confounding divides[47] about how prosecutors should best handle domestic violence cases. For some, the best hope for victims is to bring to bear the full weight of the criminal justice system upon batterers with mandatory interventions such as mandatory arrest, "no-drop" prosecution, and compelled victim testimony.[48] For others, mandatory interventions that displace victim prerogatives are far more harmful than helpful to victims and to the movement to combat domestic violence.[49] Attempting a sort of middle position, Bruce assumes prosecutors will not (and should not) cede prosecutorial discretion to victims; but he implores them to thoroughly consider and place high value on victim impacts as a factor in deciding whether and how to prosecute a case.[50]

Short of settling the matter in this context, Bruce suggests how a TJ/preventive mindset might look at a legal process and take fuller account of its harmful impacts. Indeed, there is much that a prosecutor (even in a "no-drop" jurisdiction) can do to ameliorate the harmful impacts of the criminal process upon victims. Prosecutors, for example, can seek to bolster their cases with physical evidence, potentially obviating the need for victim testimony.[51] They can use the rules of evidence to admit statements from victims who do not wish to testify.[52] Or they can charge batterers with ancillary crimes that do not require victim participation to prove.[53] Thus, even in the complex, emotionally-charged arena of prosecuting domestic violence cases, Bruce shows there is a role to play for the TJ/preventive model. Perhaps a prosecutor trained to think like a TJ/preventive lawyer in law school might go on to champion victim-centered policies in their offices. Perhaps a victim dealing with such a prosecutor will get a little more consideration, a little more voice, even a little more control over the process.

Omissions of Note

Bruce's manuscript notes indicate that he wanted to follow the first six chapters with three additional ones: a chapter applying the TJ/preventive model to the famous end-of-life legal struggles of Terry Schiavo; a chapter explaining how the model could be taught in law schools; and a chapter exploring how the model could be applied in a litigation context. Bruce did not get the chance to write these chapters, but fortunately, he published articles on the first two subjects.[54] These articles can help the reader round out the understanding that Bruce wanted the reader to take away from the book.

The envisioned chapter on litigation does not have a corresponding article, and Bruce did not write much about the litigation process itself, presumably because the heart of the TJ/preventive approach was to avoid litigation in most circumstances. To the extent he did write about litigation, it was to suggest how litigators can encourage settlement and counsel clients dealing with the emotional landmines of litigation.[55] While one might wish that we had Bruce's wisdom on the subject of how lawyers can prepare themselves to conduct litigation in accordance with therapeutic values in an adversarial world, the topic offers up new frontiers for TJ/preventive scholars and practitioners to explore. When settlement is not an option, how do we litigate in a way that is least damaging to our clients, adversaries, and third parties who may be effected by the litigation? How can we be successful, zealous advocates for our clients in litigation without compromising our clients' or our own deeply held values of civility, professionalism, and fair play? Bruce would have cherished nothing more than to know that others would be exploring even once he was gone how to make the TJ/preventive model a vehicle for lawyers in all areas of practice to find meaning in their professional and personal lives.

Conclusion

This book is an important contribution to contemporary discussions about the changing role of law and lawyers in society.[56] These discussions have been heard for some time, but are especially salient since the economic downturn of 2008 and its profound impact on the legal profession.[57] We see both the forces of contraction and expansion at work—those calling for more narrowly-focused roles for law graduates[58] counterbalanced by those like Bruce seeking a broader role for lawyers in society. This book challenges us to seriously consider the full breadth and scope of what can be achieved in the attorney/client relationship. Here is a vision of professionals who can be more than mere technicians for our legal rights. It is a vision of lawyers bringing healing and harmony to the most serious conflicts that enter our lives.

Remarkably, there is no universally accepted theory of lawyering; no agreement on what "the" role of a lawyer is or should be.[59] Often a particular lawyer's conception of what he or she is doing is driven by the context in which they practice.[60] A litigator might work from a "zealous advocate" model, in which duty to client is seen as paramount to all other considerations.[61] A transactional attorney might prefer a "business" model of practice, in which the attorney views him or herself as primarily running a business or providing a service for profit.[62] Public interest attorneys may view their work as primarily advancing social justice issues.[63] All of these and other models might intersect, conflict, or diverge from each other.[64] They might operate simultaneously, and not always harmoniously, in a single lawyer's conception of the professional role he or she plays.[65] A role only recently gaining traction as part of this standard menu of options is one that embraces a conception of the lawyer as holistic helper, healer, and resource for those who seek to repair or avoid psychological or emotional damage. The TJ/preventive model maps easily onto the Venn diagram of these possible roles. Notwithstanding some of the natural tensions between the models, it is compatible with these and many other frameworks for lawyering.

Nor has Bruce been alone in calling for a cultural shift in the way law is seen and practiced. Over the past few decades or so, numerous alternative models to law practice have emerged to challenge the cultural status quo. Susan Daicoff describes several of these kindred lawyering models as "vectors" that converge, diverge, and draw from each other, so much that we might consider them part of a movement she calls the "Comprehensive Law Movement."[66] Others have grouped some of these vectors with several other lawyering trends under the rubric "Integrative Law Movement."[67] This growing taxonomy of kindred lawyering models easily embraces "client-centered lawyering"[68] and "social justice lawyering"[69] models along with "law and emotion"[70] scholarship, the recent "trauma-informed practice"[71] movement, and arguably many others. Each of these models emphasizes particular skills or aptitudes, or focuses on particular problems or processes, but they generally share similar goals and point in the same direction.[72] They tend to share a willingness to consider non-legal factors along with an intention to find the most optimal human outcomes in any legal encounter.[73] They tend to embrace approaches that eschew adversarial processes in favor of more durable forms of conflict resolution.[74] All of these emergent models bespeak a desire for lasting change in the legal culture. Taken together they are themselves evidence that the desired cultural changes are already progressing apace, and making an impact.[75] Bruce's unique contributions have found their place in this rich landscape of law reform, which he also helped to shape.

I have noted some areas where teaching or application of this model might be difficult, and where the model could benefit from further development. It is not a perfected model, but a vision seeking more minds, hearts, and hands to shape it. Whatever we decide to do with the ideas presented in this book, we still have choices to make. Will we do nothing—and thereby capitulate to cynical forces in the legal profession that harm its reputation and deny lawyers opportunities to express their best selves? Or will we encourage the next generation of lawyers to practice with an ethic of care,[76] and to help them develop the tools they will need to resist the pressures of a sometimes dehumanized and exploitative legal marketplace? This is what Bruce really wanted. It is why he worked so passionately, even through terminal illness, to write this book, and we should all be grateful for this parting gift.

Notes

1. *See* People v. Fitzpatrick, 32 N.Y.2d 499, 300 N.E.2d 139, 346 N.Y.S.2d 793 *cert. denied,* 414 U.S. 1033 (1973); *see also* Edward J. Maggio, *Death by Statute: the Turbulent History of New York's Death Penalty,* N.Y. St. B.J., February 2005, at 14.

2. *See* Affidavit of Expert Bruce Winick, Cernuda v. Neufeld, et al., 2007 WL 576073 (S.D.Fla.) (No. 05 Civ. 22728); *see also* Foley v. Hershey, 409 F.2d 827 (7th Cir. 1969); United States v. Wayte, 710 F.2d 1385 (9th Cir. 1983), *aff'd,* 470 U.S. 598 (1985).

3. *See* Affidavit of Expert Bruce Winick, *supra* note 2; *See also* Norm Kent, *Saluting One Life, Censuring the Next*, S. Fla. Gay News (Sept. 1, 2010, 6:25pm), http://southflorida gaynews.com/Publisher-s-Editorial/saluting-one-life-censuring-the-next.html (last visited Feb. 1, 2018) (noting impact of the Ordinance on sparking the Anita Byrant crusade, which in turn galvanized the gay rights movement nationwide).

4. *See In re* Fla. Bd. of Bar Exam'r, 358 So.2d 7 (Fla. 1978) (finding avowal of homosexual orientation did not of itself equate to lack of good moral character for bar admittance purposes); See *also* Kent, *supra*, note 3, noting the historical impact of the case.

5. *See* Haitian Refugee Ctr., Inc. v. Baker, 953 F.2d 1498 (11th Cir. 1992), *cert. denied* 502 U.S. 1122 (1992). He also contributed to briefs before the U.S. Supreme Court in support of Haitian immigrants in McNary v. Haitian Refugee Ctr., Inc., 498 U.S. 479 (1991), and Comm'r, I.N.S. v. Jean, 496 U.S. 154 (1990).

6. *See, e.g.*, Brief for ACLU et al. as Amici Curiae Supporting Respondent, Kansas v. Hendricks, 521 U.S. 346 (1997) (No. 95-1649), 1996 WL 471020 (U.S.); *see also* Kansas v. Hendricks, 521 U.S. 346 (1997) (upholding Kansas' involuntary civil commitment statute).

7. *See* Amendment to the Rules of Juvenile Procedure, Fla. R. Juv. P. 8.350, 842 So. 2d 763 (Fla. 2003) (establishing right to pre-commitment hearing and counsel for foster youth facing involuntary commitment to locked psychiatric facilities).

8. *See In re* Amendments to the Florida Rules of Juvenile Procedure, 26 So.3d 552 (2009); *see also* Bernard P. Perlmutter, *"Unchain the Children": Gault, Therapeutic Jurisprudence, and Shackling*, 9 Barry L. Rev. 1, n.2, n.96, n.293 (2007) (describing affidavits, briefs, the Juvenile Shackling Voice Project, and other contributions Bruce made to the anti-shackling campaign).

9. *See generally* David B. Wexler & Bruce J. Winick, Essays in Therapeutic Jurisprudence (1991) (introducing the discipline); David B. Wexler & Bruce J. Winick, Law in a Therapeutic Key: Developments in Therapeutic Jurisprudence (1996); and Bruce J. Winick, David B. Wexler, and Dennis P. Stolle, Practicing Therapeutic Jurisprudence: Law as a Helping Profession (2000).

10. *See* David B. Wexler, *Two Decades of Therapeutic Jurisprudence*, 24 Touro L. Rev. 17, 18 (2008); David B. Wexler, *Therapeutic Jurisprudence Across the Law School Curriculum: 2012*, 5 Phoenix L. Rev. 791, 792 (2012) (bibliography); and see Int'l Soc'y Therapeutic Juris., http://www.intltj.com/resources (last visited Feb. 5, 2018), for a clearinghouse of resources exemplifying the international reach of TJ scholarship and law reform efforts.

11. *See* sources cited *supra* note 10.

12. See, *e.g.*, Bruce J. Winick, The Right to Refuse Mental Health Treatment (1997), Bruce J. Winick, Civil Commitment: A Therapeutic Jurisprudence Model (2005), as well as Bruce's journal articles too numerous to list here.

13. Bruce received numerous awards recognizing his contribution, among other things, to the global study of law and mental health issues. For example, in 2009 Bruce was awarded the Philippe Pinel Award, the highest honor bestowed by the International Academy of Law and Mental Health. *See* David B. Wexler, *In Memoriam: Bruce J. Winick (September 1, 1944 to August 26, 2010)*, International Journal of Law and Psychiatry 33, 279 (2010); *See also* Biography of Bruce J. Winick, University of Miami Ethics Programs, https://ethics. miami.edu/about/people/in-memoriam/bruce-j-winick/index.html (last visited Feb. 7, 2018).

14. *See* News Release, *UM Law Professor Bruce J. Winick Passes Away*, University of Miami, http://web.archive.org/web/20100901042759/http://www.miami.edu/index.php/ news/releases/um_law_professor_bruce_j_winick_passes_away/; *and see In Memoriam: Bruce*

Winick, University of Miami School of Law, http://web.archive.org/web/201009090035 28/http://www.law.miami.edu:80/facadmin/bwinick_memoriam.php]; *see also* Obituary & Guest Book, *Bruce J. Winick*, The Miami Herald (Aug. 27, 2010–March 18, 2011), http://www.legacy.com/obituaries/name/Bruce-Winick-obituary?pid=144966999&view=guest book&page=3.

15. Bruce explained the technological and spiritual resources he relied upon to surmount his vision obstacles in the following video: Cuttingedgelaw, *Bruce Winick Part 6*, YouTube (Sept. 10, 2009), https://www.youtube.com/watch?v=r73kE_tG-JM&list=PL322CED1065 E4ECC3&index=6 (last visited Feb. 7, 2018).

16. Christopher Slobogin, *Therapeutic Jurisprudence: Five Dilemmas To Ponder*, 1 Psychol. Pub. Pol'y & L. 193 (Winter, 1995).

17. Allegra M. McLeod, *Decarceration Courts: Possibilities and Perils of a Shifting Criminal Law*, 100 Geo. L. J. 1587, 1612 (2012); Susan Stefan & Bruce J. Winick, *A Dialogue on Mental Health Courts*, 11 Psychol. Pub. Pol'y & L. 507 (Dec. 2005); James L. Nolan, *Redefining Criminal Courts: Problem-Solving and the Meaning of Justice*, 40 Am. Crim. L. Rev. 1541 (Fall, 2003).

18. *See* sources cited *supra* note 10.

19. Mae C. Quinn, *An Rsvp to Professor Wexler's Warm Therapeutic Jurisprudence Invitation to the Criminal Defense Bar: Unable to Join You, Already (Somewhat Similarly) Engaged*, 48 B.C. L. Rev. 539 (2007); Tamar M. Meekins, *"Specialized Justice": The Over-Emergence of Specialty Courts and the Threat of a New Criminal Defense Paradigm*, 40 Suffolk U. L. Rev. 1 (2006).

20. *See* Quinn, *supra* note *19,* at 579 n.19.

21. *See, e.g.,* Meekins, *supra* note 19, at 2–14, 33–51 (2006) and Quinn, *supra* note 19, at 547 n.45, 568 (2007). Quinn suggests the rehabilitative focus of TJ approaches may be fundamentally inconsistent with counsel's duties to be zealous and unbiased, to practice within one's area of expertise, and that it may interfere with client trust. *Id.* at 569–573, 577. *But see* Susan Daicoff, *Law As A Healing Profession: The "Comprehensive Law Movement"*, 6 Pepp. Disp. Resol. L.J. 1, 60 (2006), suggesting this and similar new lawyering approaches are fully compatible with existing professional responsibility codes.

22. *See* Quinn, *supra* note 19, at 577–586.

23. Susan Swaim Daicoff, *Expanding the Lawyer's Toolkit of Skills and Competencies: Synthesizing Leadership, Professionalism, Emotional Intelligence, Conflict Resolution, and Comprehensive Law*, 52 Santa Clara L. Rev. 795, 796–818 (2012).

24. *See, e.g.,* Tom R. Tyler, Why People Obey the Law (1990); A. Allan Lind & Tom R. Tyler, The Social Psychology of Procedural Justice (1988).

25. *See, e.g.,* Howard B. Beckman & Richard M. Frankel, *The Effect of Physician Behavior on the Collection of Data*, 101 Annals Internal Med. 692 (1984), http://annals.org/aim/article-abstract/699136/effect-physician-behavior-collection-data [doi:10.7326/0003-4819-101-5-692] (last visited Feb. 13, 2018); *see also* Gay Gellhorn, *Law and Language: An Empirically-Based Model for the Opening Moments of Client Interviews*, 4 Clinical L. Rev. 321, 335 (1998).

26. *See* Barry D. Silverman, MD, *Physician behavior and bedside manners: the influence of William Osler and The Johns Hopkins School of Medicine,* 25 Proc. Bayl. U. Med. Ctr. 58 (2012 Jan); Sandra G. Boodman, *How to Teach Doctors Empathy*, The Atlantic, March 15, 2015, https://www.theatlantic.com/health/archive/2015/03/how-to-teach-doctors-empathy/387784/ (last visited Feb. 13, 2018).

27. *See* Boodman, *supra* note 26.

28. *See* Gellhorn, *supra* note 25.

29. *See* Katherine R. Kruse, *Fortress in the Sand: The Plural Values of Client-Centered Representation*, 12 CLINICAL L. REV. 369 (2006).

30. Of course, understanding what client "autonomy" is and then figuring out how to ensure its protection can itself be the subject of considerable complexity. "Autonomy," for example, can be as narrow a concept as "letting the client make the decision" to as broad as "helping the client become the person they want to be." *See* Kruse, *supra* note 29, at 413–427 (elucidating how various client-centered lawyering approaches may help or hinder the goal of respecting client autonomy).

31. High theorists of autonomy and lawyering scholars alike seem to have difficulty articulating the precise point at which various methods of persuasion become coercive. *See* Kruse, *supra* note 29, at 408.

32. *See* Kruse, *supra* note 29, as an example of scholarship that probes deeper into the kinds of questions that might be asked about the propriety and limits of particular kinds of counselor interventions.

33. *See* Susan S. Daicoff, *Expanding the Lawyer's Toolkit of Skills and Competencies: Synthesizing Leadership, Professionalism, Emotional Intelligence, Conflict Resolution, and Comprehensive Law*, 52 SANTA CLARA L. REV. 795, 840–845, 857–859 (2012) (summarizing the relevance of these and other skills and aptitudes to effective lawyering).

34. *Id.* at 845–848.

35. *Id.* at 818–833, 873 (summarizing empirical studies that suggest as much).

36. In contrast, lawyers' introspection into their own possible "countertransference" or their own positive or negative emotions toward clients, seems a useful tool for lawyers to manage appropriate attorney/client relationships. *See* Marjorie A. Silver, *Love, Hate, and Other Emotional Interference in the Lawyer/Client Relationship*, 6 CLINICAL L. REV. 259 (Fall, 1999).

37. *See* Quinn, *supra* note 19, at 582.

38. *See* chapter 6, Intro.

39. *But see* Quinn, *supra* note 19, at 583–585 (suggesting deferred sentencing may not be appropriate for poor and/or transient clients).

40. *See* sources cited *supra* note 17.

41. *See* Stephanos Bibas, *Regulating the Plea-Bargaining Market: From Caveat Emptor to Consumer Protection*, 99 CAL. L. REV. 1117, 1146–1148 (2011).

42. Bruce draws from the work of psychologist James Pennebaker in support of this suggestion. *See* JAMES W. PENNEBAKER, OPENING UP: THE HEALING POWER OF CONFIDING IN OTHERS (1990).

43. *See* sources cited *supra* notes 17 and 19.

44. *See, e.g.,* Leigh Goodmark, *Law is the Answer? Do We Know That For Sure?: Questioning the Efficacy of Legal Interventions for Battered Women*, 23 ST. LOUIS U. PUB. L. REV. 7 (2004); Linda G. Mills, *Killing Her Softly: Intimate Abuse and the Violence of State Intervention*, 113 HARV. L. REV. 550 (1999).

45. *See* Cheryl Hanna, *No Right to Choose: Mandated Victim Participation in Domestic Violence Prosecutions*, 109 HARV. L. REV. 1849 (1996) (outlining the history and debate over 'no-drop' prosecution policies).

46. *See* chapter 6 (3).

47. *See* Goodmark, *supra* note 44, at 31.

48. *See* Hanna, *supra* note 45 (recognizing potential harm to victims from such policies, but arguing individual harms are outwieghed by other interests and the need to send a strong message that domestic violence will not be tolerated).

49. *See* sources cited *supra note* 44.

50. *See also* Bruce J. Winick, *Applying the Law Therapeutically in Domestic Violence Cases*, 69 UMKC L. REV. 33, 79 (2000) (discussing Bruce's idea of "presumptive arrest," which similarly stakes out a middle ground in the debate over mandatory arrest laws).

51. *See* Hanna, *supra* note 45, at 1898–1907.

52. *See id.* at 1904.

53. *See id.* at 1905.

54. Bruce J. Winick, *A Legal Autopsy of the Lawyering in Schiavo: A Therapeutic Jurisprudence/preventive Law Rewind Exercise*, 61 U. MIAMI L. REV. 595 (2007); and Bruce J. Winick, *Using Therapeutic Jurisprudence in Teaching Lawyering Skills: Meeting the Challenge of the New ABA Standards*, 17 ST. THOMAS L. REV. 429 (2005).

55. Bruce J. Winick, *Therapeutic Jurisprudence and the Role of Counsel in Litigation*, 37 CAL. W. L. REV. 105 (2000); Bruce J. Winick, *The Expanding Scope of Preventive Law*, 3 FLA. COASTAL L.J. 189, 190–195 (2002).

56. *See, e.g.*, Susan Swaim Daicoff, *Expanding the Lawyer's Toolkit of Skills and Competencies: Synthesizing Leadership, Professionalism, Emotional Intelligence, Conflict Resolution, and Comprehensive Law*, 52 SANTA CLARA L. REV. 795, 796–818 (2012) (summarizing the changes); *see also* Alfred S. Konefsky & Barry Sullivan, *In This, the Winter of Our Discontent: Legal Practice, Legal Education, and the Culture of Distrust*, 62 BUFF. L. REV. 659 (2014).

57. *See, e.g.*, Eli Wald, *Foreword: The Great Recession and the Legal Profession*, 78 FORDHAM L. REV. 2051 (2010); and Alfred S. Konefsky & Barry Sullivan, *supra* note 56 at 660–669.

58. *See* Konefsky & Sullivan, *supra* note 56, at 691–745.

59. Eli Wald, *Resizing the Rules of Professional Conduct*, 27 GEO. J. LEGAL ETHICS 227, 239 (2014); *see also* Rob Atkinson, *A Dissenter's Commentary on the Professionalism Crusade*, 74 TEX. L. REV. 259, 303 (1995).

60. *See* Wald, *supra* note 59, at 228.

61. Margaret Chon, *Multidimensional Lawyering and Professional Responsibility*, 43 SYRACUSE L. REV. 1137, 1145 (1992) (citing Lord Brougham's classic articulation of the model); Katherine R. Kruse, *Lawyers Should Be Lawyers, but What Does That Mean?: A Response to Aiken & Wizner and Smith*, 14 WASH. U. J.L. & Pol'y 49, 64–71 (2004) (problematizing the model).

62. *See* Konefsky & Sullivan, *supra* note 56, at 663 n.10 and references therein.

63. *See* Kruse, *supra* note 61, at 64–67.

64. *See* Chon, *supra* note 61, at 1137; *and see* Atkinson, *supra* note 59, at 317.

65. *See* Chon, *supra* note 61, at 1137.

66. *See* Susan Daicoff, *Law As A Healing Profession: The "Comprehensive Law Movement"*, 6 PEPP. DISP. RESOL. L.J. 1 (2006) (describing the primary "vectors" as (1) collaborative law, (2) creative problem solving, (3) holistic justice, (4) preventive law, (5) problem solving courts, (6) procedural justice, (7) restorative justice, (8) therapeutic jurisprudence, and (9) transformative mediation); *see also* Daicoff, *supra* note 56, at 804 n.22 and references therein.

67. *See, e.g.*, Cutting Edge Law, *The Integrative Law Movement: An Introduction*, http://

cuttingedgelaw.com/page/integrative-law-movement-introduction) (last visited Feb. 15, 2018) (suggesting scores of new models that might be included under the umbrella term "Integrative Law Movement."); *see also* Pauline H. Tesler, *Can This Relationship Be Saved? The Legal Profession and Families in Transition*, 55 FAM. CT. REV. 38, 47, n.58, n.62 (2017).

68. *See* Kruse, *supra* note 29, at 369–374.

69. *See* Kruse, *supra* note 61, at 51–55.

70. *See* Susan A. Bandes & Jeremy A. Blumenthal, *Emotion and the Law*, 8 ANN. REV. L. & SOC. SCI. 161 (2012); Kathryn Abrams & Hila Keren, *Who's Afraid of Law and the Emotions?*, 94 MINN. L. REV. 1997 (2010).

71. *See* SAMHSA, U.S. Dept. of Health and Human Servs., *SAMHSA's Concept of Trauma and Guidance for a Trauma-Informed Approach,* HHS Publication No.(SMA) 14-4884, at 6–7, Rockville, MD (2014), https://store.samhsa.gov/shin/content/SMA14-4884/SMA14-4884.pdf (last visited Feb. 15, 2018) (describing collaborative efforts at the federal, state, and local levels to implement trauma-informed approaches); *See also* Sarah Katz, Deeya Haldar, *The Pedagogy of Trauma-Informed Lawyering*, 22 CLINICAL L. REV. 359, 363, 369–372 (2016); Samantha Buckingham, *Trauma Informed Juvenile Justice*, 53 AM. CRIM. L. REV. 641 (2016).

72. *See* Daicoff, *Law As A Healing Profession, supra* note 66 at 1–10 (describing common purpose of the comprehensive law vectors).

73. *See id.*

74. *See* Tessler, *supra* note 67, at 42 n.27 (explaining why "conflict resolution" approaches, as opposed to mere "dispute resolution" ones, better serve the needs of divorcing couples).

75. The relatively recent push to include "trauma-informed" approaches to the work of government at every level is a telling example of such impact. *See* sources cited *supra* note 71.

76. *See* Stephen Ellmann, *The Ethic of Care As an Ethic for Lawyers*, 81 GEO. L.J. 2665 (1993).

Acknowledgments

I wish to thank those who took the time to review my introduction to this book and provide feedback: Susan Bandes, Caroline Bettinger-Lopez, Donna Coker, Jeanne Haffner, Bernard Perlmutter, Scott Sundby, and Margot Winick. Special thanks to Scott Sundby for going the extra mile with his feedback. Extra special thanks to my wife Caroline Bettinger-Lopez for her commentary on several drafts and for her encouragement, support, and patience with the process.

I thank Patricia White, Dean of the University of Miami School of Law, for providing me with a fellowship in law and psychology at Miami Law, with which I was able to immerse myself in therapeutic jurisprudence and related subjects that proved indispensable for tackling this project.

Thanks to David Wexler and Judge Jeri Cohen for facilitating my presentation and discussion of Bruce's manuscript at the 2011 International Congress on Law and Mental Health in Berlin. I also thank the various unnamed members of the "TJ community" who provided robust feedback at that event which helped me better understand and contextualize this project.

I wish to thank all those involved in the production of this book at Carolina Academic Press.

Last but definitely not least, I wish to thank Margot Winick. Margot was the engine that powered this project from the very beginning. Her vision, passion, and limitless patience for getting her father's final work published and available to all has been steadfast. I thank her for entrusting me to shepherd this book through to the finish line.

—Sean Bettinger-Lopez, Miami, 2018

The Reimagined Lawyer

Chapter 1

Lawyering and Its Discontents: Dissatisfaction with the Profession among Clients and Lawyers

Lawyering as a profession has gotten a bad name. Lawyers are the butt of all those horrible lawyer jokes, and the public laughs at the jokes, because they contain a kernel of truth. They portray lawyers as dishonest street fighters who will lie, cheat, and steal with impunity in order to win their cases. They are seen as warmongers and mercenaries, fomenting and prolonging litigation that may be unnecessary. They are viewed as sometimes placing their own pecuniary interests above the interests of their clients.

If even a fraction of this is true, it is not surprising that clients feel uncomfortable hiring lawyers, and fear that they will be overcharged and otherwise taken advantage of. The public generally seems to rank the profession on the low side of the scale of occupational respect, placing lawyers somewhere between politicians and used car salesmen. Moreover, given this public and client attitude, it is not surprising that many lawyers have a low view of their profession and wonder whether they have made the right professional choice.

All across the country, numerous surveys, from the 1990s to the present day, show that lawyers are dissatisfied with their careers, would not choose the same career path, or would switch careers if they had a reasonable alternative. In summarizing the vast majority of findings, Professor Susan Daicoff concluded that significant portions of lawyers in most cities, regions, and across the country were not only dissatisfied with their profession, but also displeased with their personal lives. An important American Bar Association study that

surveyed lawyer attitudes in 1984, 1990, and 1995 found increasing dissatisfaction among lawyers with their practice. This finding was consistent whether
the lawyers worked in private, corporate, or government practices. In 1984,
19 percent of lawyers reported themselves as dissatisfied, very dissatisfied, or
neutral. In 1990, this percentage had increased to 24 percent, and in 1995, it
increased again to 27.5 percent. In more recent years, the work demands of
the profession have increased dramatically. Moreover, partnership in a law firm
once constituted a form of job tenure with assured income. This has changed
in recent years with the increased dissolution and consolidation of law firms,
exacerbated by the recent economic downturn. If anything, we can assume
that these more recent changes in the profession have produced even more
professional dissatisfaction. In general, professionals report higher job satisfaction than do non-professional occupational groups. Thus, the fact that
lawyers so frequently question their professional choices is particularly
surprising and distressing. Moreover, as Professor Andrew Benjamin's work
shows, lawyer dissatisfaction with the profession increases over time.

1. Evidence of Distress among Lawyers

The stress and emotional costs of being a lawyer have produced predictable
negative psychological effects for many in the profession. Psychological distress
and dysfunctional patterns of behavior certainly exist across the professions,
yet lawyers suffer these effects at higher rates than members of other
professions, including doctors, nurses, and teachers. Many lawyers feel disen-
gaged from family and friends, regularly procrastinate in meeting deadlines,
and feel trapped in their practice. Moreover, many experience a pathological
degree of psychological distress.

Research has found that 20 percent of lawyers suffer from a clinically significant psychological problem severe enough to warrant intervention. Thus,
a high percentage of lawyers are "walking wounded," practicing their profession
while experiencing serious psychological difficulties. Moreover, they suffer
from the additional distress of having to hide their problem from the rest of
the world. As Susan Daicoff has noted, lawyers in general experience
depression, anxiety, alcoholism, and other psychological problems at a rate
that is often twice that found in the general population.

In fact, law is ranked as one of the top three occupations for serious depression. A 1990 study found that lawyers have the highest incidence of depression
among 104 occupational groups. Almost every study has found that the rates
of depression are much higher among lawyers than for other professionals or

the general population. Yet, as Professor Daicoff shows, studies do not support the hypothesis that distressed, dissatisfied, or impaired individuals self-select into the law school. In fact, most law students at the outset of law school appear to be normal compared to the general population. The general rates of clinical depression are probably no more than 3 to 4 percent, yet the term sometimes is defined more broadly to encompass as much as 9 percent of the population. Professors Sheldon and Krieger estimate that the rate of depression among entering law students is around 10 percent. However, studies by Professor Benjamin and his colleagues of students and alumni in one law school (University of Arizona) show that by the spring of the first year of law school, 32 percent of students were depressed. By the end of the third year, this percentage had increased to 40 percent. This rate seems to reduce within two years of graduation, but only to about 18 percent, significantly higher than rates of depression in the general population and in other professions. Given the difficulty in estimating rates of depression, resulting in part from the lack of agreement concerning the contours of the category, this 18 percent finding may be somewhat high. However, an empirical study of a random sample of lawyers in Washington by Benjamin and his colleagues found that 19 percent of lawyers suffer from depression, a percentage that remained constant no matter how many years an attorney practiced law. This represents a rate two to five times higher than the general rate of depression in the Western world. Lawyers also seem to exhibit higher suicide rates than any other profession.

As Daicoff shows, many lawyers suffer from other types of psychological distress at higher than normal levels. These include global psychological distress and specific symptoms such as anxiety, stress, anger, obsessive-compulsive features, marital discord, social alienation and isolation, insecurity, self-consciousness, paranoia, and hostility. As professors Beck, Benjamin, and Sales have noted, surveys of thousands of lawyers have shown that more than one-third report high enough levels of clinical distress to warrant professional help. Such distress is in the area of interpersonal sensitivity, a measure of self-esteem and security based on the need to compare favorably to others. This represents some fifteen times the level of such distress in the general population. This shows that lawyers experience a high level of insecurity and possess an unhealthy need for status. If anything, the recent economic decline has increased the extent of the negative emotions experienced by attorneys, including depression.

2. Methods of Coping with Distress among Lawyers

In general, many attorneys cope with the emotional distress they experience in the profession through substance abuse, social isolation, and working harder. Studies show that some 18 percent of attorneys suffer from alcoholism, which is twice the rate of the general population. These estimates may be low because drinking is seen as a non-problematic way of dealing with stress, many lawyers hide their drinking, and lawyers often cover-up for one another. The ABA Survey referred to above showed that in 1984, less than half of 1 percent of those surveyed reported consuming six or more drinks a day. In 1990, however, some 13 percent of lawyers were in this category, including 20 percent of female lawyers. If anything, the work demands and uncertainties within the profession occurring since 1990, exacerbated by the recent economic decline, would make us think that these percentages have since increased. In addition, the rate of alcoholism is much higher among longer practicing attorneys, which demonstrates the progressive nature of the problem. More frightening still, Beck and her colleagues' study of alcohol-related problems among lawyers indicates that nearly 70 percent of lawyers are candidates for alcohol-related problems at sometime during their careers.

Daicoff quotes one estimate that the incidence of chemical dependence within the profession may be as much as twice that of the general population. Alcoholism and substance abuse themselves are psychiatric disorders that are related to a wide variety of health, mental health, family, social, and occupational problems. These coping mechanisms themselves can exacerbate existing psychological problems and can result in unethical behavior. Alcohol and drug use release anger and aggression, and may be responsible for some of the excessive combativeness that many attorneys display. Moreover, they inhibit self-control mechanisms in ways that may be conducive to professional misconduct and ethical violations. Substance abuse can result in the neglect of clients or cases. It has been shown to be involved in approximately 27 percent of disciplinary actions nationally and 100 percent of disciplinary actions in some states. These estimates may be low, as disciplinary agencies rarely go beyond the presenting violation to determine its causes. As with alcoholism, lawyers engaged in substance abuse are often in denial about having a drug problem or minimize their drug dependency. A report of the Association of American Law Schools estimated that from 50 to 75 percent of bar disciplinary actions and as many as 60 percent of legal malpractice claims were the result of substance abuse.

Social isolation and immersion in one's work are additional ways of coping with the distress of law practice. Social isolation can foster unprincipled behavior because of the lack of peer review of and feedback about the attorney's actions. Many lawyers live an unbalanced life. The ABA survey, discussed above, showed that in 1984, 35 percent of respondents reported that they worked 200 or more hours a month. By 1990, that figure had increased to 50 percent, and 13 reported that they work more than 240 hours. Anecdotal reports suggest that work demands have increased in more recent years. Many lawyers lose themselves in their work at the expense of family, social, and recreational aspects of living. Their marriages are more likely to fail and their relationships with children and friends suffer. Their neglect of exercise and the non-work pleasures that are an essential part of life itself can cause physical and emotional problems. Many consider that work and success in their lawyering supersedes all else. Unchecked ambition may degenerate into uncivil, discourteous, unduly competitive or aggressive actions, if not outright ethical violations.

Lawyers often deal with distress by exhibiting hostility. John Barefoot's research study followed University of North Carolina graduates as they practiced law over a 30-year period. One of every six lawyers studied scored over one standard deviation above the mean on hostility measures. These lawyers were over four times as likely to die as a result of cardiovascular disease compared to those who displayed significantly lower levels of hostility.

Increasing lawyer distress may be responsible for the progressive de-professionalism that has characterized the legal profession over the past generation or so, and, in turn, such deprofessionalism has undoubtedly increased lawyer distress and dissatisfaction. Lawyering once was more of a guild in which attorneys treated one another with respect and civility. Sadly, this has changed dramatically. Disciplinary actions against lawyers and ethics code violations by attorneys have increased. Malpractice suits against lawyers by disgruntled clients have become more frequent. Professional meetings lament the uncivil, discourteous, and aggressive behavior displayed by attorneys towards other attorneys and non-lawyers. Rambo-style litigation tactics, with their win-at-all-costs mentality, are decried. Lawyers complain about the increasing commercialization of the profession. In many ways, it has become more a business than a profession. Becoming a partner in a law firm once meant a stable professional life working with fellow partners. Now, everything seems to be measured by the bottom line. Partners who do not generate sufficient income are squeezed out, and venerable firms are the subject of mergers, acquisitions, and disintegration. This lack of stability and predictability has led to an every person for himself mentality, with accompanying deterioration of professional

relationships and their replacement with a pervasive sense of distrust. The ca-
maraderie and loyalty that once prevailed in the profession have broken down.
Law firm partners and associates increasingly feel that they are employees of
corporations, rather than members of firms. Moreover, many come to regard
the work they spend a great majority of their waking hours on as meaningless
and unsatisfying. Like Herman Melville's fictional lawyer, Bartleby, they see
their work as a "dull, wearisome, and lethargic affair" and experience the firm
as rendering them voiceless and invalidated.

Deprofessionalization is also evidenced by the blatant and offensive adver-
tising engaged in by some attorneys. This underscores the transition of
lawyering from a professional undertaking to a commercial enterprise. In short,
there has been a marked deterioration in professional life, which further exacerbates lawyer dissatisfaction and distress.

3. Factors Contributing to Lawyer Distress

As Daicoff shows, lawyer distress is statistically correlated with several
factors. These include work environment, stress level, anger, marital dissatisfaction, failure to use social support systems when experiencing stress, and
conflicts between the demands of personal life and career. Interestingly,
however, she concludes that attorney distress is not statistically correlated with
the number of hours worked, passing the state bar examination, the size of
one's law practice, or 'feeling in control of one's work.' This latter factor may
seem surprising. Both doctors and lawyers feel out of control in regards to
their work, but doctors suffer from a near-zero depression rate. Lawyers who
experience professional satisfaction report high autonomy in selecting and performing their work and in choosing their clients, no conflict between career
and personal demands or conflict of roles, and a strong social support network.
As with people in general, attorneys experience higher professional satisfaction
with increased age and income level.

Professor Benjamin has analyzed three factors that contribute to lawyer dissatisfaction: pressures of a deteriorating work environment, increased levels
of mental and physical distress (depression, anxiety, interpersonal problems,
and stress-induced physical illness), and a decreased ability to cope with distress
by using social support, relaxation, exercise, or humor. These factors affected
the lawyers' quality of work, productivity, relationships with their families,
firms, and clients, and level of dissatisfaction with the profession. Other factors
that are likely to contribute to lawyer distress include excessive workload, financial rewards that are felt to be incommensurate with work effort, the high

conflict of litigation or political conflicts within the law office, the feeling that the attorney's work is under-appreciated or too heavily criticized, lack of peer support, and unrealistic expectations.

Attorney Sofia Yakren blames lawyer distress on the principles of "zealous advocacy and moral non-accountability." These principles, whether used in litigation or transactional work, represent the dominant view in the profession, which is reflected in the bar's disciplinary codes, the case law on lawyer discipline, and the commentary on professional responsibility. According to Yakren, these values make lawyers a "mere instrument of the client," regardless of whether they seem just to the lawyer. As a result, loyalty to the client is the predominant professional duty, subordinating any moral duty to respect the interests of third parties and the public. Instead of considering the interests of others as imposing a moral claim upon the lawyer, he or she sees these others as a means to the accomplishment of the client's objectives. A form of moral tunnel vision results, which becomes a rationalization for conduct that many would regard as morally reprehensible.

This moral myopia may actually start in law school. Although many students enter law school with idealism and a sense of morality, the first year of law school soon strips away their values and presents them with a vision of the lawyer as an aggressive litigator who aims to win at all costs. Law school still relies heavily on the case method of legal education, the dominant teaching approach for 140 years, in which students read appellate cases and dissect them under the Socratic questioning of the professor in order to understand the appellate courts' decisions. The law schools' over-reliance on the case method as a teaching device, its emphasis on teaching trial and appellate advocacy skills, and its deification of the adversary system as a mode of resolving disputes shape attitudes about what it means to be a lawyer.

Law school thus indoctrinates students with a view of lawyering char - acterized by excessive adversarialness. Young lawyers grow up within a professional culture that regards litigation as first class lawyering, and relegates counseling, problem solving, and prevention to a second-class status. However, the high cost, lengthy delays, emotional stress, and moral challenges of participating in litigation make it a singularly inappropriate method of dispute resolution for most clients. Even so, too many students come to see litigation as the appropriate role of the lawyer, a vision reinforced by pervasive media portrayals of lawyers. The role model many aspire to is the aggressive, take no prisoners, Rambo-like vision of the lawyer reflected in popular culture.

In a provocative social criticism of modern life, Georgetown linguist Deborah Tannen describes what she calls "the argument culture." She portrays our unfortunate culture of argument and critique and shows how it limits genuine dialogue, understanding, and creative problem solving. Tannen illustrates her point in several contexts of modern American life, including politics, journalism, academia, and most relevant for our purposes, law. The excess adversarialness of the legal system implicitly regards all issues as having only two sides and represents a zero-sum game in which one party must win, and the other lose. Often, however, there is some merit in both positions and the best resolution of the controversy would be compromise. Litigation becomes a polarizing winner-take-all war in which the attorneys cast all issues in black or white terms, ignoring the fact that in reality many can more appropriately be seen as nuanced shades of gray. This excessive adversarialness seems central to much of American lawyering, and to the conception of lawyering fostered by both legal education and the media.

Yet, this role may be emotionally and morally damaging to the lawyers who play it, "requiring them to put aside their consciences and natural inclination toward human compassion." Lawyers thus rationalize and justify conduct and legal practices that are disturbing, if not deplorable. These include such discovery abuses as attempts to conceal the truth and to make the process so burdensome and costly that the adverse party will give up. They also include badgering cross-examination of an adverse party designed to discourage many victims of wrongdoing (a rape victim or victim of child molestation, for example) from pursuing their remedies. Lawyers also learn to instruct their clients not to apologize even if their responsibility for an accident, crime, or breach of duty is clear. Often, the lawsuit, rather than redressing grievances, exacerbates suffering and prevents the parties from getting on with their lives. In some areas of practice, matrimonial law, for example, many lawyers fan the flames of the client's anger and desire for revenge, and push the client into a disastrous litigation that imposes severe psychological and financial costs on the divorcing couple and their children.

Some lawyers seem to thrive on being aggressive pit bulls in the no-holds-barred war that litigation has become. Many, however, experience inner conflict and psychological distress. Psychologist Martin Seligman posits that the "deepest factor" contributing to lawyer distress is this conception of law as an ultra competitive win-loss game. This role and the excess adversarialness that the profession fosters themselves can produce psychological difficulties, encouraging the development of suspiciousness, hostility, and aggression.

Law school not only glorifies excessive adversarialness, but also does an insufficient job of teaching healthy professional values. It subjects students to an acculturation process that often causes them to set aside human values in favor of external symbols of success. Anthropologist Elizabeth Mertz studied the educational process used in law schools to teach students to "think like lawyers."

This process involves replacing one set of thinking skills and language with another. Students first learn to search through cases for facts and arguments. They learn to set aside their sense or morality, fairness, and sensitivity to human suffering, and filter the facts through legal concepts. Students then parse legal authority and form strategic arguments around these central issues utilizing a combative dialogue. These basic findings were consistent across law schools, even when accounting for differences among teachers and teaching styles. The way law school teaches students to "think like a lawyer" may diminish creativity and overemphasize consistency, rules, and rationality over ambiguity, social context, and emotion.

Many professors still use a rigorous form of the Socratic method, calling upon students publicly to state and defend their views of the case under consideration. The professor's mission is to teach legal analysis and advocacy skills by demonstrating that any position is arguable and that, implicitly, none are necessarily correct. Students are taught that they can argue both sides of an issue. In their legal practice, they will need to figure out how best to advocate on their clients' behalf. Using the Socratic method to analyze an appellate case, the professor calls upon students, asking them to state the issues, describe the court's holding, and either defend or criticize it. Whatever the student responds, the professor demonstrates the inadequacy and flaws in the student's answer, sometimes embarrassing the student in the process, and thereby reducing the student's self-esteem and feelings of self-efficacy.

When the student defends a position by invoking fairness and justice, the professor laughs sarcastically and asks what these values really mean. The point of this exercise may be a good one—the sharpening of analytical and advocacy skills—but the result may be to induce a sense of ethical relativism. There is no right answer, the student soon learns. It's all about making arguments on behalf of a position, no matter how credible.

Moral values thus are stripped away, and the student soon learns the implicit message that they are largely irrelevant in lawyering. As the Carnegie Foundation's report on legal education concludes, the teaching methods used in the first year of law school teach students "to set aside their desire for justice." They are taught that their moral concerns and compassion for the people involved in the cases under discussion should not "cloud their legal analysis." Legal education's almost exclusive focus on abstraction and neglect of social context may be a good way to teach legal analytical skills, but does so at the expense of "developing the ethical and social dimensions of the profession."

Thus, the student's intrinsic moral values are worn away by what occurs in their first-year classes. A moral vacuum results. What really is important, the law student may wonder. The answer that most come to, and that the law school may implicitly support, is that winning, success, prestige, and wealth are the important values. This message is reinforced by cinematic and television depictions of lawyering. *L.A. Law*, for example, glorifies winning, partnership in a prestigious firm, and becoming wealthy—illustrated by the L.A. Law license plate on a Mercedes Benz. TV shows like *Boston Legal* and *Shark* celebrate a "no-holds-barred," aggressive vision of litigation often unhampered by ethical norms. Winning is everything, these shows demonstrate, not how you play the game.

The extrinsic values of winning, power, prestige, and wealth thus replace the intrinsic ones that many students possessed when they entered law school. What results is a loss of idealism and a cynical attitude that defines professional success narrowly and artificially. If these extrinsic exemplars of success are all that count, it becomes easy to justify creative billing practices, and soon other forms of dishonesty, in practice. When an individual's actions are based largely on extrinsic motivation, as Professor Larry Krieger shows, he or she predictably will experience "decreased well-being, sense of meaning, and personal integration." In contrast, when an individual's actions are based on intrinsic motivation, he or she experiences the inherent satisfaction of acting consistently with one's deepest convictions and beliefs, "enhanced well-being, increased meaning, and increased personal and social integration."

This moral resocialization that begins in law school inevitably produces psychological distress in all but the sociopathic members of the profession. The moral sense that almost all students develop before law school cannot be so easily suppressed. When our professional lives are incongruent with our inner values, the result is inevitably psychological distress. Lawyers practicing without a moral compass will predictably experience intense dissatisfaction, stress, and a variety of psychological and physical maladies.

Other aspects of legal education contribute to professional dissatisfaction and distress. Former Dean Daisy Floyd has reported on law student reactions to various aspects of their education drawn from several classes she taught on legal education and on ethics. The highly competitive environment of the law school, these students reported, hampered interaction with fellow students. Peer pressure to excel makes many classroom environments actively hostile. Students compete for the prizes of law school—high grades, law journal membership, and large law firm and judicial clerkship employment during law school and after graduation. Students who do not achieve these markers of success experience feelings of failure and inadequacy.

The value placed by the law school culture on rational, analytical thought almost to the exclusion of other qualities, is seen by Floyd's students as devaluing emotional life and relationships. Indeed, law school was viewed as diminishing the ability to sustain relationships with family and friends. Law school is seen as fostering social isolation and discouraging collaboration. Law school, they report, also causes students to lose the sense of purpose that brought them to the law and the passion they had hoped to find in professional life. As a result, they suffer reduced expectations about professional life and are willing to accept unfulfilling work because they expect there are no other options. The fears and vulnerabilities that legal education inevitably engenders are not tolerated by the law school culture, with the result that students soon learn to hide their self-doubts and anxieties under a mask of self-assuredness. This may lead to a professional life in which lawyers learn to be insincere and artificial.

Law school and then the profession itself teaches lawyers that they must be zealous representatives of their clients' interests. The model is one of passionate, fervent, and often aggressive advocacy, sometimes involving trickery, intimidation, and emotional bullying of an adverse witness, a party, or another lawyer. Attorney Sophia Yakren shows that when these outer displays of zealousness conflict with a lawyer's inner feelings, the professional role contemplates a form of emotional detachment. However, this form of detachment imposes moral and psychological costs, which Yakren seeks to capture through use of the sociological theory of "emotional labor." The concept of emotional labor describes the psychological stress that workers experience when organizational norms or rules of conduct require workers to act in ways that are inconsistent with their genuine emotions. We cannot divorce our professional from our personal lives without suffering feelings of inner conflict and emotional dissonance. Yakren posits that legal norms requiring zealous advocacy and emotional detachment cause lawyers at times to suppress their true feelings and personal notions of justice, which imposes emotional costs. These costs, she shows, include "drug and alcohol abuse, headaches, absenteeism, burnout, poor self-esteem, depression, cynicism, role alienation, and self-alienation."

4. The Role of Lawyer Personality Traits in Lawyer Distress

Given the size and diversity of the legal profession, it would seem hazardous to analyze personality traits across lawyers generally. Moreover, almost no systematic research has been done in this area. Nonetheless, professor Daicoff speculates about lawyer personality traits and their relationship to lawyer dissatisfaction and stress. In attempting to generalize about lawyer personalities,

Daicoff stresses competitiveness and aggressiveness, especially among trial lawyers. These are historically masculine traits, but the increasing number of female lawyers may find it necessary to adopt these traits in order to succeed within a male-dominant profession. Daicoff also points to an achievement-orientation among lawyers, the need to compete against an internal or external standard of excellence. She suggests that lawyers are more materialistic, as a result, and possess less altruism, humanitarianism, and desire to help others. Using personality categories associated with the Myers-Briggs inventory, Daicoff suggests that lawyers demonstrate a particular decision-making style. They emphasize rational analysis, rather than feeling. They have a preference for a "rights orientation" in making moral decisions (as opposed to an "ethic of care" or "care orientation"). They emphasize obligations over emotions, interpersonal harmony, and relationships. Daicoff sees lawyers as more pragmatic than altruistic, and suggests that they are likely to lose their altruism and idealism as they practice. To the extent that they start out in non-traditional careers, such as public interest work, they seek to move to higher-paying private or corporate practice. More than in other fields, women lawyers may tend to forego an ethic of care in favor of achievement-oriented, competitive, and aggressive professional work.

Daicoff's work suggests that before law school lawyers exhibit a preference for dominance, leadership abilities, outgoingness, an interest in school and reading, and a de-emphasis on emotional or interpersonal matters. The law school's emphasis on external rewards and de-emphasis on internal desires tends to mold the lawyer personality. Daicoff concludes that law students lose their intrinsic values and become less idealistic, introspective, and interested in public service work, community, intimacy, personal growth, and inherent satisfaction. The external rewards that law students covet include appearance, attractiveness, the esteem of others, and an increased interest in private practice. As a result, students become more realistic and practical. They are more likely to be competitive, task-related, and professional in tone. Those who are people-oriented and who care about interpersonal relations tend to receive lower grades in law school. Students who came to law school with an ethic of care tend to shift toward a rights orientation.

The norms and practices of the legal profession also mold lawyer personality. As Professor Daicoff shows, the legal profession emphasizes extroversion, thinking, and judging. These manifest themselves through a preference for logical analysis, cool and impersonal reasoning, cost benefit analyses, tolerance of conflict and criticism, structured work, scheduling and planning, finality of decisions, a 'cut-to-the-chase' approach, and elevation of a client's rights over other concerns. The profession reinforces traditional masculine traits, including aggression, dominance, autonomy, action, competition, decisiveness, persistence, self-confidence, superiority, and ability to withstand pressure. It de-emphasizes traditional feminine traits, including an ethic of care, community, awareness and understanding of the feelings of others, emotion, gentleness, kindness, helpfulness, and interpersonal warmth. Non-competitiveness, altruism, lack of materialism, and feelings are disfavored, and lawyers possessing these traits may feel they do not fit within the profession, with resulting career dissatisfaction.

As mentioned above, it seems hazardous to generalize about lawyer personality traits. Assuming there to be some validity to this notion, however, we might speculate about the impact of such personality traits on lawyer dissatisfaction and distress. The answer probably depends on the inner values that the people who become lawyers possess. To the extent that lawyers are brought up believing that community, caring about others, kindness, and integrity are important values, they may find traditional modes of lawyering dissatisfying. To the extent they adopt the extrinsic values and accompanying personality traits that law school and the profession reinforce, they may experience inner conflict and resulting unhappiness in their professional roles. To the extent they follow the extreme work ethic of the profession, working 60 to 80 hours per week or more, they may inevitably neglect family, friends, and physical and cultural activities that may be essential to having a balanced personality.

Some lawyers are, of course, happy within the profession. Their values are more in-line with the extrinsic symbols of success that the media and the profession celebrate. Some are untroubled by the moral challenges that the profession sometimes imposes. Other lawyers will tolerate the professional norms and practices of existing concepts of lawyering, suppressing the concerns and conflicts that others will find intolerable. Members of this segment of the profession will experience varying degrees of distress, sometimes coping with it in unhealthy ways. Those who find the conflict between professional life and their personal values intolerable will experience even greater distress and professional burnout, and ultimately will leave the profession or create a more satisfying niche within it.

Conclusion

Considerable anecdotal evidence suggests that many lawyers are unhappy within the profession and experience emotional distress and serious psychological problems. The existing survey literature concerning lawyer attitudes and distress largely confirms this view. Much of it, however, is based on limited sample sizes and low response rates. A more recent study by professors Monahan and Swanson—a longitudinal study of the class of 1990 University of Virginia Law School graduates that had a response rate of 72 percent—reached a contrary conclusion. Overall, 81 percent of respondents reported satisfaction with their choice to become lawyers. Levels of distress were not inquired into. While this study points in a different direction, it has its own limitations. It studies only one class of students from one of the nation's preeminent law schools, and, therefore, cannot be generalized to the profession as a whole. Although non-response rates in the studies reporting lawyer dissatisfaction and distress are high, they are more consistent with the anecdotal reports. Moreover, they may actually underreport the extent of dissatisfaction and distress. Lawyers who leave the profession may not be reached by these surveys or may be less likely to respond. Those who do respond may tend to be more successful and probably are not suffering from high levels of distress. Plainly, there is need for more solid empirical research. However, it seems fair to conclude that there is much dissatisfaction by lawyers with their career choices, and considerable emotional distress and psychological problems within the profession.

The remainder of this book seeks to set forth a new model of lawyering designed to make professional life more satisfying and less distressful for those entering and who already are within the profession. This model also seeks to increase client satisfaction with their attorneys. Chapter 2 sets forth this emerging model of lawyering, a model heavily influenced by therapeutic jurisprudence and preventive law. The remainder of the book describes several areas of law practice and shows how they can be transformed by the model proposed. Chapter 3 examines the initial attorney/client interview. It shows how to conduct it in order to establish a foundation of trust and confidence for the professional relationship. Chapter 4 describes the lawyer's role as problem avoider. It suggests how a therapeutic/preventive approach can help keep a client out of legal trouble. Chapter 5 examines the role of the lawyer as peacemaker, analyzing ways that lawyers can resolve disputes for their clients without resorting to litigation. Finally, chapter 6 analyzes the role of the lawyer as healer. It illustrates how in a variety of civil and criminal contexts the lawyer can help improve the client's emotional well-being by counseling the client on ways to achieve healing and reconciliation, and when needed, rehabilitation. The book sets forth a revolutionary agenda that is much needed and that can help refashion the legal profession into one that more effectively meets the needs of its clients and produces a greater measure of both client and attorney satisfaction.

References

American Bar Association. *At the Breaking Point: The Report of a National Conference on the Emerging Crisis in the Quality of Lawyers' Health and Lives, and Its Impact on Law Firms and Client Services.* Chicago: ABA, 1991.

Association of American Law Schools. "Report of the AALS Special Committee on Problems of Substance Abuse in the Law Schools." 44 *J. Legal Educ.* 35 (1994).

Barefoot, John C., K. Dodge, B. Peterson, W. Dahlstrom, and R. Williams Jr., "The Cook-Medley Hostility Scale: Item Content and Ability to Predict Survival." 51 *Psychosomatic Med.* 46 (1989).

Beck, Connie, Bruce D. Sales, and G. Andrew H. Benjamin. "Lawyer Distress: Alcohol-Related Problems and Other Psychological Concerns Among a Sample of Practicing Lawyers." 10 *J.L. & Health* 1 (1996).

Benjamin, G. Andrew H. "Reclaim Your Life, Reclaim Your Practice." 44 *Trial* 31 (2008).

Benjamin, G. Andrew H., Alfred Kaszniak, Bruce Sales, and Stephen B. Shanfield. "The Role of Legal Education in Producing Psychological Distress Among Law Students and Lawyers." 11 *Law and Soc. Inquiry* 225 (1986). First published online in 2006. doi: 10.1111/j.1747-4469.1986.tb00240.x.

Daicoff, Susan. "Asking Leopards to Change Their Spots: Can Lawyers Change? A Critique of Solutions to Professionalism by Reference to Empirically-Derived Attributes." 11 *Geo. J. Legal Ethics* 547 (1998).

Daicoff, Susan. *Lawyer, Know Thyself: A Psychological Analysis of Personality Strengths and Weaknesses.* Washington, D.C.: American Psychological Association, 2004.

Eaton, William W., James C. Anthony, Wallace Mandel, and Roberta Garrison. "Occupations and the Prevalence of Major Depressive Disorder." 32 *J. Occupational Med.* 1085 (1990).

Floyd, Daisy Hurst. "The Development of Professional Identity in Law Students." (June 2002). Accessed December 2, 2014. http://www.law.fsu.edu/academic_programs/humanizing_lawschool/images/daisy.pdf.

Krieger, Lawrence S. "Institutional Denial About the Dark Side of Law School, and Fresh Empirical Guidance for Constructively Breaking the Silence." 52 *J. Legal Educ.* 112 (2002).

Melville, Herman. Bartleby, the Scrivener: A Story of Wall Street. Salt Lake City: Project Gutenberg Literary Archive Foundation, 2004.

Mertz, Elizabeth. *The Language of Law School: Learning to "Think Like a Lawyer."* New York: Oxford University Press, 2007.

Monahan, John and Jeffrey Swanson. "Lawyers at Mid-Career: A 20-Year Longitudinal Study of Job and Life Satisfaction." 6 *J. Empirical Legal Stud. 451* (2009). First published online August 20, 2009. doi: 10.1111/j.1740-1461.2009.01150.x.

Ronner, Amy D. *Law, Literature, and Therapeutic Jurisprudence.* Durham, N.C.: Carolina Academic Press, 2010.

Schiltz, Patrick J. "On Being a Happy, Healthy, and Ethical Member of an Unhappy, Unhealthy, and Unethical Profession." 52 *Vand. L. Rev.* 871 (1999).

Seligman, Martin. *Authentic Happiness: Using the New Positive Psychology to Realize Your Potential for Lasting Fulfillment.* New York: Free Press, 2002.

Sheldon, Kennon M. and Lawrence S. Krieger. "Does Legal Education Have Undermining Effects on Law Students? Evaluating Changes in Motivation, Values, and Well-Being." 22 *Behav. Sci. & L.* 261 (2004).

Sullivan, William M., Anne Colby, Judith W. Wegner, Lloyd Bond, and Lee S. Shulman. *Educating Lawyers: Preparation for the Profession of Law.* San Francisco: Jossey-Bass/Wiley, 2007.

Tannen, Deborah. *The Argument Culture: Moving from Debate to Dialogue.* New York: Random House, 1998.

Yakren, Sofia. "Lawyer as Emotional Laborer." 42 *U. Mich. J.L. Reform* 141 (2008).

Chapter 2

The Therapeutic Jurisprudence/ Preventive Law Model of Lawyering

This book proposes a model of lawyering based on an integration of two scholarly law reform movements—therapeutic jurisprudence and preventive law. Therapeutic jurisprudence is an interdisciplinary approach to law that builds on the basic insight that law is a social force that has inevitable (if unintended) consequences for the mental health and psychological functioning of those it affects. It is an interdisciplinary approach to legal scholarship and law reform that sees law itself as a therapeutic agent. This field was initiated in the late 1980s by Professor David Wexler and myself, and has since expanded dramatically. Therapeutic jurisprudence suggests that the positive and negative consequences imposed by law on the emotional life of the individual and society be studied with the tools of the behavioral sciences. It further posits that, consistent with considerations of justice and other relevant normative values, law be reformed to minimize anti-therapeutic consequences and to facilitate achievement of therapeutic ones. Therapeutic jurisprudence suggests that law should value psychological health, should strive to avoid imposing anti-therapeutic consequences whenever possible, and when consistent with other values served by law, should attempt to bring about healing and wellness.

Although the approach originated in the area of mental health law, it has quickly expanded beyond that context, and has become a mental health law approach to law generally. As illustrated by the book that Wexler and I co-edited in 1996, *Law in a Therapeutic Key*, the therapeutic jurisprudence perspective has now been applied in the contexts of criminal law, family law, juvenile law, disability law, discrimination law, health law, evidence law, tort law, contracts and commercial law, labor arbitration, workers' compensation law, probate law, and the legal profession. It since has expanded to include judging and the use of courts to solve psychosocial problems, civil and criminal procedure, criminology, immigration law, bankruptcy law, public health law, international human rights law, and alternative dispute resolution. The approach has provoked an entire field of original interdisciplinary work by law professors, psychologists, sociologists, criminologists, philosophers, lawyers, and judges. Moreover, it has emerged as a global scholarly movement, and now includes scholarship not only by Americans, but by scholars, judges, and practitioners from every continent except Antarctica. In recent years, there has been growing interest in a dimension of therapeutic jurisprudence that takes the law as given and explores ways in which existing law might be most therapeutically applied. This aspect of therapeutic jurisprudence explores the ways in which various legal actors (such as judges, lawyers, police, administrators, and expert witnesses testifying in court) play their roles.

Over the last twenty years, a number of new conceptions concerning the lawyer's role have emerged. All seem to share a more humanistic orientation that seeks to lessen lawyering's excessively adversarial nature, improve clients' well-being in general, and enhance clients' psychological well-being in particular. Professor Susan Daicoff calls these the "vectors" of the "comprehensive law movement"—therapeutic jurisprudence, preventive law, creative problem solving, holistic law, restorative justice, the increasing array of alternative dispute resolution mechanisms, including collaborative law, and the emergence of problem solving courts. These models all seek to move beyond an exclusive focus on clients' legal rights or interests, in favor of approaches that value clients' human needs and emotional well-being. These models represent a broadened conception of the lawyer's role; they call for an interdisciplinary, psychologically oriented perspective and enhanced interpersonal skills.

With its psychological orientation and focus on emotional well-being, therapeutic jurisprudence is a common thread running through these various movements. Therapeutic jurisprudence brings a more theoretical and interdisciplinary perspective to lawyering than these other models. As a result, therapeutic jurisprudence can be viewed as an organizing framework for these emerging movements.

An important direction in therapeutic jurisprudence scholarship has been its concern with how law is applied. Not only can the rule of law itself be regarded as a therapeutic agent, but even when legal rules remain static, the way they are applied can have important therapeutic consequences for those affected. Judges, lawyers, police officers, expert witnesses testifying in court, and governmental officials at every level have a wide range of discretion in how they apply the law and how they function can impact the psychological well-being of the individuals whose lives they touch. It therefore is important that these legal actors understand that, among their other roles, they function as therapeutic agents. It is hoped that this understanding will be transformative. If they know that their actions either can impose psychological harm or facilitate emotional well-being, they should strive to minimize the anti-therapeutic consequences of their conduct and maximize its therapeutic potential.

This book focuses on the role of the lawyer as a therapeutic agent. Therapeutic jurisprudence has spawned a reconceptualization of the role of the lawyer. It envisions lawyers who practice their profession with an ethic of care, enhanced interpersonal skills, a sensitivity to their clients' emotional well-being as well as their legal rights and interests, and a preventive law orientation that seeks to avoid legal problems. This has been described as the therapeutic jurisprudence/preventive law model of lawyering.

Therapeutic jurisprudence explicitly values clients' psychological well-being and recognizes that their legal involvement, including their interaction with their lawyer, will produce inevitable psychological consequences for them. As a result, lawyers functioning within this model are inevitably therapeutic agents in the manner in which they deal with their clients. Once this insight is absorbed, it should change the conception of lawyering held by lawyer and client alike. Lawyers embracing this broadened conception of the professional role strive to avoid or minimize imposing psychologically damaging effects on their clients. They unambiguously value their clients' emotional well-being, and in their problem analysis, problem solving, and litigation efforts they seek not only to protect and promote their clients' rights and economic interests, but also to improve, or at least preserve, their clients' emotional lives. These lawyers are psychologically oriented and apply insights and approaches drawn from the behavioral sciences.

Lawyers applying a therapeutic jurisprudence approach practice law animated by the value of caring for the client's emotional life. This ethic of care, however, disavows paternalism. Therapeutic jurisprudence work has often stressed self-determination's psychological value and has criticized paternalism as anti-therapeutic. Therapeutic jurisprudence is committed to client-centered counseling. The lawyer may have her own views about the client's best interest and certainly should discuss these views with the client when appropriate. In so doing, however, she should avoid paternalistic or manipulative attitudes and approaches and should always remember that it is the client who makes the ultimate decision. Although the client is the ultimate decision maker regarding the course to follow, the attorney/client dialogue shapes that decision, and sometimes it is appropriate for the attorney to question a client's position to ascertain whether a preferable alternative exists in terms of accomplishing the client's underlying interests. The client, thus, sets the course, but does so via counsel's client-centered guidance.

Therapeutic jurisprudence's integration with preventive law has enlarged their collective contribution to improving the lawyering process. Preventive law originated in the early 1950s through Professor Lewis Brown's work at the University of Southern California Law School and was further developed by Professor Brown and former Dean Edward Dauer of the University of Denver College of Law. It is an approach designed to minimize the risk of litigation and other legal problems and to bring about greater certainty for clients concerning their legal affairs. Preventive law is a proactive approach to lawyering, emphasizing the lawyer's role as a planner.

Preventive law has much in common with preventive medicine. Indeed, the attorney/client relationship has many analogies to the doctor/patient relationship. Preventive medicine is premised on the concept that keeping people healthy is better and more cost effective than providing treatment for them once they become ill. Analogously, preventive law is based on the idea that avoiding legal disputes is inevitably better for the client than costly, time-consuming, and stressful litigation.

Just as physicians and other healthcare professionals can prevent future illness through periodic check-ups, screenings, inoculations, and nutritional counseling, attorneys can use a variety of techniques to identify and avoid future legal difficulties for their clients. The preventive lawyer, working in collaboration with a client, seeks to identify the client's long-term goals and to accomplish them through means that minimize exposure to legal difficulties and related emotional problems. Through creative problem solving, creative drafting, and the use of alternative dispute resolution techniques, the lawyer seeks to accomplish the client's objectives and to avoid legal problems. The preventive lawyer periodically meets with the client, conducting "legal check-ups" to receive updates on the client's business, personal, and family affairs, to keep the client out of trouble, to reduce conflict, and to increase the client's opportunities for success in life. Under the preventive framework, the legal relationship's goal is to maintain the client's legal health.

Moreover, just as physicians and other healthcare professionals must cultivate a "bedside manner" to properly play their preventative roles, preventive lawyers must develop a "desk-side manner" to function as effective preventive lawyers. Therapeutic jurisprudence can work in tandem with the preventive model to further a shared set of lawyering goals. It calls for an attorney/client relationship involving increased psychological sensitivity, an awareness of basic psychological principles and techniques, enhanced inter-personal and interviewing skills, and approaches for dealing with the emotional issues that are likely to arise just before or during a legal encounter.

In 1997, the principle originators of therapeutic jurisprudence and preventive law, together with Dennis Stolle, who at the time was a graduate student in the University of Nebraska, Law & Psychology Program, decided that there was considerable value in integrating these two fields to develop a new and more comprehensive model of lawyering. We did this through meet-ings, a program held at the Law & Society Association, and jointly authored writing. Integrating therapeutic jurisprudence and preventive law has broadened and reconceptualized each approach. This integration enhanced the potential of each to achieve its objectives. Therapeutic jurisprudence alone lacked the practical procedures for law office application. Preventive law alone lacked an analytical framework for justifying emotional well-being as a priority in legal planning. Bringing the two fields together served to remedy these de-ficiencies. Through a synthesis of preventive law and therapeutic jurisprudence, preventive law provided a framework for the practice of therapeutic jurispru-dence. And therapeutic jurisprudence, in turn, provided a rich and rewarding 'human aspect' and interdisciplinary orientation for a preventive lawyer to use in everyday law practice.

Viewed as one, the therapeutic jurisprudence/preventive law model consti-tutes a new method of lawyering that brings insights from the behavioral sci-ences into legal practices to improve clients' psychological well-being, to further clients' legal interests, and to minimize legal difficulties. It embraces both a therapeutic and a preventive orientation and sees law as a "helping profession." The therapeutic jurisprudence/preventive law model involves practical law office procedures, client counseling approaches, and an analytical framework for justifying emotional well-being as an important priority in legal planning and prevention. This combined model—which is already grounded in a rich body of social science and legal research—brings a much-needed interdisci-plinary perspective to the legal representation context. This integrated approach humanizes lawyering to a greater extent and provides lawyers with the enhanced interpersonal skills needed to be more effective interviewers, counselors, and problem solvers. Practicing law in this way results in happier and more fulfilled clients and produces a greater sense of personal and professional satisfaction for the lawyer.

Two concepts drawn from the therapeutic jurisprudence/preventive law model are especially helpful. The first is the "psycholegal soft spot"—a concept that refers to any aspect of the legal relationship or legal process that is likely to produce a strong negative emotional reaction in the client.

Sometimes the legal problems the clients face, or even the process of discussing it in the attorney's office, produces anger, stress, hard or hurt feelings, anxiety, fear, or depression. These feelings may impede attorney/client dialogue, thus preventing the lawyer from eliciting the entire story, understanding the client's real needs and interests, devising an appropriate strategy to solve the problem, or counseling the client in ways that the client is able to understand and follow. Sometimes these emotional issues precipitate legal problems or exacerbate them. Sometimes the anxiety the legal encounter induces causes the client to adopt a form of psychological resistance, denial, minimization, rationalization, or another psychological defense mechanism. Sometimes these defense mechanisms produce or escalate legal problems. The therapeutic jurisprudence/preventive lawyer understands how to identify these psycholegal soft spots and is able to apply various strategies to deal with them.

The lawyer is psychologically-minded and brings to the lawyer/client relationship a heightened sensitivity to the client's emotional state. These skills have not traditionally been taught in law school, although many attorneys have an intuitive grasp of the interpersonal skills required. Some law schools have begun to teach these skills, and indeed, skills training in these areas should be offered as an essential part of legal education. This book, in presenting a therapeutic jurisprudence conceptualization of law practice, discusses these interpersonal skills and illustrates their application in various aspects of law practice.

Another important therapeutic jurisprudence/preventive law technique is the "rewind exercise"—a good technique for teaching clients about how to avoid future problems and for teaching lawyers about how to see legal problems from a preventive perspective. The idea is a simple one: once a legal problem has become manifest, the task at hand is to solve it. This calls for the usual lawyering skills—e.g., negotiation or re-negotiation, settlement, and sometimes litigation. At this stage, the preventive lawyer is interested both in ending the controversy and in preventing its reoccurrence. In helping the client avoid a future reoccurrence of the problem, it is helpful for the lawyer to assist the client in understanding why the problem originally occurred. It is also a helpful technique for analyzing the possible alternative approaches the lawyer could have used to avoid the legal problem or the litigation that ensued, or to minimize any related negative emotional consequences for the client. The rewind approach can be expressed along these lines: "Let us 'rewind' the situation back in time to the period prior to the occurrence of the critical acts or omissions to determine more preferable approaches to solving the legal problem then at hand." What could the client have done at this point to avoid the problem? What can he or she do now to avoid its reoccurrence? What could the lawyer have done or suggested that might have prevented the problem or litigation?

Thinking about the problem in this way is analogous to performing an autopsy after a patient has died. Once the doctors identify the cause of death, they may learn something about how to avoid similar problems for their other patients or how to avoid any mistakes that may have contributed to the patient's death. Rewinding the legal problem can provide both lawyer and client with important insights regarding how to avoid or minimize future problems and their accompanying anti-therapeutic consequences.

The rewind approach should become an essential tool in legal education. Few law schools currently use this technique, although some professional schools in other areas—medical and business schools, for example—use similar approaches. Law students traditionally dissect appellate judicial opinions in Socratic discussion in the classroom. Many law schools have traditionally used assigned problems in connection with the reading of such appellate cases. This problem-method approach is a good one because it brings the case and the legal principals sought to be taught to life. Using the case method exclusively, in which the class analyzes a series of appellate opinions in order to understand the legal principles they reflect, does not go far enough. The traditional case method approach is extremely helpful in developing analytical and advocacy skills and the ability to "think like a lawyer." However, it provides little if any insight into the human relations that underlie the case and how the lawyers acted or should have acted in dealing with their clients and adversaries. A problem-solving approach brings more reality to the development of these skills by requiring the students to think about how to solve particular problems (based on hypothetical or actual fact patterns) and by focusing much of the classroom discussion on how lawyers can use legal materials—statutes, regulations, and judicial opinions—to solve these problems. Even this, however, does not go far enough. It too fails to focus on the underlying human relations and behavior that bring about legal problems or contribute to their solution.

Law schools should more explicitly address these human aspects of legal issues. The rewind exercise is an excellent technique for doing so. Like the problem method approach, it focuses the student's attention on actual legal problems and gets them to think about how to solve them. These techniques are a good device for developing creative problem-solving skills. But the rewind technique also includes the human aspects and emotional components of the problem. And, it focuses attention on how the problems could have been avoided, prevented, or minimized. Rather than exclusively relying on the reading of appellate opinions and developing an understanding of the court's reasoning in its decision and the legal arguments that were or should have been made by the lawyers, the rewind technique includes an analysis of the human context of the dispute. It asks law students to engage in a thought experiment. What would they do if they were the lawyer at the inception of a case or were consulted by the client before the dispute occurred (perhaps learning information in a legal checkup about the client's future plans)? By asking the student to think about what could have been done, and by discussing the various options in class, the students acquire a preventive orientation that sharpens their interpersonal skills. In rewinding the case, students are asked to think about the psycholegal soft spots that might occur and how they can deal with avoiding or minimizing the negative impact that the legal problem often imposes on the client's emotional well-being. Students and lawyers and continuing legal education programs that are taught with this approach acquire a heightened sensitivity to the emotional aspects of legal practice, a preventive orientation, and creative problem-solving skills.

This book frequently uses the rewind technique to present the therapeutic jurisprudence and preventive law skills that are needed if we are to re-imagine lawyering as the book proposes. The book teaches these skills in a variety of legal contexts. We have defined the therapeutic jurisprudence/preventive law approach to lawyering in this chapter, though by its nature the description of the approach is rather abstract. The remaining chapters of the book attempt to put meat on the bones of the approach by illustrating its specifics in a variety of legal practice contexts. In this way, it seeks to bring the approach to life and demonstrate its feasibility and advantages over existing models of lawyering. And so we are ready to illustrate how this evolving approach would work in the everyday practice of law.

References

Brown, Louis M. "The Law Office—A Preventive Law Laboratory." 104 *U. Pa. L. Rev.* 940 (1956).

Brown, Louis M. and Edward A. Dauer. *Perspectives On The Lawyer As Planner.* Mineola, N.Y.: Foundation Press, 1978.

Hardaway, Robert M. *Preventive Law: Materials On A Non-Adversarial Legal Process.* Cincinnati: Anderson Pub. Co., 1997.

Patry, Mark W., David B. Wexler, Dennis P. Stolle, and Alan J. Tomkins. "Better Legal Counseling Through Empirical Research: Identifying Psycholegal Soft Spots and Strategies." In *Practicing Therapeutic Jurisprudence: Law as a Helping Profession*, edited by Bruce J. Winick, David B. Wexler, and Dennis P. Stolle, 69–79. Durham, N.C.: Carolina Academic Press, 2000.

Stolle, Dennis P., David B. Wexler, Bruce J. Winick, Edward A. Dauer. "Integrating Preventive Law and Therapeutic Jurisprudence: A Law and Psychology Based Approach to Lawyering." 34 *Cal. W. L. Rev.* 15 (1999).

"Symposium: Therapeutic Jurisprudence and Clinical Legal Education and Skills Training." 17 *St. Thomas L. Rev.* 403–896 (2005).

Wexler, David B. and Bruce J. Winick. "Putting Therapeutic Jurisprudence to Work." 89 *A. B. A. J.* 54 (May 2003).

Wexler, David B. and Bruce J. Winick. *Law in a Therapeutic Key: Developments in Therapeutic Jurisprudence.* Durham, N.C.: Carolina Academic Press, 1996.

Winick, Bruce J. "A Legal Autopsy of the Lawyering in Schiavo: A Therapeutic Jurisprudence/Preventive Law Rewind Exercise." 61 *U. Miami L. Rev.* 595 (2007).

Winick, Bruce J. "The Expanding Scope of Preventive Law." 3 *Fla. Coastal L. J.* 189 (2002).

Winick, Bruce J. "Client Denial and Resistance in the Advance Directive Context: Reflections On How Attorneys Can Identify And Deal With A Psycholegal Soft Spot." 4 *Psychol. Pub. Pol'y L.* 901 (1998).

Winick, Bruce J., David B. Wexler, and Dennis P. Stolle. *Practicing Therapeutic Jurisprudence: Law as a Helping Profession.* Durham, N.C.: Carolina Academic Press, 2000.

Winick, Bruce J., David B. Wexler and Edward A. Dauer, guest eds. "Special Theme: Therapeutic Jurisprudence and Preventive Law: Transforming Legal Practice and Education." 5 *Psychol. Pub. Pol'y & L.* 793–1210 (1999).

Chapter 3

Starting Off the Relationship: The First Client Interview

The first time an attorney meets a new client is an opportunity for the attorney to establish trust and confidence and to begin to build the relationship. First impressions are always important, and tend to color the way the client regards the attorney and the nature of the professional alliance. This chapter makes some suggestions on how to conduct the initial interview with the client and the aims that the attorney should have in doing so.

For the client, the first encounter with the lawyer may be fraught with stress. It is probably safe to assume that most, if not all, clients experience some degree of anxiety when meeting an attorney for the first time. The very fact that they require the services of an attorney is likely to be the result of a stressful situation that the client is unable to resolve on his own. If it is the client's first time hiring a lawyer, he may be unsure about what to expect. Certain types of legal problems will likely produce greater levels of stress, such as criminal accusation, discharge from employment, divorce, imminent eviction, and the loss of food stamps or other benefits.

The attorney in such a situation has a variety of tools at his disposal to put the client at ease, to inspire confidence, and to gain trust. This starts even before the two ever meet face to face. It often will start when the client telephones the lawyer to make an appointment. As this is the first opportunity for attorney/client interaction, it is crucial that the attorney make a good first impression. The lawyer should ascertain the reason why the client would like an appointment, and in a friendly but authoritative manner should attempt to reassure the client and establish rapport. The attorney should demonstrate interest in the client's problem, request that he bring to the appointment any pertinent documents, and ask him if he has any immediate questions, all of which will begin to build the client's confidence that he is in the right hands. The attorney also should, at least in a general way, reveal his fee policy to the client when they speak over the phone. If the initial consultation is without charge, he certainly should say so; if not, the client also should know the expenses he will be incurring at the initial appointment. A fuller discussion of fees can occur at the appointment itself. The lawyer himself should have this conversation, not a secretary or associate. It is not too early, in this initial telephone conversation, for the attorney to focus on building trust and confidence.

When the client comes to the office, the layout of the waiting room may have an impact on the client's initial perceptions. What does the waiting room in the law office look like? Is it organized and welcoming or cluttered and in disarray? A professional, welcoming environment allows the client to feel confident in the quality of service the lawyer will provide. A non-professional environment does not.

The same concern applies to the set up of the attorney's office—how is the furniture arranged? The traditional set-up, with the client's chair positioned several feet in front of the attorney's desk, is the most authoritative arrangement and conveys the message that the attorney is the boss and is the one in control of the relationship. Rather than this conception of the attorney's role, the lawyer should strive to present himself as the client's ally, counselor, and advisor whose mission it is to help the client solve his problems in ways that defer to the client's autonomy.

For a client who is already uncomfortable and anxious, the traditional office setup may be an unattractive layout that may call to mind a school principal's office. A better, less intimidating option is to conduct the client interview away from the attorney's desk altogether, preferably at a group of chairs arranged around a coffee table. This arrangement is the most intimate, the least threatening to the client, and works especially well when there are multiple clients. However, if space considerations do not allow this, the attorney can help to put the client at ease simply by moving the position of the chairs around the attorney's desk. Positioning two chairs across a corner of the desk, rather than at each end, increases the intimacy of the environment. The arrangement of the office also communicates that the attorney is a trusted ally in helping the client deal with his problem, rather than a paternalistic, domineering authority figure who will tell the client what to do.

Shortly before the client arrives, the attorney should instruct his staff to hold all calls and not to interrupt the interview. He should put away his Blackberry and other items that might make the client feel that his concentration is diffused. He wants to give his client his undivided attention, and not appear distracted by other matters. He should clear his mind of any suppositions or expectations. He should be oriented in the present and open to what the client may present. His focus should be on what he can learn from the client and how he can serve his interests, legal and emotional. Some attorneys spend a few minutes meditating in order to clear their minds of extraneous chatter and to become present oriented.

Where the attorney chooses to greet the client also matters. Most often, the choice will be between the waiting room and the attorney's office, with most attorneys preferring the latter. Most clients, however, prefer to be met by the attorney in the waiting room, and led back to the attorney's office personally. This communicates to the client that the lawyer is not too busy and important to greet them personally and allows the attorney to put the client at ease through small talk during the walk to the office. The attorney should greet the client by name and introduce himself. He also should offer the client a coffee or soft drink. These initial comments, simple as they may be—did you have any trouble finding the office, for example—communicate to the client that they mean more to their attorney than a legal problem to be solved (and paid for), and provide a transition to the interview itself.

These preliminary interactions also serve a much more important, and often overlooked, purpose. Professor Gay Gellhorn's study of videotaped attorney/ client interviews has shown that initial statements by the client, either in response to the attorney's use of ice-breakers or at the outset of the interview, frequently contain information that is essential to the case. These revelations are often emotional, and provide both useful facts and context to the issue at hand. For instance, during the chitchat portion of one interview, the client, who was somewhat reluctantly seeking disability benefits, spoke emotionally about his eight younger sisters, for whom he had spent much of his life caring. This statement was a clue that the client's sense of self-worth had been disrupted by his switch from the role of caregiver to someone who is now being cared for, and explained his reluctance to achieve financial independence through being labeled "disabled."

Gellhorn's study found that many lawyers do not pay sufficient attention to these initial moments, assuming that they represent only inconsequential small talk. Several study participants who were watching interviews on tape literally fast-forwarded past this portion of the interview. This behavior has predictable and negative consequences for both interviewer and client. Some clients will repeat the information again and again until they are finally heard. Others will not repeat the information, perhaps assuming that the lawyer does not want to hear it, and will leave the interview feeling dissatisfied or hurt. For both client and lawyer, this is a waste of valuable time, and potentially, of valuable information, and may set the relationship off in the wrong direction.

Gellhorn's research showed that clients come to the first interview with a need to speak about specific things that they feel are important, and that it is critical for the attorney to recognize this, and allow their clients to tell their stories. This finding is consistent with a dissertation study that administered a questionnaire to clients of a university student legal service and of a legal aid society. The study found that clients approach the initial attorney interview with two basic goals—to be given the space to tell their story and to gain a legal perspective and interpretation of their situation. The study identified three factors that were highly correlated with client satisfaction with the initial interview: 1) the ability to raise all of the issues that the client wanted to, 2) an explanation from the lawyer of the legal aspects of the client's situation, and 3) the ability to be able to say everything that the client felt was important without undue interruption. The study further found that clients want to be able to control what is talked about, not necessarily how it is discussed. For instance, beyond the basic question, "What am I supposed to do?" clients were generally unconcerned with asking their own questions of the interviewer. Rather, they were willing to allow the attorney to take control of the interview, in terms of asking the questions, ascertaining facts, and then explaining the law to the client. This was true both for clients who stated that they preferred high levels of control in personal interactions and for clients who preferred less control. The authors concluded that the clients' need for a legal perspective outweighed the need for control of the conversation because the legal perspective allowed the clients to feel more in control of their own role in reaching a resolution to their problem. The major focus of the initial interview, this study suggests, is the client's need to reassert control over the situation that has produced the legal difficulty that brought him to see the lawyer. The lawyer therefore should attempt to frame the problem appropriately for the client, and in a reassuring way, suggest that there will be several possible ways of dealing with it that they will explore together. The lawyer should attempt to make the client feel that he is in the right hands and that a knowledgeable, experienced professional will help to guide him through the problem.

Unfortunately, aside from these few studies, little research has been conducted on how attorneys and clients interact in their initial meetings. The theoretical research on "procedural justice," however, would seem to have direct application to the attorney/client dialogue. Empirical studies of how litigants experience judicial and administrative hearings have led to the development of a literature on the psychology of procedural justice. This literature indicates that the process or dignitary value of a hearing is important to litigants. People who feel they have been treated fairly at a hearing—dealt with in good faith and with respect and dignity—experience greater litigant satisfaction than those who feel they were treated unfairly, with disrespect, and in bad faith. People highly value "voice," the ability to tell their story, and "validation," the feeling that what they have to say is taken seriously by the judge or other decision-makers. Even when the result of a hearing is adverse, people treated fairly, in good faith and with respect are more satisfied with the result and comply more readily with the outcome of the hearing. Moreover, they perceive the result as less coercive than when these conditions are violated, and even feel that they have voluntarily chosen the course that is judicially imposed. Such feelings of voluntariness rather than coercion tend to produce more effective behavior on their part. For many litigants, these process values are more important than winning.

These procedural justice considerations apply not only to the hearing or trial, but also to interactions between the attorney and client. In the initial client interview, the attorney needs to provide the client with "voice" and "validation." The client needs to tell his story and have the attorney listen attentively. A brief discussion of the confidential nature of attorney/client communications can reassure the client that he is free to share this information with his lawyer without fear of disclosure. "Tell me what brings you here today," the attorney can say, and then afford the client a full opportunity to tell his story. The lawyer can use open-ended questioning to encourage the client to tell his story in his own words and way, rather than feeling compelled to present the facts within the framework of the lawyer's more specific questions. The attorney can use the technique of active listening, punctuating the client's story with "Ah ha," and shaking his head "Yes." He should try not to interrupt the client's narration and either remain silent or say "go on," when there is a lull in the conversation. The attorney also can use reflective listening, occasionally summarizing what the client has said and adding comments that display empathy, such as "that must have made you feel upset," or "I'm sorry to hear that."

The attorney should encourage the client to relate the facts of the events in question and his reasons for visiting the lawyer. In addition, the lawyer can ask the client to relate his feelings about those events. The lawyer should at all times treat the client with dignity and respect and convey a sense of empathy and caring. I am your ally, and am here to help you, the lawyer's verbal and non-verbal modes of communication should stress.

Many lawyers are not good listeners. They are short on time and somewhat impatient, tending to jump quickly to conclusions at the early stages of the attorney/client dialogue, cutting the dialogue off because it is thought to be unnecessary to continue. But when the client is cut off in this way, the feeling may be created that the lawyer doesn't truly care about the client or about hearing the client's full story. Clients have a human need to tell their stories and to feel listened to by their lawyers in a way that is non-judgmental and empathic. The lawyer needs to convey sympathy and understanding. The lawyer needs to encourage the client to "open up," to communicate what has occurred and the feelings it produced. This is particularly important where the client has been the victim of a crime, accident, or other traumatic event. In such instances, the need to talk about the event with a trusted, sympathetic, and understanding confidant, if fulfilled, can do much to help the individual get past the event.

The lawyer therefore needs to understand the important lessons of the literature on procedural justice and how to apply them in the attorney/client interview. The therapeutic jurisprudence/preventive lawyer needs to develop his interpersonal skills so that he can make the client feel understood and appreciated. When the client is telling his story, the attorney needs to listen with rapt attention. He needs to convey, both verbally and non-verbally, that he practices law with an ethic of care and sees his role as serving his clients' interests and well-being. He needs to establish rapport with the client and forge an emotional bond. Other chapters in this book contain more specific details on psychological insights and approaches that can be used in the attorney/client relationship. These include: how to convey empathy; the forms of client questioning that are best calculated to elicit information and induce a climate of comfort in the relationship; how to deal with client denial and other psychological defense mechanisms; how to deal with anger and other strongly expressed emotions brought about by the legal problem; problems of transference and counter-transference; the social psychology of persuasion and motivation; and ways of increasing the likelihood of compliance by the client with the attorney's advice. These skills and topics are addressed within the context of dealing with specific kinds of problems in the legal relationship and performing specific roles—helping the client to avoid future legal problems, functioning as a peacemaker, helping to achieve healing and rehabilitation for the client, and dealing with the special stressors that litigation produces. The focus of this chapter is on the initial client encounter.

A developed literature exists in other professional contexts, particularly in that of the doctor/patient initial interview. Much of the rest of this chapter reviews that literature. It then draws insights from it that are applicable to the lawyer/client interaction.

Neither physicians nor lawyers are good listeners. They often start the process of analyzing the problem before the interviewee can finish his response, and cut off the response with additional questions. This conveys to the interviewee that he will not be able to relate fully what had occurred. It is insulting and shows an uncaring attitude and communicates that the professional will dominate the conversation. When the professional asks the client or patient a general question designed to prompt the individual to tell his story ("Tell me what happened" or "Tell me why you are here today"), he must remain silent, thereby signaling to the interviewee that he now should respond.

Although little research exists concerning the lawyer/client interview, a body of work probes the parallel context of the physician/patient dialogue. How do physicians conduct the first patient interview? What differing styles of interviewing do physicians use, and which are most effective? A study by Beckman and Frankel, which explored the relationship between physicians' interview styles and the collection of information about the patient's medical situation, found that the doctor's choice of interview technique at the beginning of an interview determines, in part, what the outcome will be. The authors found that open-ended questioning at the beginning of an interview is beneficial because it encourages patients to identify and elaborate on what they think is important, which leads to the collection of valuable information. It also may give the patient a greater feeling of control and validation. A question such as, "What brings you here today?" allows the interviewee to self-select what they will speak about and gives the impression that the doctor cares about what they have to say. However, the study also found that physicians often interrupted patients while they were speaking—in the study, 77 percent of interviewing physicians interrupted their patients before they could finish their initial statements. The authors concluded that these interruptions led to longer interviews, a loss of valuable information, and a feeling of dissatisfaction on the part of the patient. These conclusions mirror the results that Gellhorn found with regard to lawyers not paying sufficient attention to clients' opening comments.

Beckman and Frankel identified three basic types of medical interviewer styles. Elaborators listen to what the patient has stated, then encourage them to continue speaking in that same vein ("Tell me more about your headache."). Recompletors repeat the concern that the client has voiced back to the client, which encourages elaboration about the stated concern, but discourages disclosure of other concerns ("Your head is killing you?"). By contrast, neutral utterers say little, tacitly encouraging their patient to say whatever is on his or her mind. These interviewers, for instance, insert phrases like "mmhm" or "go-on" periodically.

The authors criticize the first two techniques because of their tendency to interrupt the patient before his full story can be told, thereby cutting short some relevant information and leading the physician to frame a premature hypothesis that may be unwarranted. By contrast, the authors suggest that neutral utterances can be most effective.

This method encourages the interviewee to identify and expand on whatever he thinks is important, which has two major benefits. First, for the physician, this style will often bring to light valuable information that the physician may not have thought to ask about. This helps to ensure that nothing is missed and that the doctor does not waste time on hypotheses that only fit part of the relevant information. Second, this type of conversation provides patients with a greater sense of satisfaction with the overall encounter, makes them more likely to remember what the physician said, more likely to follow a treatment plan, and less likely to sue the doctor for malpractice.

This technique resembles passive listening. Passive listening encourages the interviewee to continue his story. Yet, it lacks some of the value of active or reflective listening.

Active listening is an effective way to demonstrate that the interviewer has understood the interviewee. The interviewer summarizes what he thinks the interviewee's response was and reflects back to him its emotional content. The interviewer is careful not to interrupt the response or the interviewee's story, but to wait until a suitable pause occurs in the conversation. The interviewer does not repeat the response verbatim, but puts it in his own words. This response is based not only on the interviewee's verbal answers, but also on his non-verbal modes of communication—body language, tone of voice, etc. The interviewer is neutral, and does not convey a value judgment about the interviewee's responses. This technique allows confirmation of the accuracy of the interviewer's understanding, and also serves to convey empathy. Active listening also constitutes a good technique for establishing trust and confidence. It communicates to the interviewee that the interviewer is really understanding what the interviewee is saying and feeling.

Attorneys need to consider the parallels between the physician/patient first meeting and that of the attorney and client. Which of these styles is most effective in the lawyer/client context? Which techniques are preferable? Active or reflective listening would seem to have clear benefits for affording the client a sense of voice and validation, and for establishing the trust and confidence that are an essential ingredient of the professional relationship.

Research on the doctor/patient interview also examines the function of the interview and proposes ways of increasing its effectiveness. Lawyers also need to consider the extent to which the function of the lawyer/client interview has similar aims, and therefore calls for similar approaches. In their book *The Medical Interview*, Lipkin, Putnam, and Lazare reviewed approximately 25 years of medical interviewing research. The book identified and explored three core functions of the physician/patient interview: 1) determining the nature of the problem, 2) developing the therapeutic relationship, and 3) patient education.

The first function of the interview, determining the problem, is perhaps the most basic. The authors suggest several tasks to assist with this goal that translate well to the attorney/client relationship. First, the physician needs to possess a base of knowledge about the relevant diseases and disorders. In the attorney/client context, the equivalent step would be for the attorney to educate himself about the client's unique legal issue. If a client comes to the lawyer with a landlord/tenant problem, for instance, then the attorney needs to become an expert on landlord/tenant law if he is not already.

The next step in determining the nature of the problem is to become familiar with any psychosocial problems that the patient may have developed as a way to cope with his medical problem. In other words, how does the patient understand his disease and its impact on his life, and how is the patient behaving in the role of a patient with this particular problem? This step is no less important for the attorney. As was discussed in the beginning of this chapter, clients generally seek a lawyer's services as a response to a stressful situation that they have been unable to solve on their own. The very fact that they need a lawyer often adds to the stress. The lawyer can play a helpful therapeutic role simply by being aware that this stress may influence the client's behavior. In a divorce and child custody case, for example, a client who had thought himself to be happily married may behave in a way that seems irrational if he has not yet come to terms with the fact that he is soon to be divorced.

The final step in determining the nature of the problem is to create and test different hypotheses about the patient's disease and appropriate treatment. For a physician, this involves probing the patient's symptoms, conducting any needed medical tests, matching them to possible medical problems, ruling some out along the way, and deciding on a course of treatment. For the attorney, this may mean eliciting increasingly detailed information from the client in order to fully diagnose the client's legal problem and possible solutions. In an auto accident case, for instance, ascertaining who was likely at fault will assist the lawyer in deciding how to proceed. In a criminal case, the lawyer needs to make at least a preliminary assessment of whether the client is factually guilty, and if so, whether there are defenses that can be raised. If the client was at fault for the accident, or guilty of the crime charged, he may be unwilling to admit this at the outset. The lawyer should gently probe the client's description of what occurred. If he thinks the client is concealing the central facts that might render him liable or guilty, he should not press the client too much during their first encounter. If the client tells his lawyer a lie at the outset, it may be difficult for the client to later feel comfortable revealing this to his lawyer, and the lie and its concealment can undermine the client's comfort with his lawyer and the effectiveness of the entire relationship. The lawyer can probe the client's story in a more detailed way in subsequent meetings, and thereby provide the client with an opportunity to be fully forthcoming.

Aside from this potential dilemma, the lawyer should elicit from the client at least a brief description of what occurred so that he can properly diagnose whether there is liability or guilt and the existence of possible defenses. The lawyer will also need to explore different strategies for dealing with the problem. In a tort case, for example, these would include negotiation and settlement, various modes of alternative dispute resolution, and potential litigation. In a criminal case, it would involve a discussion of plea options (including possible plea bargaining), enrollment in a diversion program of rehabilitation, and the pre-trial and trial defense strategy. At this initial meeting, the lawyer also should get a sense of the client's goals, desires, and values. The lawyer is the agent of the client, and he therefore must understand his principal's basic objectives.

A serious potential problem that hampers both physician/patient and lawyer/client communication occurs when the patient is of a different background from that of the professional. If the interviewer can recognize these barriers to effective communication, he can overcome them and create a stronger relationship and one more likely to accurately elicit the nature of the problem. Physicians are cautioned to be alert to these differences and to reflect on the extent to which they may impact effective communication, the accuracy of diagnosis, and treatment decision making.

Common barriers include inconsistencies in the patient's verbal and nonverbal messages, resistance to the treatment, or the doctor's own discomfort with the patient. Is there a social or cultural difference that is making the patient or the physician uncomfortable, or that hinders effective communication? Are race, ethnicity, social class, gender, sexual orientation, or age differences creating the problem?

The physician needs to understand these areas of difference and to develop cross-cultural competence. He needs to be conscious of these potential hindrances to effective communication. Once he has identified the source of the problem, he can overcome it by discounting the biases that he may have, consciously or unconsciously, concerning these areas of difference, and by providing targeted emotional support. The physician needs to understand the insights of medical anthropology. How patients perceive their illnesses and decide about treatment options is culturally mediated. Moreover, how physicians diagnose illness, make treatment recommendations, and communicate to their patients about these matters may be based, in part, on the physician's perhaps mistaken understanding of the patient's culture (as well as these other sources of difference). Culture sometimes determines how and whether symptoms are interpreted as normal or abnormal. In some cultures, for example, diarrhea may be seen as normal, whereas in others, it is a distressing symptom of serious illness. Culture may also provide erroneous causal explanations for symptoms. Patients may be culturally predisposed to blame their symptoms on deviant behavior or some presumed physiological attribute, like bad blood. In America, medical practice presumes a patient with autonomy who will absorb the medical information provided by the physician and make a treatment decision based on informed consent. In other cultures, however, medical decision making resides more in the family. Physicians need to understand these cultural differences and avoid the potentially biasing effects on diagnosis and treatment that failing to take them into account can produce.

These concerns and challenges apply equally to attorney/client communications. Both the medical and legal literature discuss this problem of difference and how to acquire cross-cultural competence.

The second core function of the medical interview is developing the therapeutic relationship. This is perhaps the most important task of the initial interview. If the physician does this properly, it will lead to a variety of benefits for both the patient and the doctor, including successfully eliciting needed information from the patient, patient compliance with treatment recommendations, a reduction in the patient's stress, and increasing satisfaction in the professional relationship for both parties.

In many respects the doctor/patient relationship itself has an important therapeutic value. The concept of the therapeutic alliance, originated in the context of the psychotherapist-patient relationship, now is recognized to apply more generally to the physician-patient relationship. The actual caring, human relationship between therapist and patient is itself transformative or curative, and the professional relationship can itself therefore be regarded as a therapeutic agent. To reach its therapeutic potential, the therapist must establish an environment of safety and trust. A real and open patient-physician dialog concerning treatment planning and decision making is necessary to bolster the patient's faith in the physician and in the physician's dedication to the patient's best interests.

For this to occur, the physician, during the first interview, must engage the patient's trust and confidence. The physician, of course, should discuss the confidential nature of the professional relationship. Absent patient authorization, information gained in the relationship may not be disclosed to third parties. This is the foundation of the doctor/patient alliance because it facilitates open and frank discussion with the physician, which is necessary to the administration of proper medical care. The physician should explain that he has a fiduciary duty to the patient. He must act in the patient's best interests, and is enjoined to "do no harm." The physician should communicate any pertinent medical specialty and experience that he may possess, so as to assure the patient that he is in the right hands. He also should display his ability to ask relevant questions, give meaningful feedback, and to project an air of confidence.

The physician needs to explicitly elicit the patient's perspective on his symptoms and treatment options. The patient isn't an abstract disease, but a person suffering from a particular problem. The physician needs to understand the patient holistically, and therefore needs to know his basic values and relevant behavior patterns. Research on physician/patient interviews also shows that eliciting the patient's perspective is a valuable method to establish trust and develop a successful relationship. When patients believe that they have been genuinely listened to, they are more likely to comply with the physician's directions and are more likely to have a positive view of the relationship. As a result, physicians should ask their patients for their own definition of the problem, their own theory about its cause, any fears they may have related to moving forward with treatment, and their preferred methods of treatment.

At the initial meeting, the physician needs to demonstrate his interest in, respect for, and empathy with the patient. Forging a true therapeutic alliance requires that the physician take all of these essential steps at the outset. An important focus of the first lawyer/client interview similarly is the establishment of an effective professional relationship. The attorney, therefore, will need to take parallel steps at the first meeting in order to succeed in this endeavor. The need to create an effective relationship and the steps necessary to do so are strikingly similar for both professions. Both require a full measure of trust and confidence to achieve their potential. This may be more essential for the doctor/patient relationship because the relationship itself is an important ingredient in the patient's healing. However, this consideration applies as well to the attorney/client relationship. While this may not be its traditional conceptualization, under the re-imagined role for lawyers that this book calls for, the therapeutic jurisprudence/preventive lawyer also functions as a therapeutic agent and healing becomes an important dimension of the lawyer's role.

The expression of empathy is an essential ingredient in both the doctor/patient and lawyer/client initial interview. Empathy is the ability of the professional to enter the client's or patient's feelings and to see the world through that person's eyes, to walk in his moccasins, so to speak. As Atticus Finch, the attorney-hero of Harper Lee's *To Kill A Mockingbird*, puts it: "You never really understand a person until you consider things from his point of view—until you climb into his skin and walk around in it."

Empathy has both cognitive and affective components. The professional needs to convey both the intellectual response that he thinks the same way as the individual, and the emotional response that he feels the individual's pain and other emotions. The patient or client is experiencing a serious problem that prompts him to seek professional advice. When the professional listens to the client's problems with empathy, the client's anxiety level is reduced and his feeling of being understood increased. An empathic response, therefore, may be essential for establishment of the climate of comfort and trust that may be necessary to the formation of an effective professional relationship.

The problem likely has provoked various emotional reactions that cannot be ignored by the professional. These may include fear, anxiety, sadness, anger, and depression. In the legal context, client problems or stages in the legal process that tend to generate such emotions are known as psycholegal soft spots. The professional must listen to the client's story and encourage him to express the feelings he has about the predicament he is facing.

As mentioned earlier, a good technique for accomplishing this is active listening, in which the attorney reflects back to the client the essential features of his story and the emotions it likely has produced. When the client doesn't discuss his emotional reactions, the lawyer can attempt to encourage their expression through statements like, "That must have made you angry," or "I'm sure you're anxious about how to deal with the problem." Some clients will have difficulty expressing their emotions, but to comprehend the situation with all its complexities, the professional needs to understand its emotional aspects. Only then can he fully diagnose the problem and explore possible solutions. Empathy and the creative use of active listening therefore can help to accomplish both the aim of determining the nature of the client's problem and creating an effective professional relationship. Moreover, the expression of the feelings his predicament has prompted can have an important therapeutic value for the client.

When the client expresses emotions, the professional needs to be accepting and non-judgmental. When the individual feels a sense of shame about his legal problem or medical condition, he is likely to be more sensitive to the way his lawyer or physician communicates with him and more likely to experience humiliation as a result of the professional's responses. In the medical context, research demonstrates that patients who experience shame and humiliation in their relationship with the physician are more likely to complain to hospital administrators or bring malpractice actions.

The third core function of the medical interview is patient education. This component can have a significant impact on patient satisfaction with the physician/patient relationship, and is essential for patient compliance with the physician's medical advice. A major challenge in medical practice is how to get the patient to understand his medical condition and engage the patient in ways that will increase treatment compliance. The physician may be a world authority on the patient's medical condition, but unless he can communicate effectively to the patient and persuade him of the value of the treatment recommended, his expertise will not translate into a successful therapeutic relationship.

Although this function of the medical interview is crucial, it is the most often insufficiently performed or overlooked altogether. Studies have shown that physicians grossly over-estimate the amount of time they spend giving patients information and under-estimate the amount of information their patients want. When doctors do give information, research shows that they do not communicate effectively, and that their patients are frequently confused about what the physician has said. One reason for these problems is that doctors see themselves as treatment providers, not as educators. They are there to solve the problem, not to talk about it. However, giving more information and being mindful of effective communication has several proven benefits, including an overall positive effect on patient attitudes, reduced anxiety, better coping skills, and increased healthcare compliance.

Several techniques can be employed by the physician in order to ensure that he is providing adequate information and increase the likelihood of achieving treatment compliance. The physician should avoid being distant, seeming distracted or busy with other matters, reading case notes instead of having eye contact with the patient, using jargon, asking patients questions that call for a yes or no answer, and interrupting the patient, thereby preventing the patient from telling his story in his own words. He should eschew a paternalistic or judgmental attitude, avoid having a desk or other obstacles between him and the patient, and in other ways communicate that the relationship is one of allies in the patient's fight against his illness. The interview should not be terminated abruptly.

The physician should probe potential differences with the patient about the problem. Patients may not reveal such areas of difference unless asked. In language the patient can easily understand, the physician should communicate the basis for his diagnosis, information about the origins, effects, and treatment of the condition, and the prognosis of the illness in the future. He should fully consider the patient's concerns, beliefs, and fears. He should involve the patient fully in treatment decision making, presenting the various options and their risks and benefits, and assuring the patient that the choice is up to him. If asked, as is likely, he should provide his view of what is best. However, he should avoid pressuring the patient. If the patient experiences elements of coercion, he may not comply or comply fully with the treatment plan. Only if he participates in treatment decision making, will he feel that the choice of treatment is his own. This feeling will trigger the patient's intrinsic motivation to succeed, thereby setting up a self-fulfilling prophecy effect that will help to increase treatment compliance and likelihood of success.

Attorneys have much to learn from this literature as they too are concerned with increasing the client's understanding of his problem and the likelihood that he will fully consider the attorney's advice. He therefore should avoid the problems occurring in many physician/patient interviews that hinder effective communication and the likelihood of appropriate compliance. He should communicate clearly and persuasively, but avoid pressuring the client. He can help to guide the client's decision making process, but should remember that the choice is ultimately up to the client and that respecting the client's autonomy will improve the functioning of the attorney/client relationship and the likelihood that it will solve the client's legal problem in a way that conforms to the client's wishes and desires.

The initial interview is essential to the formation of the relationship that a professional shares with the individual who seeks his services. This first encounter defines the relationship and sets up ground rules and expectations that color how both parties will subsequently see it. This chapter has described the doctor/patient interview and some do's and don'ts for how medical professionals should conduct it. The lessons have obvious applications for attorneys.

Therapeutic jurisprudence/preventive law attorneys need to master the techniques that are successful in other professional settings. They need to avoid the problems that hinder success in these other professional contexts. These attorneys need to improve their interviewing and counseling skills in order best to understand, avoid, and solve their clients' problems. Moreover, they need to do so with the special sensitivity to the client's emotional well-being that therapeutic jurisprudence so highly values.

References

Bastress, Robert M. and Joseph D. Harbaugh. *Interviewing, Counseling, and Negotiating Skills for Effective Representation*. Boston: Little, Brown, 1990.

Beckman, Howard B. and Richard M. Frankel. "The Effect of Physician Behavior on the Collection of Data." 101 *Annals Internal Med.* 692 (1984). Accessed Dec. 3, 2014. doi:10.7326/0003-4819-101-5-692.

Binder, David A., Paul Bergman, and Susan C. Price. *Lawyers as Counselors: A Client Centered Approach*. 2d ed. St. Paul, MN: Thomson/West, 2004.

Gellhorn, Gay. "Law and Language: An Empirically-Based Model for the Opening Moments of Client Interviews." 4 *Clinical L. Rev.* 321 (1998).

Lee, Harper. *To Kill a Mockingbird*. Philadelphia: Lippincott, 1960.

Lipkin Jr., Mack, Samuel M. Putnam, and Aaron Lazare, eds. *The Medical Interview: Clinical Care, Education, and Research.* New York: Springer-Verlag, 1995.

Meichenbaum, Donald & Denise C. Turk. *Facilitating Treatment Adherence: A Practitioner's Guidebook.* New York: Plenum Press, 1987.

Olsen, Scott J. *Client Satisfaction and Control in the Initial Attorney Client Interview.* PhD diss., University of Denver, 1985.

Pennebaker, James W. *Opening Up: The Healing Power of Expressing Emotions.* New York : Guildford Press, 1997.

Silver, Marjorie A. *The Affective Assistance of Counsel: Practicing Law as a Healing Profession.* Durham, N.C.: Carolina Academic Press, 2007.

Sternlight, Jean R. and Jennifer Robbennolt. "Good Lawyers Should Be Good Psychologists: Insights for Interviewing and Counseling Clients." 23 *Ohio St. J. on Disp. Resol.* 437 (2008).

Thibaut, John and Laurens Walker. "A Theory of Procedure." 66 *Calif. L. Rev.* 541 (1978). Accessed Dec. 3, 2014. Available at: http://scholarship.law.berkeley.edu/californialawreview/vol66/iss3/2.

Tyler, Tom R. *Why People Obey the Law.* New Haven: Yale University Press, 1990.

Winick, Bruce J. and Alina M. Perez. "Aging, Driving, and Public Health: A Therapeutic Jurisprudence Approach." 11 *Fla. Coastal L. Rev.* 189 (2010).

Chapter 4

Lawyer as Problem Avoider

Introduction

An important role of the therapeutic jurisprudence/preventive lawyer is to keep the client out of legal trouble. Helping the client to avoid legal difficulties is far superior than helping him to deal with legal dilemmas after they have arisen. This is essentially the mission of preventive law, the accomplishment of which is greatly facilitated by the integration of preventive law and therapeutic jurisprudence.

As noted in chapter 2, preventive law has been defined as "a branch of law that endeavors to minimize the risk of litigation or to secure more certainty as to legal rights and duties." Preventive law provides a framework in which the practicing lawyer may conduct professional activities in a manner that both minimizes his or her clients' potential legal liability and enhances their legal opportunities. In essence, preventive law is a proactive approach to lawyering. It emphasizes the lawyer's role as a planner and proposes the careful private ordering of affairs as a method of avoiding the high costs of litigation and en-suring desired outcomes and opportunities.

An analogy is often drawn between preventive law and preventive medicine. Just as preventive medicine works from the premise that keeping people healthy constitutes a better allocation of resources than treating people who become sick, preventive law works from the premise that preventing legal disputes is less costly than litigation. Furthermore, preventive law promotes a client cen-tered approach, just as preventive medicine promotes a patient centered ap-proach. In preventive law, the lawyer and client engage in a joint decision making process regarding legal strategies. The focus of the legal meeting is not limited to a particular dispute or legal issue, even if this is why the client sought legal help. The focus is considerably broader, going beyond the particular problem to include the client's long term goals and interests and how best to achieve them while minimizing exposure to the risk of legal difficulties.

The preventive lawyer meets periodically with the client, at least on a yearly basis. This is analogous to the medical checkup. Medical checkups allow the physician to prevent future illness through examination of the patient, medical testing, inoculations, and medical and nutritional counseling. In a similar way, the legal check up can allow the attorney to use a variety of techniques to identify and avoid future legal difficulties for the client.

Working in collaboration with a client, the preventive lawyer identifies his long-term goals and seeks to accomplish them through means that minimize exposure to legal problems. The lawyer facilitates the client's aims through careful planning. He uses creative problem solving, creative drafting, and alternative dispute resolution techniques to accomplish the client's goals while avoiding legal dilemmas, litigation, and criminal and regulatory violations.

The preventive lawyer holds periodic meetings with the client, either in person or over the phone, conducting legal checkups to receive updates on his business and personal affairs. The aim is to keep the client out of legal trouble, to reduce potential conflict, and to increase his opportunities for the successful accomplishment of goals. To succeed, the preventive lawyer needs to monitor the inevitable changes that may occur in the client's business and personal arrangements.

The client initially contacts the lawyer in order to obtain his professional help in the accomplishment of a particular objective. He probably does not understand the requirements of the law, and may be oblivious to potential legal pitfalls. The lawyer, on the other hand, is an expert on the accomplishment of legal goals and understands potential legal risks. Indeed, the lawyer is risk averse. He has an instinctual pessimism that allows him to identify potential risks, even esoteric ones, and to worry about how to avoid them or what to do if they come about. He therefore is in a good position to help the client stay out of trouble. Once he understands the client's business and personal life, he can function as a primary physician would, attempting to maintain his legal health. He can encourage periodic meetings with the client, or at least phone calls, so that he can keep abreast of changing circumstances. He can remind the client, perhaps by letter, of future requirements and looming deadlines.

This approach requires reeducating the client about the nature of the lawyer/ client relationship. Most clients will think that they should see a lawyer only if they are in or are threatened with legal difficulty or about to take a step that they know will require legal advice or drafting. Similarly, most patients will consult a physician only if they experience illness. To keep the patient medically healthy, and to keep the client legally healthy, requires an on-going relationship with a professional who can knowledgeably monitor the individual's ever-changing situation. The patient will know when he has a broken leg or an obvious sign of illness, but will not know about conditions that are not immediately apparent. Periodic blood tests, blood pressure readings, and physical exams can detect conditions that the patient may be unaware of but which present serious potential problems. These problems may often be avoided by early detection, medical counseling, and treatment. As a result, increasing numbers of individuals recognize the need for an on-going relationship with a primary physician and the need for a yearly check up. Given the complexities of the law and the increased litigiousness of our society, it would similarly be advantageous for individuals to have an on-going relationship with a lawyer and undergo periodic legal checkups.

"But I only came to see the lawyer for a particular reason," the client will think, "and I didn't think I would be undertaking the on-going expense of periodic legal visits." "Is it really necessary or worth it?" To overcome this obvious concern, the legal profession needs to educate clients and potential clients about the value of preventive lawyering. We can use proverbs in this connection: "A stitch in time saves nine." "An ounce of prevention is worth a pound of cure." This may be a hard sell, in view of the low esteem that lawyers are held in by many people. This is why we need to change our professional role and its accompanying image. Lawyers once described themselves as "counselors and attorneys at law." But the role of lawyer as counselor has seemed to diminish markedly in recent years. The integration of therapeutic jurisprudence and preventive law into the model of lawyering advocated by this book seeks to reclaim this lost ground. It seeks to reshape the everyday practice of law in ways that emphasize this counseling function and that give this counseling function real structure and substance, rather than merely paying it lip service or describing it in amorphous and often unhelpful ways.

We need to educate the public about the therapeutic jurisprudence/ preventive law model of lawyering and its differences from the existing model of lawyering it is designed to replace. This will take time, of course, but this is the mission of this book. Clients understanding the real value of therapeutic jurisprudence/preventive lawyering will see the justification for this rearrangement of their legal needs and expenses. Indeed, if properly educated, they will demand that their lawyers practice in this fashion.

This chapter illustrates how a therapeutic jurisprudence/preventive lawyer can function as a problem avoider. It does so through several examples involving both private practitioners and in-house counsel. An example follows drawing from elder law practice, a variation of which we have used in previous articles explaining the preventive law approach.

1. Preventive Approaches in Private Practice

A. Elder Law

Contrary to popular opinion, most lawyers are not litigators. Most have an office practice helping their clients with their business and personal affairs. A significant aspect of such a practice is planning and problem-solving. The lawyer needs to identify the client's objectives and alternative ways of accomplishing them, taking into account legal limitations and requirements, economic concerns, tax consequences, and social issues including how a client can best relate to others in his business or personal life. Many lawyers are generalists, although the trend is in the direction of narrow specialties. The lawyer may be a solo practitioner or work with other attorneys in a law firm environment. The likelihood of specialization is greater in a law firm, particularly a large one, where the economics of scale justify having lawyers or departments specializing in such areas of law as corporate law, real estate, trust and estates, tax, bankruptcy, entertainment, and litigation. Lawyers practicing in a small firm or solo practice are more likely to be generalists. They can be compared to family doctors who can treat most problems, and when needed, can refer patients to specialists in various areas of medicine. Whatever area of practice they may be in, the therapeutic jurisprudence/preventive law model can be helpful and is likely to increase both client and professional satisfaction.

Let us assume that a general practitioner is visited by two new clients, a married couple who schedule an appointment to discuss the preparation of a will. They each are 61 years of age, and have been married for 35 years. Neither has ever consulted with a lawyer before. Most lawyers would treat their consultation in a relatively straightforward way, regarding somewhat narrowly the client's needs, in accordance with their stated goal to be the drafting of a simple will. In many instances, they would leave the office with a will and nothing more.

The first step for a therapeutic jurisprudence/preventive lawyer is to consider the couples' immediate purpose for seeking out legal advice while looking beyond that to determine whether they have additional legal needs and the extent to which their emotional or psychological well being will be affected by the legal arrangement or consultation. The preventive lawyer should be able to use client counseling skills to quickly bring out information regarding their age, health conditions, family structure, vocations, and avocations, all of which may prove to be critical information in drafting a document to distribute their assets in accord with their intent, and also may trigger the need to address other legal or practical issues beyond their simple request. Furthermore, this information can be used to alert the preventive lawyer to any potential emotional concerns. As a therapeutic jurisprudence/preventive lawyer, the attorney views the client holistically and is sensitive to the psychological aspects of the client's situation. The clients probably are not expecting to receive much more than a simple will, and so the lawyer needs to be sensitive to not offending them or appearing to raise issues they may regard as irrelevant to their reason for seeking legal advice.

An initial conversation might reveal that the couple has recently become concerned with setting their affairs in order as they approach their later years of life. They have three children, two of whom are married daughters with children of their own. Their third child, a twenty eight year old son, has a history of drug and alcohol abuse for which he periodically receives treatment. They wish to treat their children fairly and equally in the distribution of their assets upon death. They are concerned, however, with how to provide for their son, who although desirous of remaining drug and alcohol free, periodically falls off the wagon. They don't want to contribute to his problem and are fearful that, should he receive a large sum of money, the temptation may be great for him to spend it on drugs.

The lawyer needs more information and a better understanding of his client's life situation and expectations for the future. He certainly needs to understand their assets, and because they still are young (61), what their economic situation will be following their retirement. The lawyer should elicit information about their existing assets and liabilities. He learns that the wife has always been a homemaker who never worked. The husband, until two years ago, managed a service center for a Chevrolet dealership, earning $75,000 a year. Unfortunately, the dealership closed two years ago as a result of the downturn in the economy and the particular problems encountered by General Motors and other American automobile manufacturers.

He receives a pension of $2,800 per month. The lawyer's questioning reveals that he is nervous about what might happen to his pension now that General Motors is in bankruptcy. He relies on his pension for the couples' monthly expenses. The lawyer knows (or his research reveals) that under the Employee Retirement Income Security Act (ERISA), his pension will be protected even if his former employer is in bankruptcy, although not if the company is liquidated. In view of the US government bailout of the auto industry, liquidation seems unlikely, and in fact, GM is now doing better financially. This information is reassuring to the couple, who breathe a sigh of relief.

After a period of unemployment, he succeeded at obtaining a job at a local supermarket about three miles from their house as assistant manager, earning $28,000 a year. The couple owns their home outright, but the present market value, although once higher, now is about $200,000. They make car payments of about $500 on two automobiles. They have savings of about $30,000, and stocks worth $40,000 that were inherited by the wife when her mother died several years ago. The clients display considerable anxiety. They are worried about the future and what will happen if the husband were again to lose his job.

They announce that they are planning to start to collect the husband's social security benefits upon his 62nd birthday. He is happy that he finally qualifies for social security and thinks this will be a good supplement to his income. He has calculated that this would add approximately $1,452 per month. The lawyer knows (or his research reveals) that there is a problem with this plan. Although eligible for social security at age 62, the benefits received when the individual earns income in excess of $14,160, are reduced. For every $2 earned in excess of this amount, the beneficiaries' social security benefits are reduced by $1. At his assistant manager position making $28,000, this means that his benefits will be reduced by $6,920 per year or $849 per month. Thus, instead of receiving the $1,452 he anticipates, he only would receive roughly $603 per month.

On the other hand, if he waits until age 66, he would receive considerably more per month and there would be no reduction for income earned. He also can wait until age 70 and collect a still higher monthly benefit. By informing his clients about how the law operates in this area, the lawyer can avoid what would turn out to be the mistake of electing to collect social security benefits at age 62 while employed at his level of income. Should he start collecting at 66 or 70? It's too early to say as the decision may turn on their needs at the time and how they assess the value of foregoing social security benefits for six years in order to collect a higher monthly benefit at age 70. It depends in part on their assessment of their likely longevity. How they weigh these relative consequences is up to them, and they need not decide this question as yet.

This is a fairly obvious point that any elder lawyer would know, but being a therapeutic jurisprudence/preventive lawyer, the attorney is alert to the potential emotional impact that this advice is likely to produce for his clients. This is a psycholegal soft spot, and the lawyer should anticipate it and how he will break the news in a way that will reduce their anxiety and stress. They presently are paying their bills without social security, so as long as the husband's job at the grocery store continues, and they maintain their expenses at existing levels, they should be able to get by without invading their assets.

The supermarket business, he can point out, is not as vulnerable to the economic problems that befell the auto industry, as even in bad economic times, people continue to visit the supermarket, and may even do so more frequently as the cost of eating out becomes more difficult for many people to bear.

Should they have a will or a trust? What tax consequences, if any, will affect their planning? The estate of the first to die will go to the surviving spouse as a result of the marital deduction. At their asset level, they will not be subject to federal estate tax, but may need to pay state estate taxes. The marital deduction will allow the deferral of these tax consequences until the death of the surviving spouse.

Given the concerns the couple has about their son, a trust will have advantages over a simple will that distributes the estate equally among the three children. It also will avoid the expense of probate. A trust will build in flexibility concerning the distribution of the assets. A trustee will be named, either someone known and trusted by the couple, or perhaps an institutional trustee like a bank, and the trustee will be given power of distribution subject to standards set forth in the trust instrument. It may be that the couple would like to give their two daughters their shares upon death of the surviving spouse, but protect against the risk of contributing to the son's addiction problem by allowing the trustee to give him his share over time in ways that they may provide direction for. But what would the psychological or emotional ramifications of this be? This differential treatment could provoke family quarrels and even alienate the son from his sisters. This is an additional psycholegal soft spot, and the attorney should anticipate it and think about ways of handling it that can reduce negative emotional consequences for the family.

How can this problem be avoided? Perhaps the couple's decision should be explained to the three children in advance, or at least in an explanation that will be provided to them following their death, perhaps in the form of a letter or a video delivered posthumously. The son is less likely to resent his sisters or hate his parents for treating him differently in this regard if he understands their thought processes and that the decision was made out of love and the desire to protect him from his addiction problem. Should he experience sufficient recovery at some point during their lifetime that lessens their concern about this, the trusts always can be amended. Indeed, this is the type of topic that the lawyer can raise with his clients each year at a legal check up, a meeting to discuss how things are going in their lives and whether their legal needs have changed in any regard.

Another issue is who should be named as trustee should they decide to establish a trust, or executor should they decide to have a will. This issue also has the potential for provoking family conflicts. Will it in this situation? Is there a potential risk that existing rivalries between one of the daughters who might be named trustee and the son might result in a conflict of interest that leads to unfairness in the administration of the trust? Should someone who is neutral, perhaps, an uncle, cousin or friend who can be counted on in this regard be appointed? If not, should they appoint an institutional trustee like a bank? Thinking through the emotional components of this simple legal issue can prevent many problems for the family in the future.

The couple appears to be in good physical and mental health. However, during the course of several meetings, the lawyer notices that the husband appears to have a serious vision problem. When asked to sign some papers, his signature strayed considerably from the signature line. When going over their expenses, he learns that their auto insurance has gone up considerably and when he inquires, he learns that the husband has been involved in several accidents during the preceding year. With great sensitivity, the lawyer should inquire about whether he does have a vision problem and about its nature. The attorney needs to be careful to approach this issue in ways that don't make the clients feel it is an inappropriate subject for the lawyer's inquiry. It would be, for example, inappropriate for the lawyer to gratuitously observe that the wife is fat and should lose some weight. But the inquiry about vision is more germane to the attorney's role of providing legal advice and estate planning.

The lawyer also will be concerned with preventing potential future legal problems resulting from the husband's vision problems. Is this a progressive condition that makes it inadvisable for the husband to continue to drive? Might it affect his present employment? The client appears anxious in dealing with this topic. This is not surprising, and the attorney should be aware that the psychological defense mechanisms of denial and minimization may affect the client's understanding of his vision problem and his willingness to deal with it effectively. The husband admits that he recently was diagnosed as having macular degeneration. This should immediately raise therapeutic and preventive law concerns. Macular degeneration is a chronic, degenerative disease of the macula that can contribute to future vision problems. It increasingly is common among the elder population. Sharp, clear, straight-ahead vision is processed by the macula, and damage to it results in blind spots and blurred or distorted vision. Those affected by macular degeneration find many daily activities such as driving and reading increasingly difficult. Furthermore, the severity of this condition is related to a decline on some measures of psychological well being.

Here, the husband's macular degeneration may impact his ability to drive and future employability. This can have a particularly detrimental impact on his psychological well being. While studies show that many elderly drivers self-limit or cease to drive on their own as they lose their ability to be safe drivers, many continue to drive putting themselves and others in danger. They may minimize their limitations, or be in denial about them. Driving cessation has been associated with feelings of diminished self-worth and self-esteem as well as depression because many elderly drivers, particularly men, regard it as the cornerstone of their autonomy, mobility, and independence. The husband may fear that giving up driving may have devastating consequences for his ability to meet many of his basic needs and for its impact on his family dynamics. Particularly since he spent most of his working life in the automobile industry, giving up driving may impose a serious blow to his feelings of self-efficacy and may lead to feelings of uselessness and lack of purpose. Indeed, he may feel that he won't otherwise be able to get to work.

This presents a challenge for the therapeutic jurisprudence/preventive lawyer. How can he persuade his client to reduce or give up driving without offending him and in ways that reduce these potentially serious, negative effects on his emotional well-being? In his conversations with his clients, the lawyer also notices that the wife is concerned with the safety of her husband's driving and would like him to drive less or give it up altogether. The lawyer needs to allow the husband to express his feelings about what would happen if he were to give up driving. He needs to be a good listener and to convey empathy. Having sensitive conversations with the client about emotionally volatile issues is something that every therapeutic jurisprudence/preventive lawyer needs to master. Chapters 5 and 6 elaborate on how to have such sensitive conversations with the client.

The lawyer can use a technique known as motivational interviewing, discussed in detail in chapter 6, to attempt to get the husband to see for himself the value of eliminating his driving. What are his goals and objectives for the next few years, and what impact would a serious accident have on these? He should allow the client to see the point for himself, rather than providing advice in a paternalistic and overbearing way. Even if the client acknowledges that a serious accident could be devastating for his future plans and goals, he will be unable to act on this insight if he believes that he can't get by without driving. The lawyer can meet these concerns by making a number of practical suggestions. Can he take the bus to work or can his wife drive him there? Can he get a ride with a fellow employee or take a cab? Even if this would add expenses, it would reduce the expenses of owning, maintaining and operating an automobile. He already has been involved in a few minor accidents, and sometimes drives with his wife, children, and grandchildren as passengers. How would he feel if his driving were to lead to their injury?

When will his present driver's license expire, and what are the renewal requirements? Will he be required to take a vision test as a condition for renewal?

How will he feel if he is stopped by a police officer who, following an accident or observing erratic driving, confiscates his license and refers him to the motor vehicles bureau? How will he feel if a clerk at the motor vehicles bureau upon his failing a vision test confiscates his license? Wouldn't it be better for him to make the decision for himself rather than being made to give up driving in one of these ways? The lawyer can empower his client to make his own decision rather than having them imposed on him coercively by the government. Having his license suddenly taken away could lead him into serious depression and other negative emotional problems.

The benefits of taking a voluntary approach to giving up driving are illustrated by the author's own experience. I suffer from a congenital visual deficit that has progressed over time. A little over twenty years ago, I began to reduce my driving and avoided driving at night as a result of the increasing visual deficits I was experiencing. At the time, my state law required drivers to renew their licenses every six years by appearing in person at the DMV and receiving a vision test. I barely passed the previous vision test, and realized the chances I would fail were high. As the time for renewal approached, I thought about the consequences of failing the test and having my license taken away. I believed having my license involuntarily taken away could have extremely negative psychological effects, including resentment, anger, lowered self-esteem, and depression. I decided it would be better for me to avoid these negative effects by deciding for myself to relinquish my license. Having done so, I felt good about this exercise of choice and was more able to accept the end of my driving than if it had been imposed upon me involuntarily. The lawyer can use my example or similar ones experienced by other clients, friends, or family members, in a gentle effort to persuade the client that he would be better off making the decision for himself.

The wife volunteers that her husband wants to read the newspaper, but has been doing so less frequently as a result of his decreasing vision. This too will have obvious negative consequences for his psychological well-being. The lawyer can make a number of suggestions to remedy this problem, however. He can refer a client to an organization like the Lighthouse for the Blind that provides retraining and remediation for people with visual problems, or he can find out for himself the kinds of things available to those with vision problems that can help them continue an active life. The National Federation for the Blind operates a free telephone number that allows people with vision problems to hear newspapers read over the phone in a life-like computer voice. The husband can easily learn how to use this approach to reading the newspapers, and will discover that it increases his access to hundreds of newspapers and magazines that he can selectively read portions of in voices and rates of speed that he can choose.

In addition, there is computer software available that allows an individual with vision problems to operate a computer differently. This software allows the screen to be read to an individual in a computer voice and to operate the computer through keyboard entries that make the use of the mouse unnecessary for those who lack the visual ability to operate the computer normally. Another useful device is a handheld personal data assistant that contains a GPS that, using a computer voice, allows the individual to identify his location and to establish walking routes for locations of his choosing. Still another is a talking cell phone that contains a small camera that can take a picture of typewritten or printed text and read it back within seconds in a computer voice.

It is unlikely that the husband will know about these and similar other assisted technology devices that are available to people with vision problems. He probably has some denial or minimization about his problem and the anxiety of facing it and exploring for himself these alternative options would produce sufficient psychological stress that he is unlikely to undertake it. The preventive lawyer, however, can provide a real service to the client by explaining these options or referring him to agencies or experts in the community who can provide him with this information and training. In short, the lawyer can help the client to adjust to his increasing vision problem. Is this an appropriate role for the lawyer, or should it be reserved for expert consultants in vision? It might be better for the client to consult with such a specialist, but he may not do so because of the psychological stress that coming to grips with his problem may produce. Many people with vision problems never discover their alternative options which can allow them to live a full and productive life notwithstanding their problem. The client's problem is brought to the law office, however, and so it is entirely appropriate for the lawyer to provide this kind of assistance, even if it is outside the domain of traditional legal advice.

In response to questioning by the lawyer, he learns that the wife's mother suffered from Alzheimer's disease since her early 80's, and died at the age of 85. The wife has several sisters and brothers. However, sharing the burden of her mother's care stirred up controversy among the siblings. The wife displays considerable emotion in talking about this subject. Here is another psycholegal soft spot.

The lawyer understands that there is some evidence suggesting that Alzheimer's disease may have a hereditary component. Although the wife displays no noticeable current symptoms of dementia, this is a future risk, and one that the therapeutic jurisprudence/preventive lawyer will encourage his client to plan for. Does she have home health insurance? If not, she should investigate the insurance premiums which probably are quite high at her age. At some point, a patient with Alzheimer's disease may need to be admitted to a nursing home. Was this the case with her mother? Has she thought about how she would want such an issue to be handled should Alzheimer's disease befall her? This is an extremely sensitive conversation likely to produce anxiety, fear, and perhaps even depression. How should the attorney approach the subject?

He needs to convey considerable empathy, perhaps relating the story of someone in his family or a friend or client who had Alzheimer's disease or another condition needing nursing home admission. He needs to observe her closely, listening not only to her words, but reading her non-verbal communication. Should he get into the subject now or at a later date, perhaps scheduling a talk about it for a later time? Ultimately, he needs to have a frank discussion with her about care and residential options. He needs to understand what she would wish to happen under various scenarios. He then can suggest the use of an advance directive instrument to express her preferences and seek to accomplish them.

An advance directive instrument is an excellent preventive law planning device. It allows a person, while competent, to make or guide decisions in the future when he or she might become incompetent. A living will is a popular example, but advance directive instruments can be used for a variety of purposes, including future nursing home admission. Alzheimer's disease progresses along several different stages, and ultimately causes death. During the beginning stages the individual has a considerable degree of competency, and can live at home requiring, perhaps only minimal care. As the condition deteriorates, more care is required, and at some point, the care burden becomes so overwhelming that nursing home admission may be required. She should be able to think about the possibility of entering the nursing home at some point, and how she would like that issue handled. Does she wish to delegate it to her husband or one of her children? Does she want to guide their actions by stating her standards in the instrument that will govern how her health care surrogate will proceed? Does she wish simply to state some of the relevant values that she would like to govern the decisions?

As her mother's experience shows, parental care can often cause conflict within the family. Does she foresee such a possibility involving her daughters and son? Should her husband be named as health care surrogate? If he should predecease her, would she want to name one of their children? Placing a close relative in the position of making key decisions in this area, including nursing home admission or even discontinuation of treatment or nourishment, is bound to cause great stress within the family, particularly for the individual charged with making the decision. How does her husband feel about playing this role? The more she can specify standards or preferences, the easier it will be for the surrogate to make the decision. There won't be room for any family conflict about what mom would like if competent because she has already expressed her preferences. When a surrogate has to make a difficult decision of this kind without guidance from an advance directive, the decision is very likely to cause tremendous stress and feelings of guilt. These can be relieved, at least somewhat, by an advance directive instrument.

Indeed, both clients should have advance directive instruments governing future health care in the event of incapacity and also how decisions should be made about their property and finances. The advance directive should cover the issue of when and whether life sustaining treatment or nourishment should be discontinued. Some people would like that to occur should they be in a coma without likelihood of recovery. Some would like it to occur in other situations involving great pain and no likelihood of distress abating. Some would like it to occur in the event of advanced Alzheimer's disease. These are questions she should think about and discuss with her family and clergyman. Her decision can then be reflected in an advance directive that the lawyer will prepare. The law is in flux concerning when a patient can elect to decline life-sustaining treatment or nutrition. A patient may refuse treatment necessary to keep him alive, but may not elect euthanasia or physician-assisted suicide. Creative drafting solutions can be used here to achieve as many of a client's objectives as is or may be possible at the time. As long as the individual is competent at the time, he may elect to refuse treatment even if the illness is minor. However, once he becomes incompetent, he cannot make health or other decisions for himself absent an advance directive instrument executed while competent that specifies under what conditions he will elect to decline treatment or nutrition. In most jurisdictions not even the family can make this decision for the individual, at least absent delegation of authority to do so.

If a client executes an advance directive instrument while competent, she can elect to decline treatment or nutrition in the event of even pneumonia or urinary tract infection. What would his client prefer if she were in an advanced stage of Alzheimer's? While people may not legally be able to choose euthanasia, they are able through the use of advance directives to make treatment decisions, including refusal of treatment that is necessary to prolong life. Would she prefer to be kept alive or to decline treatment or to be allowed to die? If the latter, she would be able to achieve the same with a creatively drafted advance directive instrument. These are impossibly difficult decisions, but the attorney can assist her to plan for the future by presenting the options that advance directives make possible. The advance directive instrument allows a competent person to make such a choice for a future time when she will become incompetent. How does his client feel about these issues? These are, of course, difficult emotional decisions, but it is better to think them through now and make a decision than to wind up in a state when death would be preferable to continued suffering and she or her family may not be able legally to discontinue needed treatment. Although these are difficult decisions to face, not facing them now may place her and her family in a position that would be much worse. Creative drafting can allow the preventive lawyer to help the client to accomplish many of her objectives even when the law imposes significant obstacles.

The management of the couples' property during a period of future incompetence can also be dealt with through creative drafting. The potential exists, in the absence of an appropriate instrument, that family will become concerned that their elder relative is incompetent and is spending her money or managing her property inappropriately. They may do this for selfish reasons, which have been described as "premature probate." The family (or a family member) may file a petition in probate court seeking to declare their relative incompetent and to have themselves appointed as guardian of her person and property. There are noteworthy examples of abuses in this area, one involving Brooke Astor, the widow of Vincent Astor. Being required to be evaluated for competency by a court-appointed physician is embarrassing and degrading and the guardianship proceeding frequently is a public one. Even though the individual may be marginally incompetent, the process alone and the official attachment of an incompetency label may be psychologically devastating to the individual, diminishing her self-esteem and self-efficacy in ways that accelerate her descent into incompetency.

One solution is a power of attorney vesting a surrogate with the management of the individual's property in the event of incompetence. Moreover, the concept of incompetence can be defined in accordance with the individual's preferences, rather than left to a legal standard or court decision. At what point would the individual want to delegate the management of her property to another? Partial guardianship, in which the individual and the surrogate both participate in the decision-making, is possible. Perhaps the individual's ability to make decisions involving more than a particular amount of money can be delegated with the power to make decisions involving smaller expenditures retained. These are all issues for the client to think about and decide. The lawyer, of course, can be helpful by making suggestions or describing how other clients or family members have dealt with these issues.

The client will need to decide to whom to delegate the power to decide on his behalf. This decision can cause family turmoil. Like the naming of an executor in a will or trustee in a trust, it therefore requires careful consideration of the emotional dynamics of the family.

Everyone should have a power of attorney, but few do. The cost of not having one, both financial and emotional, can be considerable. This simple planning device can avoid many legal and emotional difficulties.

This elder law example well illustrates the power and benefits of a therapeutic jurisprudence/preventive law approach in office practice. Some lawyers would simply provide a will or trust and not unearth the potential legal and psychological problems that the couple may face. They see their role as providing a piece of legal work, and don't go much beyond the clients' expression of the need that brought them to the law office. As the example illustrates, the therapeutic jurisprudence/preventive lawyer goes considerably further in interviewing and counseling his clients. Many conventional lawyers would discover some of these issues, but the preventive orientation of the therapeutic jurisprudence/preventive lawyer broadens the scope of his inquiries and the services he can offer. Rather than waiting for a future legal problem to befall his clients, the preventive lawyer anticipates future legal troubles and uses creative solutions to avoid them. Moreover, he does so with sensitivity to the psychological impact of the legal issues on the client and the family dynamics that might arise as a result.

B. Business Planning

Another example of how lawyers can be problem avoiders is provided by business law. Many clients visit a lawyer to help them establish a business or achieve some business purpose such as drafting a contract or lease. Good business lawyers are well-versed in the relevant business, real estate, and tax issues. The therapeutic jurisprudence/preventive lawyer also will address his client's needs with a preventive orientation and an emotional sensitivity.

Take, for example, the establishment of a new business venture by four individuals having diverse interests and needs. Assume that a husband and wife seek legal advice about opening a small, family run bake shop. They plan to bake pastries and cakes on the premises, sell them to go, and to have table service. They also will sell coffee and tea. The couple has $10,000 they saved up in order to start the business. The husband's brother, a wealthy investor, plans to contribute $30,000 to the business, but will not be involved in operations. The wife's best friend wishes to contribute $5,000 to the business, and plans to be a full-time hostess and waitress.

The situation presents many legal and psycholegal issues. At the outset, the attorney needs to determine the client's objectives, interests, and needs in order to effectively meet them. It is not sufficient to respond to the client with a cursory assessment of their legal needs, without further dialogue. For example, they may want to operate the business as a sole proprietorship. What are the tax, business, and potential liability issues of conducting their business in this way? Should they consider alternative devices—a closely held corporation, a partnership, a subchapter S corporation, or a limited liability company? The attorney should engage in the usual business planning discussions with the client, exploring the legal and tax consequences of these options. Moreover, the client's interests are likely to evolve over time. "What are your dreams about the future of the bake shop," the attorney might ask the clients. "What would you like to see happen in five or ten years, or even more?"

After the clients' interests are clearly in focus, the lawyer can begin to consider what legal arrangements might best accomplish them. What kind of business entity should be used? Will the husband and wife retain overall decision making authority, or will the brother-in-law and friend also be permitted to participate in decisions? This scenario provides a classic example of a situation in which advance legal planning will be critical to the success of the business. There are differing expectations and levels of capital contribution from the four individuals and there are different family and social relationships. How can a structure of corporate (or partnership) control and internal dispute resolution that satisfies the needs and expectations of each of the principals be established?

This scenario also demonstrates the need for periodic legal checkups because the relationships and the business itself will not remain static. As the relationships change and the business grows and prospers, and as changes occur in the legal or regulatory environment, alterations of the business structure may become appropriate. Moreover, periodic legal checkups or attorney/client contact is often essential to the continued attainment of business ends. Assume, for example, that the bake shop has an advantageous lease at a good location. The lease is for two years, and the tenant bake shop is given an option to renew after two years at a rental that is ten percent higher. Exercise of the option, according to the lease, must be done by certified mail to the landlord by a specified date. Will the client be aware of these exercise terms when the lease approaches the exercise date? Many clients will not have these issues on their radar screens, and as a result, may find that the landlord refuses to renew their lease. Their advantageous lease terms and location would be lost. The preventive lawyer, however, will have made note of this exercise date and will check in with the client sufficiently beforehand to avoid this potentially disastrous consequence. Many lawyers would see their roles as simply assisting the client to set up its business, and would not focus on its future legal needs. The therapeutic jurisprudence/preventive lawyer, however, would regard keeping in touch with the client through periodic checkups or contacts as an essential part of his service. Ultimately, a well drafted corporate agreement that takes into consideration not only the financial investment of the shareholders, but also their social and emotional investment, could avoid future disputes, which have the potential to tear apart the corporation, friendships, and family relationships.

The clients have identified space for the bake shop that previously had been occupied by a restaurant that was about to close. The new owner would take over the lease and purchase some of the fixtures and restaurant equipment. What kinds of provisions should the lawyer consider including in the contract with the former restaurant owner? What kinds of things as the bake shop's lawyer should the lawyer check before drafting the contract? Certainly he would want to read the lease to ensure that the leasehold terms were what the client expected and that the lease was assignable. Could the fixtures be sold by the former restaurant owner or were they the property of the landlord? Did warranties exist for the restaurant equipment and were they assignable? Is any of the equipment subject to an encumbrance such as a UCC-1? Are the premises subject to any liens? Would the zoning be consistent with your client's planned use of the property and was there a certificate of occupancy that would permit this use? Would a new and larger sign be consistent with zoning restrictions and would it require the landlord's permission? Did the individual at the restaurant with whom your client had spoken own the restaurant and its equipment? Was he the tenant on the lease? If an entity was owner and tenant, did the individual with whom your client negotiated have the authority to enter into the transaction?

These questions illustrate the range of issues involved in even a simple business transaction, the importance of having the contract contain a variety of representations and warranties on the part of the former restaurant owner, and the importance of the lawyer's performing due diligence concerning a variety of issues. The lawyer's interview with his clients should also discuss ways of identifying the various risks that the new business might face, and of considering the possibility of purchasing insurance of various kinds to minimize or avoid at least some of these risks, including "key man insurance" to protect against the possibility that one of the critical employees might become disabled or die. How should these risks be conveyed to the clients without scaring them away from the deal? An additional issue to explore is what will happen in the future should one or more of the parties wish to withdraw from the business. Should there be a buy-out agreement? What methods should be used for assessing the business' value in the future? The lawyer should consider a contract provision calling for alternative dispute resolution among the four principals should conflict arise in the future.

These are just some of the issues that a bake shop scenario raises. Probably few were thought of by the clients. If not dealt with adequately, legal problems could arise in the future. The mission of therapeutic jurisprudence/preventive law is to avoid these problems and to do so with sensitivity to the psychological issues that may arise. The four principals can envision nothing but success and a bountiful future. Yet, reality doesn't always turn out this way. Getting the clients to focus on these potential problems may stir up a host of psychological reactions, possibly including anxiety, jealousy, and suspicion. As a result, the lawyer needs to move into this terrain slowly and carefully, watching the clients closely to observe their emotional reactions to the issues and risks they may never have previously considered. Future difficulties can arise, and the lawyer should plan for the future in order to minimize the likelihood or extent of these problems. The preventive lawyer is by nature risk averse, and dealing with these issues may be emotionally painful for the clients. However, if not dealt with, dealing with the future legal problems and emotional difficulties that may arise can be even more painful.

2. Preventive Approaches for In-House Counsel

Lawyers functioning as in-house counsel to corporations and other associations, including governmental agencies, are essentially playing a preventive law role for their clients. A significant aspect of their representation of their clients involves keeping them out of legal troubles. The clients have business, associational or governmental interests that they wish to achieve. How best can they accomplish these interests? In the process, how can they avoid violating the law? Properly understood, lawyers in these contexts are serving as preventive lawyers. And in accomplishing this mission, the interpersonal skills that therapeutic jurisprudence brings to the lawyering process can significantly improve their ability to deal effectively with their clients. Although their clients are entities, they are run by individuals who are their officers, directors, or officials. The preventive lawyer in this context therefore needs to understand human nature and how to deal with individuals.

In this era of increasing concern with white collar crime, attorneys will more frequently find themselves representing corporations and other organizations that are or could be involved with criminal prosecution. Keeping such organizations from violating criminal prohibitions through counseling on the requirements of the law, conducting periodic legal checkups, and compliance monitoring is the hallmark of the preventive lawyer. If the lawyers representing companies like Enron, British Petroleum, and Goldman Sachs were preventive lawyers, we might remember their clients for their favorable accomplishments rather than the fraud, securities manipulation, and environmental disasters we've come to associate with them.

Developments over the past 20 years involving the adoption of special sentencing guidelines for organizations give this role added importance and provide new opportunities for attorneys to keep their clients out of trouble and to minimize their difficulties when criminal charges have been filed. With increasing frequency, state-end federal prosecutors are targeting corporations and other organizations, as well as their executives, for the suspected criminal acts of their employees. These include securities and antitrust violations, regulatory and environmental transgressions, fraud, money laundering, and even murder and manslaughter. A corporation or other organizational entity may be held criminally responsible for acts of misfeasance, malfeasance, or nonfeasance even though the act complained of requires a specific intent or was accomplished through unauthorized conduct.

Although vicarious criminal liability tends to be broad in scope, until recently the penalties imposed on corporations were not particularly large. Corporations typically were subject to the same penalties as individuals. This began to change in the mid-1980's when Congress amended the Federal Sentencing Guidelines to increase corporate criminal sanctions against associations, corporations, joint stock companies, partnerships, pension funds, trusts, governments, and unions.

The setting of fines includes a multiplier that reflects the corporation's level of culpability. Under the Alternative Fines Act (18 U.S. Code § 3571(d)), an organization may be fined twice the gain or loss associated with an offense. Unless the corporation demonstrates entitlement to relief under the Guidelines' mitigation provisions, fines can be exceedingly high. However, mitigation of the fine is available for organizations that have effective monitoring programs and report violations promptly to the government. The Guidelines were an innovative attempt to provide incentives to organizations to maintain internal mechanisms for preventing, detecting, and reporting criminal conduct. The fine depended in part on the level and extent of involvement in or tolerance of the offense by the association's officials. These Guidelines governing the sentencing of organizational offenders, as well as parallel federal and state statutory provisions, provide a number of opportunities for the therapeutic jurisprudence/preventive lawyer to offer significant services to the organizational client. An organization will have its fine reduced if it reports the unlawful conduct, cooperates in the investigation, and accepts responsibility for the criminal activity. Having an effective compliance plan in place at the time of the unlawful conduct is a significant factor.

The preventive lawyer therefore will encourage his client to develop an effective compliance program. Preventive lawyers can assist their organizational clients to understand the "carrot and stick" approach of these provisions, can provide them with the tools to anticipate illegal activity, assist them to implement procedures to identify and prevent it, and affect sentencing when conviction of the organization has occurred. Development of a compliance program, however, may produce a risk of disclosing offenses that would not have been detected and of waiving confidential communications. Counsel should point out to the client both these advantages and risks. They should, however, suggest that the minimization or avoidance of the risk of criminal liability argues strongly for the adoption of such a plan.

To be effective, a compliance plan must demonstrate that the organization exercised due diligence in seeking to prevent and detect criminal conduct. The organization must have: adopted standards and procedures that are reasonably capable of reducing the prospect of criminal conduct; not delegated substantial discretionary authority to someone whom the organization knew or should have known had a propensity to engage in illegal activities; effectively communicated the standards and procedures of the compliance program to all of its employees; enforced the program through monitoring and auditing systems; and, taken reasonable steps to respond to the offense and to prevent further similar offenses.

The therapeutic jurisprudence/preventive lawyer should counsel the client about these requirements. However, counsel should not simply prepare the plan for the client. Rather, he should involve the client and its employees in the process of the plan's development. The lawyer practicing therapeutic jurisprudence will be aware that psychological principles of compliance and relapse prevention suggest that allowing the client to develop the plan will more likely achieve its purposes. Counsel can play a role, but the setting of standards and procedures should be done with the active participation of the client's officers and employees.

In the case of large organizations, counsel can suggest the use of survey teams in the development, implementation, and maintenance of compliance programs. These teams, composed of outside and in-house counsel and the members of the organization's human resources department, can identify potential problem areas, review past civil and administrative difficulties experienced by the organization, and consider problems confronted by other industry members. However the plan is developed, counsel should impress on the client that merely designing a compliance plan is not sufficient. It must be implemented with policies and procedures that provide constant monitoring and review.

Counsel should be aware of a number of potential problems in the implementation and maintenance of compliance programs. Major problems can occur when top management is not committed to the compliance program. In this situation lower level employees sense the lack of commitment, thus ensuring the program's failure. When this occurs and prosecution results, federal investigators are quick to assert that the compliance program was a "sham" or just "window dressing" from the start. Problems also can occur when the appointed compliance officer has no background in compliance issues or does not regularly communicate with the board of directors, thereby undermining the effectiveness of the compliance program. Other problems to avoid include when the policies and procedures are not circulated to all employees and when the organization does not regularly re-evaluate the program.

In-house counsel can play a major role in impressing upon employees the seriousness of the compliance plan, ensuring the plan is distributed to all employees, and seeing to it that training programs concerning the plan occur periodically. How can mechanisms be put into place to assure that this occurs? Counsel can help put in place practices and procedures that ensure the corporate culture embraces the plan.

Ensuring compliance is a subject that also arises in the medical context. Patient noncompliance with the recommendations of their health care providers is a significant problem that has provoked much discussion in the medical literature. The field of behavioral medicine has much to contribute to the resolution of this problem. Preventive lawyers can adapt healthcare compliance principles to the job of counseling their clients about legal compliance, thus avoiding a repetition of any past wrongdoing.

A technique of behavioral psychology known as behavioral contracting or contingency management captures many of these compliance principles and may be helpful in ensuring that employees of the organization adhere to the compliance program. This approach is based on an explicit, formal agreement where the contracting parties obligate themselves to achieve specified goals. Motivation to achieve the goal is facilitated through contract terms providing for a combination of agreed-on rewards for success and penalties or aversive consequences for failure. Indeed, the Organizational Sentencing Guidelines themselves can be viewed as a form of contingency management in which the government offers to enter into an agreement with its citizen corporations by providing special incentives, including a reduction in sentence, in exchange for the organization's commitment to implement and monitor a compliance program. To assure compliance with the plan by its employees, the organization can enter into a behavioral contract with them by providing motivational incentives. For example, monetary bonuses may be offered periodically to divisions, sectors, or other identifiable subgroups that remain in compliance for a specific period of time. Non-monetary incentives may be even more effective. These can include time off from work; points accumulated toward a larger office, new desk, or file cabinet, or a faster computer; installation of a coffee or soda machine at the workplace; tickets to sporting events, movies, or concerts; added discounts on the company's products; and other creative possibilities. The employees might agree that if violations of the compliance plan occur by them or under their watch, they suffer a penalty, such as a fine, extra duty, or loss of certain benefits.

The combination of positive reinforcement to encourage compliant behavior and aversive conditioning to decrease or extinguish noncompliant behavior can be quite effective and serves as the basis for behavioral contracting, a technique frequently used in clinical practice. Moreover, the office behavioral contract can provide not only rewards or penalties for achievement or non-achievement of a long term goal (like compliance for a five year period), but also on the occurrence or nonoccurrence of intermediate goals. Behavioral contracts between the organization and its employees that contain these features can be an effective means to increase employee commitment and motivation to adhere to the plan.

The therapeutic jurisprudence/preventive lawyer can thus offer a variety of significant services to the organizational client designed to keep it out of legal trouble. The lawyer can audit the client's operations to insure that the organization is in compliance with various legal requirements and assist the organization to develop, monitor, and maintain effective compliance plans. Increasingly, the violation of a wide variety of federal and state legal requirements can expose the client to serious criminal liability. All in-house counsel should strive to identify and prevent or minimize risk. The psychological sensitivity and preventive orientation of this developing type of lawyering can help even an organizational client to reduce risk more effectively.

Some clients may object that they do not think they need such a compliance audit and do not want to pay for it. Preventive lawyers need to educate their clients concerning the high value of such preventive services. Compliance audits and the adoption of such plans can be justified not only by the interest in avoiding criminal liability, but also by the interests of the directors of the organization in avoiding their own potential civil liability. Repairing a stitch in the hem of one's clothing also may cost money, but far less money than nine stitches. Business clients and other organizational clients need to understand the costs and burdens of being involved in legal proceedings with the government, and criminal proceedings in particular. The legal fees involved in fighting such proceedings can often be astronomical, far more than the cost of compliance audits.

There are other, even more serious costs as well. Defending against criminal charges can drain organizational resources by complying with discovery requests, attending meetings with lawyers, making appearances in court, and responding to press inquiries. Moreover, there are often serious emotional costs. Legal proceedings are intensely stressful and can create feelings of fear, anger, anxiety, and depression. In short, they are highly anti-therapeutic. In addition, being publicly charged by the government with unlawful activity can be highly damaging to the reputation of the organization. Indeed, accusation of serious wrongdoing and criminal violations can produce a lasting stigma that may seriously diminish the organization's business and other activities. Mending a bridge or a highway in need of repairs can also be expensive, but society justifies the expense as necessary to prevent disaster. Being a defendant, even an organizational defendant, in a criminal prosecution is nothing less than a disaster.

There still will be clients who do not see the light and decline their attorney's suggestion of the need for a compliance audit and the development of a compliance plan. Perhaps they fully are in compliance, and their compliant behavior is already adequately assured by procedures that are well in place or by some other viable review mechanism. If this is so, there may be no need to have the attorney double-check their compliance. Other clients simply do not want to spend the money, or may wish to remain in denial concerning their non-compliant behavior or about procedures within the organization that might (even inadvertently) encourage such behavior. Sometimes it is the duty of lawyers to make their clients face their denial. Doing so may often require a degree of psychological skill, understanding, and sensitivity, particularly if their denial has a psychological basis, as it often does. Dealing with clients about such issues is challenging work. It demands a considerable amount of judgment and the ability to listen to the client, to make the client feel comfortable, to communicate empathy, and to understand the social psychology of persuasion and motivation.

Conclusion

These are skills that therapeutic jurisprudence brings to the attention of lawyers. This chapter illustrates the advantages of their integration into a model of lawyering that champions the principles of preventive law and the psychological-mindedness of therapeutic jurisprudence. A primary function served by the therapeutic jurisprudence/preventive lawyer is the avoidance of legal problems for his client. He contemplates an on-going relationship with periodic legal checkups so that the lawyer can keep abreast of changes in his client's business, personal and family affairs. This is a return to the role of lawyer as counselor and wise problem solver.

Keeping clients out of trouble is a noble undertaking. It is one that the lawyer's issue-spotting, analytical, and creative problem-solving skills well equip him for. To perform this function effectively, the lawyer needs to develop heightened interpersonal skills. He needs to understand his clients and develop a relationship of trust and confidence. He needs to develop his communication skills and the psychological sensitivities needed to identify and deal with any psycholegal soft spots that arise. He needs to develop excellent interviewing and counseling skills so that he can understand the full picture of his client's affairs and provide advice that the client will comply with.

This is a reorientation of the usual expectations that clients have about seeking legal advice. Lawyers need to solve problems that the client brings to the law office, but helping to prevent problems can save the client considerable time, expense, and emotional turmoil. The lawyer can help the client to plan his affairs and achieve his goals efficiently and with a minimization of risk.

For most clients, this is a new model for the use of lawyers. Corporations, associations, governmental agencies, and other organizations that hire in-house counsel have a better understanding and appreciation of this role, and on the whole, appreciate the benefits of having their lawyers play this role. Individual clients have a lesser understanding of the importance of this role and a lesser appreciation of the value of using lawyers in this way. This book is designed, in part, to re-educate clients about the roles their lawyers can play and the value of using lawyers and periodic legal checkups to stay out of trouble. Not all clients will see the value of retaining counsel when they do not have an obvious legal problem staring them in the face. The therapeutic jurisprudence/ preventive lawyer can maintain their legal health and help them avoid looming problems they may be unaware of. This is a cost effective way of using lawyers, and one that is considerably more satisfying than hiring lawyers only when the client already is in deep legal difficulties. The analogy to preventive medicine is apt. Having an annual checkup with a primary physician with whom the individual has a long-standing relationship can succeed in preserving their health and avoiding many medical problems. It is time for lawyers to adopt such a preventive orientation and for clients to develop the habit of using their lawyers to maintain their legal health.

References

Alexander, George J. "Advance Directive Instruments For End-Of-Life And Health Care Decision Making: Durable Powers of Attorney as a Substitute for Conservatorship: Lessons for Advance Directives." 4 *Psych. Pub. Pol. and L.* 653 (September 1998).

Brown, Louis M. and Edward A. Dauer. *Perspectives On The Lawyer As Planner.* Mineola, N.Y.: Foundation Press, 1978.

Gruner, Richard S. and Louis M. Brown. "Organizational Justice: Recognizing and Rewarding the Good Citizen Corporation." 21 *J. Corp L.* 731 (1996).

Hardaway, Robert M. *Preventive Law: Materials On A Non-Adversarial Legal Process.* Cincinnati: Anderson Pub. Co., 1997.

Kapp, Marshall B. Kapp. "'A Place Like That': Advance Directives And Nursing Home Admissions." 4 *Psychol. Pub. Pol'y & L.* 805 (1998).

Meichenbaum, Donald & Denise C. Turk. *Facilitating Treatment Adherence: A Practitioner's Guidebook.* New York: Plenum Press, 1987.

Re, Honorable Edward D. "The Lawyer as Counselor and the Prevention of Litigation." 31 *Cath. U. L. Rev.* 685 (1995).

Stolle, Dennis P., David B. Wexler, Bruce J. Winick, and Edward A. Dauer. "Integrating Preventive Law and Therapeutic Jurisprudence: A Law and Psychology Based Approach to Lawyering." 34 *Cal. W.L. Rev.* 15 (1997).

"Symposium: Therapeutic Jurisprudence and Clinical Legal Education and Skills Training." 17 *St. Thomas L. Rev.* 403–896 (2005).

Winick, Bruce J. and Alina M. Perez. "Aging, Driving, and Public Health: A Therapeutic Jurisprudence Approach." 11 *Fla. Coastal L. Rev.* 189 (2010).

Winick, Bruce J. "Using Therapeutic Jurisprudence In Teaching Lawyering Skills: Meeting The Challenge Of The New Aba Standards." 17 *St. Thomas L. Rev.* 429 (2005).

Winick, Bruce J. "Redefining the Role of the Criminal Defense Lawyer at Plea Bargaining and Sentencing: A Therapeutic Jurisprudence/Preventive Law Model." 5 *Psychol. Pub. Pol'y & L.* 1034 (1999).

Winick, Bruce J. "Harnessing the Power of the Bet: Wagering with the Government as a Mechanism for Social and Individual Change." 45 *U. Miami L. Rev.* 737 (1991).

United States Sentencing Guidelines §8B2.1, 18 U.S.C.A. (Effective Compliance and Ethics Program).

U.S. Sentencing Guidelines Manual §8B2.1 and Amendment 744 (2013).

United States Sentencing Guidelines §8B1.2, 18 U.S.C.A. (Remedial Orders—Organizations (Policy Statement)).

U.S. Sentencing Guidelines Manual §8B1.2 and Amendment 422 (2013).

18 U.S. Code §3571(d) (Alternative Fines Act).

Chapter 5

Lawyer as Peacemaker

Introduction

Among his many roles, the traditional attorney and counselor at law functioned as a peacemaker. Few lawyers still so regard themselves. This book seeks to revive that role.

An important function of the therapeutic jurisprudence/preventive lawyer is the settlement of disputes. This chapter explores the role of the lawyer representing a client in a potential or actual civil dispute. Faced with the client involved in such a conflict, the lawyer either can resort to litigation or can consider alternative approaches that might avoid it. A client is embroiled in a controversy or sees one looming on the horizon. If the controversy has reached the point that consultation with a lawyer is deemed necessary, it is likely that the client will be experiencing a high degree of emotional turmoil. How can the lawyer interview and counsel the client so as to reduce this turmoil? Can litigation be avoided? Is negotiation and settlement possible, and how can successful settlement be facilitated? What alternative method of dispute resolution might be best suited to resolve the problem? What psychological obstacles to settlement might arise, and how can the lawyer overcome them? How should the lawyer discuss settlement possibilities and strategies with the client? How can a settlement be crafted so as to prevent or reduce the likelihood of a future controversy arising between the parties? The way the lawyer faces these questions can have an important impact on the client's emotional and legal health.

This chapter examines these issues. It analyzes how a therapeutic jurisprudence/preventive lawyer should deal with the settlement of civil disputes. It suggests how lawyers representing clients involved in civil disputes can act so as to reduce the emotional stress their clients will likely face and facilitate their ability to resolve their conflicts and experience psychological healing.

1. Avoiding Litigation as a Therapeutic Jurisprudence/Preventive Law Goal

As every lawyer knows and most clients will soon discover, litigation is an altogether disagreeable form of dispute resolution. It is expensive, much more expensive than most reasonable cost projections would suggest.[1] The taking or defending of a deposition alone can cost several thousand dollars, and this form of discovery is used more frequently today. Increasingly crowded court dockets present long and sometimes intolerable delays in the scheduling of hearings and trial. One or more appeals may follow. They alone can take several years, and typically involve additional attorney's fees and expenses that can exceed the cost of trial. During the several years that it might take to resolve the controversy through litigation, the plaintiff remains uncompensated, and interest on the verdict typically will run only from the date of the entry of judgment. A money judgment rarely will compensate the plaintiff fully for his or her damages, yet money typically is the only remedy the plaintiff can hope to receive. Moreover, during the several-year wait for judgment and the additional period of delay that may ensue until collection or enforcement, the plaintiff has lost the time-value of the amount that he or she may ultimately recover. In addition, the plaintiff may only rarely receive the full amount that he feels his injury is worth. The verdict often reflects a compromise reached by the jury that provides the plaintiff with only half a loaf, and a stale one at that.

Although the plaintiff may appear to suffer more as a result of lengthy delay, the defendant also will suffer as a consequence of the cloud of uncertainty that will persist throughout this period. This will likely result in negative effects on the defendant's psychological state and sometimes his credit. Moreover, the negative publicity that may accompany the lawsuit may jeopardize the defendant's business or personal relations. The allegations made against the defendant may drive customers away or dry up potential business opportunities. The lawsuit may injure the defendant's reputation in the community, costing friends and sometimes jeopardizing relations with spouse and family. The wounds that the conflict has precipitated will remain open during the pendency of the lawsuit, making it more difficult for healing to occur and for the parties to move on with their lives.

Moreover, being involved in a lawsuit is ethically challenging, bringing forth guile and concealment, if not outright dishonesty. Sometimes a lawsuit resembles a street fight, in which anything goes. The parties may be totally unprepared for the way a law suit may cause the controversy to escalate and for the compromises in their moral values it may produce.

The lawsuit also will absorb the energies of the parties, distracting them from fully engaging in business affairs or personal life. Meeting with lawyers, searching for and examining records, answering interrogatories, participating in depositions, and attending trial will take the parties and their employees away from more productive and enjoyable activities. The fiscal and social costs of this lost time may be hard to calculate, but they often are quite substantial.

Being involved in a lawsuit also imposes serious emotional costs on both parties.[2] A lawsuit always is vexatious and stressful; indeed, it ranks among the most stressful experiences that the individual may endure in his or her lifetime—comparable to the stress of the death of a loved one, the breakup of a relationship, or the loss of a job.[3] Judge Learned Hand, one of our best judges, with lengthy experience on both the trial and appellate court, once noted that "as a litigant I should dread a lawsuit beyond almost anything else short of sickness and death."[4]

In addition to stress, litigation predictably will produce other negative emotions. A lawsuit exacerbates feelings of anger that the party probably already will have concerning his adversary. So intense may be such anger, that wounds may never heal and the relationship between the parties may forever be severed. This may not matter in situations where the parties are strangers, for example, in a case growing out of an automobile accident. However, litigation frequently will occur between spouses or business partners or associates, suppliers and manufacturers, employers and employees, neighbors, or family members involved in estate litigation. Litigation in these contexts may rupture relationships that the client would like to preserve. The lawsuit frequently will turn nasty, producing hard and hurt feelings that may significantly impair advantageous relationships in ways that may cause serious economic or emotional losses to both parties. Such feelings may prevent the parties from dealing with one another effectively about such essential issues as the well-being of their children following a divorce. A lawsuit may cost both parties friends, who may become swept up in the controversy and forced to choose sides. Litigation between business associates, employers and employees, manufacturers and suppliers or customers, neighbors, or family members may cause a variety of non-parties with whom the litigants previously enjoyed business, family, or other personal relationships to sever their ties with one or both of them.

Litigation also may produce fear and anxiety in both parties. Many people hate being involved in controversy, and litigation often produces direct and vigorous confrontation by the adversary's lawyer. Being required to testify at a deposition or at a public trial, typically in the presence of their adversary, can provoke intense fear and anxiety, feelings that most clients will have great difficulty dealing with. Litigation also may produce strong feelings of sadness and depression, sometimes provoking a clinical depression that may require mental health treatment or even hospitalization. Moreover, these psychological difficulties may in turn produce an assortment of physiological problems that may seriously impair the individual's health or shorten his life.

These serious anti-therapeutic consequences of litigation are of special interest to the lawyer who practices therapeutic jurisprudence/preventive law. Litigation, of course, sometimes may be necessary. Sometimes the client has been seriously wronged and the wrongdoer refuses to acknowledge responsibility or to offer compensation or adequate compensation. Sometimes the client's rights have been violated and he seeks vindication as a matter of principle. Sometimes the client has been sued, and has no choice but to defend his or her position. Whether litigation is necessary is, of course, up to the client in our system, which values client-centered counseling.[5] But the lawyer should make sure that the client understands the relevant considerations, including the difficulties, costs, delays, and anti-therapeutic effects of litigation. Even when, on balance, litigation may appear to be both necessary and likely to succeed, the lawyer should point out that litigation always is risky and unpredictable. There are no sure bets in litigation, and it sometimes produces problems that may be difficult to predict. An old folk saying is that, he who goes to court, "has a wolf by the ear."[6] In short, litigation generally may be the worst alternative, except for violence, for resolving disputes.[7]

2. Alternatives to Litigation

The lawyer thus has a duty to explore with the client all possible alternatives that might render litigation unnecessary. What are these alternatives? Sometimes the client thinks that he has a valid claim, but upon examination, it turns out to be unmeritorious. Federal Rule of Civil Procedure 11 and comparable state rules require the attorney to sign the complaint and other pleadings, thereby certifying that there is a good faith basis in law and fact to support the claim. Legal research may reveal that the facts fail to add up to a claim upon which relief can be granted. In the alternative, a factual investigation may demonstrate that the client's ability to prove his claim is considerably less than he may have supposed. In either event, it may be better for the client to walk away from the claim rather than to pursue it through a lawsuit. Even when the claim is legally and factually plausible, the risks, costs, and psychological consequences of litigation may far outweigh the likely benefits. Advising the client in these circumstances to let the matter go and move on with the rest of his or her life may be advice that the client will come to appreciate.[8]

Apart from abandoning the claim, there exists a variety of alternative dispute resolution mechanisms, each of which is almost certainly superior to litigation. These include negotiation and settlement, mediation, arbitration, and collaborative law.[9] The attorney should advise the client about each of these alternatives and give serious consideration to attempting one or more of them before resorting to litigation.

Arbitration is less formal, costly, and lengthy than litigation. However, it bears many similarities to it and in some situations, claimants' attorneys regard it as less desirable than litigation. In arbitration, the parties agree to designate an individual or group of individuals to function as judges in hearing and deciding the dispute. Arbitration can be binding or non-binding on the parties. It can share some of the formalities of litigation, and often may bear many similarities to it. As a result, it may be less desirable than other alternatives. A type of arbitration that may be especially useful exists when the parties can agree to designate a mutually respected friend or relative to hear both sides of the controversy and render a decision. This can be done on a more informal basis, and closely resembles traditional dispute resolution practices involving the use of a village elder or chieftain or a family patriarch or matriarch functioning as dispute resolver and peacemaker. Thus, if there is a mutually respected and neutral family member, member of the clergy, or prominent figure in the business or profession involved who would be willing to play this role, the lawyer frequently can suggest this process as a mode of resolving the controversy.

Negotiation and settlement is perhaps the best alternative. If the parties can discuss the issues and resolve the conflict themselves, they will avoid the difficulties that litigation presents and most likely will feel considerably better about deciding the matter for themselves rather than having a resolution imposed from outside by an authority figure like a judge or arbitrator. As Gerald Williams notes, negotiation can itself be a "healing process, bringing together disputants to discuss and iron out their differences and helping them to resolve their conflicts and to achieve reconciliation."[10] In general, people prefer making their own decisions rather than having decisions imposed upon them by another.[11] Exercising a degree of control and self-determination in significant aspects of one's life may be an important ingredient of psychological well-being.[12] If the parties can come to their own solution to the controversy, they will likely be more satisfied and more willing to accept the outcome than when the judge decides the controversy for them.[13] Resolving the dispute for themselves may be transformative for the parties. It may provide them an opportunity for empowerment and to acquire dispute resolution skills that they almost certainly will find useful in the future. These skills may improve their relationship with their adversary, and reduce the likelihood of experiencing future conflicts. Successful negotiations may provide an opportunity for an apology and forgiveness, bringing about reconciliation and healing. Successfully resolving the dispute through negotiation with an adversary probably will increase the client's sense of self-esteem and self-efficacy, in the process enhancing the client's sense of psychological well-being.

Lawyers should counsel their clients that settlement will put an end to the controversy and allow the client to get on with his or her life rather than being mired in the conflict for the several year period that trial and appellate litigation might take. The lawyer should tell the client that it is unhealthy for him or her to hold on to hatred, anger, and resentment during this several year period; giving it up can allow the client to experience a degree of peace, relaxation, and joy in life that might otherwise be impossible.[14] Helping clients to understand the emotional value of settlement, and to achieve it, can thus be an enormous contribution by lawyers to their clients' psychological well-being.

Although settlement can have significant advantages over trial, it often is difficult when emotions run high between the parties. The controversy itself or the events that provoked it will likely have produced strong emotions in the client that may make it impossible to meet in the same room with his adversary to discuss their differences. In such cases, counsel can represent the client in settlement discussions conducted with opposing counsel.

In the alternative, the services of a third party mediator can be used. A skilled mediator seeks to identify the parties' interests, looking beyond their stated positions.[15] Often, by shuttling between the parties, the mediator can narrow the scope of disagreement, explore the areas in which compromise is possible, and forge creative solutions that will satisfy the interests of both. The attorney should be aware of the differing types of mediation and counsel the client concerning the most appropriate for the circumstances. Some mediators are facilitative, seeking simply to identify compromises that will satisfy both parties and see their roles as being limited to resolving the dispute.[16] Other mediators conceptualize their role more broadly, attempting to bring about not only a result that will be acceptable to the parties, but one that also is just and fair. Such mediators, applying an approach known as evaluative mediation,[17] will inform the parties about how a judge is likely to decide the matter in the circumstances, thereby shaping the negotiation process. Both facilitative and evaluative mediation are problem-solving models that focus on settling the dispute, but largely ignore relationship issues. When the dispute arises between individuals who have had a prior relationship—family members or committed partners, or those in an employment or business relationship, for example—the controversy has probably arisen out of the relationship. A dispute resolution mechanism that neglects to focus on the relationship issues may miss much of the complexity that has brought it about and the opportunities that the controversy may provide to address these issues and attempt to heal the relationship.

A third type of mediation, known as transformative mediation, places a high value on the relationship.[18] This model is more therapeutic in its orientation and involves a multidisciplinary approach to understanding and dealing with conflict and the emotions it usually produces. In this version, the mediator seeks to empower the parties by teaching them dispute resolution skills and allowing them to apply them to solve the problem that has precipitated their dispute. The mediator invites the parties to see the controversy as an opportunity to work on the relationship issues that may have produced it. The focus not only is to find a resolution to the conflict, but to transform the adversaries and their relationship in the process. This approach to mediation thus views the dispute as material for a potential transformative experience, and in this way goes considerably beyond the more limited goals of facilitative and evaluative mediation. Because of its emphasis on increasing the individual's psychological well-being, transformative mediation can be seen as more of a therapeutic jurisprudence model than the other two types of mediation. Moreover, because it seeks not only to resolve the immediate problem, but also to heal the relationship, it can be seen as a preventive law approach. The other forms of mediation can be viewed as dealing principally with the client's presenting symptoms, whereas transformative mediation seeks to address the underlying problem in ways that will prevent the repetition of similar disputes in the future.

Which model of mediation may be best in the circumstances? The answer may depend on whether the client's objective is simply to resolve the present controversy or also to work on the relationship issues that it may symptomize. The client may see only the narrow objective of resolving the controversy, but careful interviewing and counseling may reveal a wider goal and a willingness to use the dispute as an opportunity to seek growth and healing for both the individual and the relationship.

Mediation, although it frequently is a good vehicle for producing settlement, sometimes has its disadvantages. The parties sometimes find it difficult to agree on who the mediator should be, or on how to share the costs that the mediator will charge. Some jurisdictions have court-ordered mediation before trial can occur. However, in many of these, such a referral to a mediator cannot take place until after the pleadings have been filed. The complaint and answer may contain allegations that the opposing parties consider inflammatory, such as assertions in a divorce case involving child custody concerning why each party is an unfit parent. The anger that such allegations may produce may prevent mediation from succeeding. These allegations may push the parties to litigation as a means of vindicating their injured reputations and satisfying their hurt feelings. In addition, in the resolution of divorce and child custody disputes, mediation sometimes reflects and reinforces power and knowledge imbalances that exist in the marital relationship, often to the detriment of the wife.[19] Moreover, even when mediation has succeeded in producing a tentative settlement, when the parties take it back to their respective lawyers, the lawyers often seek to persuade them that they can do better in litigation. Sometimes (sadly) this advice reflects the lawyer's pecuniary interest in litigating rather than settling the case.[20] When this occurs, the lawyer may be recommending litigation to pursue his own financial interests, even if the client's interest would be best achieved by the tentative mediated settlement. Such conduct is unethical, representing a serious breach of the lawyer's fiduciary duty to the client.

One way of avoiding these dilemmas that sometimes occur with mediation is the emerging model of collaborative law. This is a technique that draws much from therapeutic jurisprudence and preventive law.[21] Indeed, I was a member of a small group assembled in the mid-1990s to expand the model, which at the time, was just beginning. The model reflects therapeutic jurisprudence and preventive law because its goal is to avoid the anti-therapeutic effects of matrimonial litigation and to prevent future controversies between the parties.

In collaborative law, which originated in the divorce and child custody dispute resolution context, the parties agree that it is in their best long-term interests to settle the dispute themselves, recognizing that their continued ability to relate to one another as co-parents is likely to be seriously compromised by engaging in divorce litigation. Under this new model, each party hires a lawyer for settlement purposes only. The lawyers and parties agree that they will use their best efforts to attempt to settle the case and will make full disclosure to the other side concerning financial and other issues. Should the case not settle, and this is, of course, always possible, the attorneys are contractually barred from participating in any ensuing litigation.

This arrangement removes the lawyers' financial incentive to push their clients toward litigation. Success for the lawyer is achieved by settling the case. Failure occurs when the case does not settle. As a result, this arrangement unleashes the attorneys' creative abilities in pursuit of crafting a sensible settlement. The parties meet with their own attorneys, and subsequently with one another with their attorneys present, typically over lunch, to begin the process of negotiating a fair settlement. As practiced in some jurisdictions, the parties also are given psychological and financial counseling, when appropriate, to help them deal with their feelings about the divorce and to understand the full financial picture.

In the divorce context, two models have emerged, one called collaborative family practice, and the other called collaborative divorce. Collaborative family practice is a referral model and collaborative divorce is a team model. In collaborative family practice, the clients hire the lawyers for the negotiation and resolution stage of the proceedings. The lawyers handle the initial consultation with the clients and explain options for the process. These options may include the use of "divorce coaches" (almost always mental health professionals) to help the parties deal with communication problems and identify underlying needs to be resolved through the negotiation process (for example, where financial issues are based upon safety concerns by the lower earning spouse). Also common are the use of neutral financial specialists (often accountants) to assist the parties in exploring a variety of property settlement and support options and what the long-term effects of those options might be, including tax consequences. The use of child experts (typically mental health professionals) to assist the parties to identify their children's needs through the dissolution process and beyond, and how to plan to best meet those needs, may also be beneficial. These experts can help parties to select the best time-sharing arrangements, with the children's needs serving as the focal point for such discussions. In this model, the attorney is the primary source for dispute resolution and the other team members are brought in by referral as the attorneys for the parties deem necessary and with the consent of the parties.

By contrast, the collaborative divorce model is a team model from its inception. Intake for this model may occur through the attorney or through coaches or a case manager (generally a mental health professional). Meetings between the parties and their attorneys (generally known as "four-way meetings") may include the presence of the divorce coaches from the beginning to facilitate healthy communication and identification of underlying needs of the parties.

Collaborative law can be seen as reflecting principles of therapeutic jurisprudence because it significantly minimizes the anti-therapeutic consequences of divorce litigation for both parties and their children. It can be seen as embodying a preventive law approach because settlements reached in this way typically will last, whereas when decisions are imposed by the divorce court, continued litigation about child custody disputes and changed economic circumstances will frequently occur. Because the collaborative law approach not only may settle the existing dispute, but also teach the parties dispute resolution skills when it is successful, it tends to prevent the myriad continued disputes that often occur in the post-divorce context.

The collaborative law model, and the negotiation and settlement skills it calls for, also may be applied in a variety of other legal contexts in which the parties, although engaged in a dispute, would like their relationship to survive the dispute. These include estate litigation, which frequently drives the surviving members of the family apart, employer/employee disputes, disputes between manufacturers and their suppliers or customers, and disputes between neighbors. An important function of the lawyer in these contexts is to find creative ways of resolving the dispute that do not do irreparable damage to the relationship. This frequently can be accomplished through use of the collaborative law model.

Lawyers need to understand each of these methods of alternative dispute resolution—arbitration, negotiation, the differing types of mediation, and collaborative law—and should discuss these alternatives to litigation with their clients. The client generally will be considerably better off if one of these methods can succeed and litigation can be avoided. Many clients may come to the law office demanding that their attorney "sue the bastards." The lawyer should listen carefully to the client's story and why the client believes litigation to be appropriate. Although litigation may be necessary, it rarely is. Helping the client to understand the costs, delays, and psychologically damaging effects that litigation usually brings and the advantages of pursuing alternative modes of dispute resolution should be the lawyer's duty.

3. Counseling the Client about Ways of Avoiding Litigation

It is never too early for the lawyer to start thinking about settlement and the various ways of avoiding litigation. And it is never too late. If earlier attempts at settlement have not succeeded, the lawyer should try, try again. At the very first client meeting, the attorney should discuss the various alternative dispute resolution approaches and explore which ones may be appropriate in the circumstances. Many clients will come to the attorney's office to interview him or her for the role of trial lawyer. They know what they want, they think, and are seeking to engage the attorney to bring a lawsuit. In their minds, they are auditioning the attorney for the role of Rambo. They may not seriously have considered the possibility of settling the dispute. They may be angry with their adversary, wanting to punish him or her by suing them and vindicating the righteousness of their cause. They may over-inflate the chances for litigation success and the amount of the recovery they think they will receive. They may overlook problems of collection. They may underestimate the possibility that their adversary might be more reasonable than assumed and might be open to a negotiated compromise.

The lawyer needs to set the client straight about these possible misconceptions at the first opportunity. The attorney's task is to reframe the purpose of establishing the lawyer/client relationship. It is not (hopefully) to litigate the controversy, as the client may have thought. The task is to resolve the conflict. Once the client can see the case in that way, it looks quite different. If either the client or the lawyer defines the problem as how to win a lawsuit, then a lawsuit will surely follow. If they instead can define the problem as how to resolve a dispute, then many creative options become possible. As Maslow once said, if the only tool you have is a hammer, then everything looks like a nail.

In discussing how law students can be taught creative problem-solving skills, Professor Edward Dauer relates an anecdote about a woman who notices a cat in her tree, and sets about to get it down.[22] She attempts use of a garbage pail with food at the bottom attached to a pulley system, hoping that she can raise the pail to the branch where the cat is located and that the cat will jump in to get the food and then can be safely lowered to earth. However, she can't seem to succeed in throwing the rope attached to the pail over the branch in question. Her husband comes outside and asks what the problem is. "I'm trying to get the cat out of the tree," she says. Whereupon the husband goes back into the house and returns with a shotgun, which he plans to use to shoot the cat out of the tree. The wife defined the problem as how to save the cat, and the husband as how to rid the tree of the cat. How they framed the problem dictated the solution each came up with. As lawyers who are creative problem-solvers, we must attempt to see the problem in different ways, rather than accepting without examination the way the client defines the problem or the way we initially think it should be defined. How we define the problem dictates the solutions we will attempt, and creativity requires flexibility in looking at the problem in different ways and in helping our clients to do so.

Once the client can redefine the problem as how to resolve the dispute, an entire range of ways of doing so enter into his field of vision. Litigation is only one mode of dispute resolution, and the lawyer should explain to the client why it frequently is the worst. The lawyer should review with the client the various modes of alternative dispute resolution, discussing the pros and cons of each in the circumstances. This calls for a careful and sensitive use of the attorney's interviewing and counseling skills.[23]

Is a direct negotiation between the client and his or her adversary possible? If direct discussions between the two have not as yet been attempted, the lawyer should explore this possibility. There may be circumstances in which it would not be appropriate—where there is a power or knowledge imbalance between the parties that might seriously disadvantage the client in such head-to-head discussions, for example. But if not, such direct discussions between parties without the participation of their attorneys may well produce an acceptable compromise. If this is to be attempted, the lawyer certainly should strategize with the client about how to conduct such discussions, seeking to ascertain the client's interest in the controversy, not merely his or her stated position. The lawyer may well be able to suggest alternative possibilities that would not otherwise occur to the client, who perhaps is too emotionally involved in the controversy to see things clearly.

After dispelling misconceptions and distortions that might stand in the way of the client's success in conducting direct negotiations with the adversary, the lawyer should explore settlement options with the client. How much is the client willing to accept at a minimum to settle the case? Is there anything other than money—an apology, for example, or a renegotiation of the contract or business arrangement—that would be acceptable to the client to supplement or even replace monetary compensation? What is the adversary's bottom line likely to be? What contentions that the client might make in direct negotiations with the adversary will be most persuasive? What are the likely counter-contentions that the adversary might make, and what are the best responses to them? What should be the emotional tone of the discussions? What are the likely savings in costs and attorneys' fees that would result from settlement rather than litigation? How should consideration of these savings be raised in the negotiation process, and how should these savings be allocated between the parties? In short, the attorney should prepare the client for the negotiating session and coach him or her on how to do it. After a negotiating strategy has been decided upon, the attorney should consider performing a role-play exercise with the client in which the attorney plays the adversary. It may even be helpful to videotape such a role-play exercise and then view it with the client. This can give the attorney an opportunity to provide comments concerning the client's performance, and provide the client with direct feedback concerning his negotiating style and the effectiveness of his verbal and non-verbal forms of communication.

If direct negotiations between the client and the adversary are not possible or would seem unproductive or inadvisable, the lawyer should explore with the client the other possible avenues to dispute resolution that could be attempted before litigation is considered. Should the attorney conduct negotiations on behalf of the client with the adversary's lawyer? Should a negotiation session be scheduled with both attorneys and their clients? Is there a mutual friend, business associate, or member of the clergy whom both parties might agree to permit to perform the role of an informal arbitrator or mediator? Is a lawyer's demand letter threatening litigation appropriate in the circumstances, or might it backfire? If a letter is to be written, what should be its tone and how explicitly or implicitly should it threaten possible litigation? Thinking about these issues is a highly contextualized matter, and the decision-making process will profit considerably from careful and sensitive interviewing of the client and a thorough dialogue.

Is a collaborative law process possible? If the client wishes to have a future relationship with his or her adversary, use of the collaborative law model may be best suited to achievement of this goal, unless, of course, the parties can resolve the controversy themselves without assistance. If they can't work it out for themselves, then the choice by the parties to enter into a collaborative law process may itself have important symbolic psychological value that can pave the way for successful dispute resolution. The willingness of both parties to use a collaborative process provides a series of mutual assurances that will increase the comfort level of both and create a psychological climate that is conducive to success. The collaborative model constitutes a mutual pledge that the parties value their relationship and wish it to survive the dispute. They thereby both attest that they will use their best efforts to attempt to resolve the matter in good faith. They will be honest in their discussions and reasonable in the positions they take. They will not be manipulative or act opportunistically, and will avoid posturing. They will share rather than conceal the information that is needed for a fair resolution of the controversy. Because they value their continued relationship, they will not act in any way to further undermine it, and indeed, wish to repair it.

Parties who decide to use a collaborative law model to resolve a dispute they seem unable to resolve for themselves, therefore, enter a process predicting, and even expecting, that it will produce a resolution of the controversy that will leave the relationship intact and that both parties will find acceptable.[24] These expectancies will help the individuals to focus their attention and energies on achieving the goal of a just settlement of their dispute, facilitating goal achievement.[25]

These positive expectancy effects thus can significantly increase the likelihood that a collaborative law model will succeed in settling the controversy. But, whether the client's decision to attempt a collaborative model will produce these positive expectancies has much to do with the attorney. One function of the attorney is to manage the client's expectations concerning various aspects of the legal process. The lawyer should explain to the client choosing a collaborative model what the commitments to the process are and how it will be conducted. Often implicit, the lawyer should make these commitments explicit. By expressly including them in the parties' written agreement, the parties can later be reminded of these provisions should they stray from their commitments. Putting them in writing triggers the goal-setting effect and sets in motion the positive expectancies that can contribute to success. The collaborative law agreement can have even better effects if executed at a formal signing ceremony and witnessed by the couple's children, parents, and friends. Indeed, whatever alternative dispute resolution mechanisms the client decides to choose to attempt, creating positive expectancies of success can be an important contribution by the lawyer to the outcome. This is especially true for modes of dispute resolution that involve the client taking an active part in the process such as negotiation and mediation. Creating positive expectancies on the part of the client about to engage in one of these approaches, therefore, should be an important goal of the lawyer/client dialogue.

A collaborative law model, of course, requires a desire on the part of both sides to settle the matter fairly and to participate in the collaborative process in good faith. This simply may not be possible in certain circumstances, and if not, the lawyer should then consider other possible avenues to settlement. Should mediation be attempted? If so, who would be the appropriate person to function as mediator? Are there individuals whom both parties trust and respect who can play this role? Should a professional mediator be used? The attorney should be knowledgeable about mediators and mediating practices in the community. What style of mediation—facilitative, evaluative, or transformative[26]—would be best suited to the client and the circumstances? If mediation is to be used, how should the client function in the mediation process? This calls for a similar exploration of interests, positions, and strategies as was discussed above in the context of direct negotiation between the parties, and perhaps use of the role-play exercise suggested there.

If mediation seems inappropriate or proved unavailing in the circumstances, the possibility of arbitration should be considered. Arbitration sometimes produces a compromise decision, perhaps providing the client with a less advantageous result than would occur in litigation. However, litigation frequently will impose significant added costs, attorneys' fees, and delays, and these must be taken into account. If arbitration is to be selected, should it be binding or non-binding? Both sides in the controversy may have unrealistic positions, and non-binding arbitration—particularly by a mutually respected friend, associate, or clergyman—may bring each a new sense of reality and create the opportunity for productive negotiation and settlement. The attorney should be familiar with professional arbitrators and arbitration practices in the community. Can one arbitrator be agreed upon? Often this is not possible, and a solution is to use a panel of three arbitrators, with each side selecting one of the arbitrators and the two arbitrators selecting the third member of the panel.

If none of these alternatives are feasible or productive, the question will be whether the client should walk away from the controversy or file a lawsuit. If the matter in controversy is sufficiently small, walking away may make a good deal of sense, just as paying a driving or parking ticket rather than taking the time off from work to fight it and to risk a higher fine and costs often is the most reasonable thing to do, even if the ticket seems unjustified. If litigation is decided upon, a demand letter sent by the attorney may bring a new sense of reality to the adversary, creating the possibility for negotiations or other alternative dispute resolution procedures to occur in the shadow of litigation.

If a complaint is filed, what allegations should it contain? Detailed factual allegations are typically not required for a complaint to survive a motion to dismiss for legal insufficiency.[27] As a result, the attorney may wish to avoid the tendency to include detailed allegations that may be insulting or inflammatory to the adversary, decreasing the possibility that the matter may be settled before trial.

4. The Timing of Settlement

Settlement possibilities should be raised with the client at the first client interview, and the various alternative dispute resolution options should be discussed. Chapters 3 and 6 contain an extensive discussion of the first client interview. Hopefully, the client will be willing to attempt at least one of the alternative dispute resolution mechanisms before a lawsuit is filed. Even if a lawsuit is filed, however, the lawyer should remind the client that settlement still is possible. In civil litigation, there is always the potential to settle before final adjudication and sometimes even thereafter. After the complaint has been filed, settlement should be explored in the pre-trial period in order to avoid costly discovery and the trial itself. Settlement is always possible even during trial and sometimes thereafter. Some cases settle during jury deliberations, and some settle after the verdict in order to avoid an expensive appeal and potential retrial.[28] The lawyer, therefore, should always be alert to the potential of settlement.

Timing is an important ingredient in the settlement process. An offer made early on in a dispute, before tempers have flared and feelings grown hard, can be a very effective settlement strategy. The earlier an offer of settlement is presented, the more likely and substantial the therapeutic benefits will be. Counseling the client about these benefits of early settlement offers should be part of the initial client interview or should come soon thereafter. As the duration of a dispute is drawn out, the legal costs are augmented, time away from the client's personal and professional life increases, pressure and stress grow, and the client's emotional, psychological, and even physical health will more likely be adversely affected. Delaying settlement negotiations to just prior to trial can prove difficult for the lawyers involved as well.

Moreover, launching a settlement process only at the eve of trial may meet with resistance by the other side. As one litigator put it, "When I am getting ready for trial, the last thing I want to do is to talk settlement. I have always felt a visceral incompatibility between final trial preparation and meaningful settlement discussions."[29]

Late offers of settlement, however, can also have significant value. An offer at any time can prevent the perpetuation of the detrimental effects that can result from ongoing litigation. Pre-discovery settlements thus can be quite advantageous. However, evaluating what would be an appropriate settlement in the circumstances is often difficult prior to discovery. Discovery may be essential to assessing the value of the case. Whether a settlement offer should be made before discovery, therefore, presents a difficult question, and will depend on the extent to which the attorney thinks that the value of the case can be adequately estimated at that point.

Prior to discovery, when the parties may lack an adequate understanding of the actual facts, their expectations about prevailing in the controversy, should it go to litigation, may diverge widely. This will hinder the prospects for settlement to be achieved. Later on, following pretrial motions and the completion of discovery, the parties will possess a much better understanding of the strengths and weaknesses of their respective cases, and at this point, their expectancies about trial outcome will begin to narrow. This narrowing, creating a smaller range within which negotiations can then proceed in earnest, will foster settlement. As a result, the timing of the initiation of settlement discussions may hinge on the ability of the parties at various points in the process to assess the range of possible outcomes with reasonable accuracy. When not enough is known, at least some discovery may be necessary before negotiations can be fruitful.

However, the attorney must bear in mind that discovery can be prolonged, costly, invasive, and nearly as stressful as trial. While a deposition may be something the attorney has done a thousand times before, for many clients it is a new and intimidating experience. One way of handling the risks of making a settlement offer before discovery has occurred can be suggested: To the extent that a settlement proposal is based upon an assumption about the facts not yet revealed in discovery, the offer can include a condition that, if the offer is acceptable, the adversary provide certain representations about the facts and documentation supporting them.

Another possibility is to negotiate with the other side the use of informal discovery or a shortened discovery schedule. What is really needed is more information that would allow each party to better understand what the likely outcome of a trial would be. In certain circumstances, the parties might agree to share the relevant information, rather than requiring that it be extracted through expensive and often time-consuming and anger-provoking depositions. The parties might also agree to propound to one another a limited number of written interrogatories that the other would be required to respond to in good faith within a specified number of days or weeks. The parties could agree to preserve their option to conduct further discovery, including the taking of depositions, after an additional period has passed. In the interval, an attempt could be made to see whether negotiations would produce a settlement.

If settlement discussions have not occurred prior to the completion of discovery, they certainly should be considered at that point. When settlement attempts between the parties have failed to produce significant progress, the judge herself may take the initiative and encourage both sides to compromise. This often occurs at the judicial settlement conference or pretrial conference, at which the judge meets with the attorneys in an attempt to resolve the dispute without trial.[30] Even if a full settlement of the controversy is not possible, the pretrial conference with the judge may make the parties more realistic and produce a stipulation that resolves or narrows at least some of the issues, limiting trial to those that remain.

An approaching trial and the horrors that it can bring can produce more realistic settlement discussions and behavior on the part of both parties. Avoidance of trial has significant advantages for everyone. It will be less costly than trial, less risky and fear-provoking, and less intrusive on personal and occupational life. Court proceedings become part of the public record, whereas settlements reached by the parties can require confidentiality to protect the privacy of all the parties involved.

Often, it is human nature not to act until given a deadline to do so. The trial date is a deadline of sorts. As trial approaches, stress and tension are likely to build for both clients and lawyers on each side. Sometimes this deadline is needed to enable or induce compromise. When the deadline is in the distant future, parties may be less likely to seriously examine their positions and to be open to making concessions. Furthermore, as the parties get closer to the trial date, they are increasingly removed from the time of the incident which spurred the litigation in the first place. The elapsed time may allow tempers to cool and healing to begin. Moreover, as the trial date grows closer, the parties and their attorneys will have a better understanding of the strengths of one another's cases, sometimes changing their expectations about the outcome of trial. While at an earlier point in the dispute, the parties estimates of the probabilities of prevailing at trial may diverge significantly, making settlement less likely, as trial approaches and the parties' understanding of the strengths and weaknesses of each other's position increases, their expectations about the outcome of trial will tend to converge, increasing the likelihood of settlement to avoid the costs of trial. Settlement discussions held at the eve of trial therefore may be quite productive.

If the case has gone to trial, negotiation and settlement remain possible during its pendency. Some cases settle while the jury is out, and some settle even post-verdict. It sometimes is the case that neither party is fully happy with the decision. For example, in a divorce case, the court's decision will likely address several issues—equitable distribution of the couple's property, exclusive occupancy of the marital home for the custodial parent for at least some period, child custody, visitation, child support, alimony, and even attorneys' fees. Each party may be pleased with the decision on some issues, but not on others. The decision thus may set the stage for further negotiations, which may result in an agreement that both can live with and which then can be offered to the judge as a replacement for the decision rendered.

Moreover, the party who lost the case may prosecute an appeal. Appeals are very costly, and may result in postponing the winning side's ability to collect the amount awarded for many years. The costs and delays of appeal may prompt post-verdict negotiation in which the victorious party may be willing to accept less than what was awarded in order to avoid the time and expense of the appeal.

5. Overcoming Psychological Barriers to Settlement: Insights from Therapeutic Jurisprudence

Often the client will not want to settle the dispute. Some clients are too angry with their adversaries to discuss anything, let alone the resolution of their dispute. Some will want to hold on to the dispute or even "punish" their adversaries through the litigation process. Some will suffer from misconceptions about the law, or about the willingness of their adversary to negotiate a reasonable settlement. Some will misperceive their adversary's motives or the realities of the situation. False conceptions of these kinds can prevent them from wanting to consider settlement.

Some clients will be plagued with denial, rationalization, or minimization—psychological defense mechanisms that will make it difficult for them to acknowledge their wrongdoing and see the appropriateness of engaging in settlement discussions.[31] Some will experience similar psychological defense mechanisms that will prevent them from accurately understanding the conduct and purpose of their adversaries. An example is the spouse in a divorce proceeding or the partner in a business who refuse to acknowledge that the marital or business relationship is over. Another is the defendant in a tort action who has harmed someone but seems psychologically unable to accept responsibility for his wrongdoing. In addition, the controversy may inspire fear and anxiety in the client that will significantly interfere with his or her ability to participate effectively in the settlement process.

How can the lawyer deal with these strong emotions, cognitive distortions, or psychological defense mechanisms that are likely to interfere with settlement discussions? When the client's desire to file a lawsuit is animated mostly by anger and the desire to punish his or her adversary, the lawyer should acknowledge the client's strong feelings, but question whether these are the client's principal motives for seeking litigation. If they are, the attorney should ask the client to think about whether these reasons should justify the high cost and other negative effects of pursuing a lawsuit. Moreover, the attorney should tell the client that pursuing litigation out of anger and a motive for revenge may be deleterious to the client's health. In this connection, the lawyer can remind the client of the saying, attributed to Confucius, "If you devote your life to seeking revenge, first dig two graves."[32]

While anger and the desire for retribution are appropriate human feelings, they may not justify the filing of a lawsuit. Going to court may be justified for the purpose of seeking compensation, preventing a future injury to the client, or vindicating the client's rights and reputation. But a lawsuit should not be considered an appropriate outlet for anger or for punishing the client's adversary. There are better and healthier outlets for anger.

Held anger is unhealthy, producing not only psychological difficulties, but possibly even illness—high blood pressure, headache, back or neck pain, and possibly even heart attack or stroke. From a therapeutic perspective, the client needs to let go of the anger, put it past him, and move on with his life. A lawsuit will only perpetuate the anger during its pendency, preventing the client from experiencing the peace and inner equilibrium that may be essential to pleasure and productivity. The client can be reminded that the lawsuit frequently will be all-absorbing, causing him to put good energy after bad. It may be best for the client to learn whatever lesson the experience of his dispute and resulting harm may have to offer, and go forward, rather than dwelling on it for the several-year period that the lawsuit is likely to last.

This is a sensitive conversation to have with the client, and the lawyer should be certain to display empathy and to be non-confrontational. It may be best, through conversation, to allow the client to identify his long-term goals. Where does the client see himself in a year or two, or even five years down the road? Will continued involvement in this dispute contribute to or hinder attainment of these goals? Will holding on to intense anger or desire for revenge or to punish his adversary frustrate the achievement of his long-range objectives? The lawyer should give the client the opportunity to answer these questions for himself, rather than telling him what he should do.[33]

This is a sensitive conversation, and may involve discussing with the client a possible referral to a mental health counselor. The lawyer should be familiar with the mental health services available in the community, and should be prepared to make recommendations, if sought, concerning psychologists, licensed clinical social workers, or other mental health counselors in the area that are known to be skilled clinicians. In having such referral conversations with the client, the lawyer should take care to avoid being insulting or demeaning. Some clients may deeply resent the suggestion that they need therapy or counseling. Rather than speaking directly about the client, the lawyer sometimes can relate anecdotes about similar problems experienced by the lawyer's family members, friends, or former clients. These can involve situations where unresolved anger produced serious additional problems, and those in which treatment or counseling proved beneficial. It may be easier for the lawyer to allow the client to himself draw inferences from these experiences of others rather than drawing the inference for him. In helping the client to understand that his desire to vigorously pursue litigation may be based on misconceptions or cognitive distortions, the lawyer may gain from an understanding of the literature on cognitive behavior therapy.[34]

When a client's stated desire to file a lawsuit is based on misconceptions or cognitive distortions, the lawyer's task is to attempt to demonstrate to the client the errors his analysis is based upon. This can provide a real challenge for the lawyer's interviewing and counseling skills, requiring careful and sensitive interviewing to uncover the client's false assumptions and skilled counseling to persuade the client to abandon them.[35] A therapist specializing in cognitive behavior therapy similarly seeks to break down the patient's cognitive distortions and to help to replace them with new, more adaptive cognitive strategies. This process is known as cognitive restructuring,[36] and in many ways the lawyer's task in helping to break down the client's cognitive distortions can be seen as closely analogous. Indeed, as previously mentioned, the lawyer can have an important role in effecting a positive cognitive restructuring of the client's attitudes toward litigation, helping him to see the goal not as winning a lawsuit, but as resolving the dispute.[37] Once the client can begin to see the objective as dispute resolution rather than litigation, he or she will be open to considering the various alternative dispute resolution options that may be available.

When the client's resistance to considering settlement possibilities seems to be the product of denial or a related psychological defense mechanism,[38] or of intense fear or anxiety, sensitive interviewing and counseling strategies are called for.[39] These psychological defense mechanisms or strong emotions may arise in the representation of clients on both sides of the controversy. They may take the form of resistance to any consideration of settlement, and may prevent effective participation in the discussion of settlement strategies and options.

One type of psychological resistance occurs when the client has acted improperly, with resulting damage to the party raising a claim against him for compensation, but seems psychologically unable to acknowledge responsibility for his wrongdoing. Many clients against whom a claim of wrongdoing has been made come to the lawyer's office with the expectation that they should deny wrongdoing, and that such a defensive posture will result in a smaller recovery against them than if they take responsibility for their actions. Moreover, this expectation often is fostered by the general practice of many lawyers in civil cases of assisting their clients in denying the wrongs they have done.

Professor Jonathan Cohen has offered a powerful critique of this general practice.[40] He documents the harmful psychological and spiritual consequences of this practice on clients. His thesis is not that lawyers should talk their clients into acknowledging their guilt, but that they should consider discussing the subject of taking responsibility with them, something they rarely do. Lawyers frequently tell their clients to deny responsibility for the harms they have done, and advise them not to apologize to their victims. This posture makes settlement much more difficult, escalates the conflict, and is more likely to result in litigation that not only is expensive, but brings forth dishonesty and concealment on the part of the client. Professor Cohen makes a compelling case that this practice presents serious moral, psychological, relational, and even economic risks to the client, and as a result, challenges the general assumption made by many lawyers that denial of wrongdoing is in the client's best interests. He argues that the lawyer's role in facilitating and even encouraging the client's denial of wrongdoing helps to produce in the client conduct that is basically immoral. Such denial, he shows, compounds the wrong done to the victim by adding a secondary injury. Not only does this impose additional and unjustified harm to the victim, but when the client and the victim have shared a prior family or business relationship, it inevitably impairs that relationship.

But is it the lawyer's role to save her client from immorality? Professor Cohen does not argue that the lawyer should impose her morality on the client. It is for the client to determine the ultimate ends of legal representation in the client-centered model of the lawyer/client relationship that our system embraces.[41] The lawyer's conduct in this regard typically is based on the assumption that it is in the client's best interests to deny wrongdoing. Professor Cohen shows that this assumption frequently is erroneous, and that also erroneous is the assumption that clients have only economic interests. Lawyers should not ignore their clients' other interests—moral, psychological, relational and spiritual interests—and unless these other interests are explored in candid conversations with the client, the assumption that denial of wrongdoing is best for the client may be false. Professor Cohen's conclusion is correct that the lawyer should openly discuss with the client whether to admit or deny wrongdoing and the consequences of both. If the client, following this discussion, expresses the willingness to accept responsibility for his wrongdoing, the next question is whether he should offer an apology to the injured party.

Raising the question with the client of whether his response to the controversy reflects denial or some other psychological defense mechanism, or whether he should accept responsibility for wrongdoing and offer an apology, may be delicate and somewhat awkward. After all, the client has come to the lawyer's office presumably to seek advice about avoiding responsibility. The lawyer may be concerned that the client will perceive his raising the questions of responsibility taking and apology as judgmental or even disloyal, perceptions that might destroy the client's trust in the attorney.

How can the lawyer have these difficult and sensitive conversations with the client? At the outset, the attorney needs to establish a relationship of trust and confidence with the client. This should be an important goal of the first client interview. The first attorney/client interview is discussed in further detail in chapter 3. Because denial and similar defense mechanisms are responses to the strong feelings of anxiety that the situation provokes in the individual, in every meeting with the client, and certainly at the initial meeting, the attorney needs to be sensitive to the client's psychological state, to be supportive and non-judgmental, and to convey empathy.[42] The attorney needs to understand that to even begin to deal effectively with such denial or resistance requires creation of a climate in which the client can feel comfortable in discussing highly personal and sensitive matters that produce intense emotional reactions. In order to establish the client's trust and confidence at the initial interview, the attorney should explain the attorney/client privilege and the confidentiality that extends to communications occurring within the professional relationship. The attorney should encourage the client to express his feelings about the conflict, his or her adversary, and the prospect of being involved in litigation. Unless the client feels that the attorney is an ally and confidant, he or she will not feel free to share thoughts and feelings with counsel in an open and forthright way.

Having sensitive conversations of this kind with the client requires heightened interpersonal skills.[43] Attorneys need to be good listeners, paying attention not only to what the client says, but also to their non-verbal forms of communication.[44] They need to develop their "emotional intelligence"[45] and be "affective" or "relationship-centered" lawyers.[46] The attorney needs to convey to the client that unless he is willing to consider and discuss with his lawyer issues relating to the lawsuit even though they may provoke intense anxiety, embarrassment, or internal conflict, the lawyer's ability to achieve the client's best interests will be undermined. In having these conversations, lawyers need to avoid acting paternalistically, respecting their clients' autonomy and persuading them of the merits of the advice offered rather than coercing them.

In dealing with denial and similar defense mechanisms that seem psychologically based, the attorney should consider using an approach adapted from the technique of motivational interviewing.[47] This technique, developed in the context of substance abuse counseling, where the interviewer seeks to help the individual to recognize the existence of a problem and motivate him to deal with it, has been suggested for use by criminal defense attorneys attempting, in connection with plea bargaining, diversion, or sentencing, to help their clients accept responsibility for their wrongdoing and understand that they have a problem they need to deal with.[48] Several basic principles underlie motivational interviewing. First, the interviewer needs to express empathy by trying to understand the individual's feelings and perspectives (through careful and respectful listening to the individual) without judging, criticizing, or blaming. Reflective listening and acceptance are essential to this process. It is often the case that the individual is reluctant and ambivalent in the beginning. Those traits should not be deemed pathological, but rather considered an ordinary aspect of human behavior.[49]

Second, the interviewer, in a non-confrontational way, should seek to identify discrepancies between the individual's present attitudes or behavior and important personal goals. The interviewer thus must elicit the individual's underlying goals and objectives, and through interviewing techniques, including open-ended questioning, reflective listening, the provision of frequent statements of affirmation and support, and the elicitation of self-motivational statements, should attempt to enable the individual to recognize the existence of a problem. It is important that the interviewer point the individual in the right direction, but it must be left to the individual to express the intention to change and the feeling he can do so on his own.[50] Only when people perceive the discrepancy between how they are behaving and the achievement of their personal goals will motivation for change be created. Third, when resistance is encountered, the interviewer must attempt to roll with the resistance rather than become confrontational. This requires listening with empathy and providing feedback to what the individual is saying by introducing new information, thereby allowing the individual to remain in control, to make his own decisions, and to create solutions to his problems. The interviewer should avoid arguing with the individual, which can be counterproductive and create defensiveness.[51]

Treating the client with dignity and respect, conveying empathy, respecting the client's autonomy and using a form of motivational interviewing can help to break through the psychological denial and resistance that may pose an insurmountable barrier to achieving a beneficial settlement for the client. These techniques also will facilitate the client's acceptance of responsibility where that is appropriate. Moreover, they can facilitate the client's willingness to offer an apology for his wrongdoing.

An apology can do much to create the opportunity for successful settlement of the dispute, and if the apology is accepted, this can do much to repair the relationship between the parties and diminish the chances that conflict between them will again arise. The injured party may desire an apology as much as or even more than compensation. An apology, especially if made publicly, can bring a much-needed feeling of vindication. The making of an apology and its acceptance by the injured party often will dissipate the anger and bad feelings that existed between the parties, restore the injured party's sense of equilibrium, and permit a healing of the relationship. By contrast, when an individual who has wronged another refuses to take responsibility for his actions and to apologize for them, the anger and bad feelings that are likely to exist between the parties can prevent clear thinking about settlement possibilities, distort the ability of the parties to be realistic in negotiations and to understand the value of settlement, and prevent them from accurately comprehending and evaluating settlement offers and making effective counter-offers. Compromise may be impossible in this climate, and the dispute is much more likely to end up in litigation.

The attorney for the party against whom a claim of wrongdoing is made, however, may be concerned that allowing the client to apologize may present risks should negotiations fail and the dispute become a lawsuit. In such an event, it is possible that the apology would be admissible in evidence, seriously undermining the defendant's ability to contest liability.[52] While the legal culture of today still discourages apology,[53] this is beginning to change as commentators extol the virtues of apology in facilitating settlement.[54] A number of jurisdictions have enacted legislation preventing an apology from being used against its maker at trial.[55] Some jurisdictions, however, only prevent the admissibility of apologies that are expressions of sympathy, providing no protection for those that acknowledge fault.[56] While such partial apologies may be effective in limited circumstances, they often may backfire, increasing feelings of resentment on the part of the injured party.

To be effective, an apology typically must acknowledge wrongdoing, offer an explanation for it, express shame and remorse, and include a willingness to make reparations.[57] Furthermore, the injured party must feel that the maker of the apology is sincere in his expression of remorse.[58] Successful apologies satisfy a number of psychological needs on the part of the injured party—the restoration of his self-respect and dignity, the assurance that both parties have shared values and that there is safety in their relationship, the desire for meaningful dialogue with the person who wronged him, the recognition that the offense was not his fault, and the feeling that the wrongdoer should suffer reparation for the harm done.[59] An apology that meets these needs, or at least many of them, facilitates the process of forgiveness.[60]

On the other hand, partial apologies—those that merely express sympathy, but do not acknowledge fault or express remorse and the desire to make reparations—are likely to be unsuccessful. An apology that seems insincere or is devoid of sympathy, sorrow, remorse, or admission of wrongdoing will not prompt forgiveness and may even fuel animosity if the injured party perceives the apology as a thinly veiled attempt to escape liability. This conclusion is supported by recent empirical research showing that not only is the likelihood of settlement substantially increased when there is a full apology, but that a partial apology reduces the likelihood of settlement to less than that existing when there was no apology at all, particularly when the injury is severe.[61] A partial apology therefore may backfire.

As a result, the attorney should counsel the client about the value of a sincere apology accompanied by an admission of wrongdoing, the expression of remorse, and an offer to make reparations for the wrong. Such an apology will significantly increase the likelihood that the apology will be accepted, that forgiveness will be granted, and that a settlement of the dispute will be reached. In addition, such a full apology may be necessary for healing of both the injured party and the client. Accepting responsibility and making amends to the injured party can be vital to the emotional well-being of the client when he knows he was at fault. Acceptance of the apology can provide needed closure for both parties, allowing them to move forward with their lives and to heal their relationship. It can diffuse the stress, anger, hostility, hatred, resentment, and fear that is associated with holding a grudge. Attorneys representing both alleged wrongdoers and parties injured as a result therefore should discuss with their respective clients the value of a full apology and its acceptance in producing forgiveness, reconciliation, settlement, and healing.

Accepting responsibility for a mistake or for negligence is difficult for some people. As a result, many clients will be reluctant to apologize. People generally are reticent to disclose their mistakes, and sometimes seem psychologically unable to admit them even to themselves. As a result, in discussing responsibility taking and apology with a client, the therapeutic jurisprudence/preventive lawyer will need to display the enhanced interpersonal skills discussed above, avoid paternalism, convey empathy, and use a form of motivational interviewing. Sometimes these techniques will allow the client to concede to himself and his lawyer that he was wrong. This doesn't necessarily mean that the client will be willing to acknowledge his wrongdoing and apologize to the injured party. The client may still wish to deny wrongdoing and attempt to avoid liability. This is his right, but the attorney should tell him that this course will likely provoke litigation, that the client's wrongdoing may be exposed in discovery or trial, and that this exposure following denial will likely make the injured party less willing to compromise the claim or lead the jury to impose a higher award. Moreover, the attorney should tell the client that it would be unethical for the attorney to participate in facilitating the client's perjury on the issue. If the client accepts wrongdoing and tenders an appropriate apology, on the other hand, the client can avoid the dishonesty that his denial will likely lead him to engage in and the feelings of guilt and inner conflict that this can provoke, and also can produce a more advantageous settlement.

6. Crafting a Settlement That Will Last: A Preventive Law Challenge

For a settlement to succeed, it must not only end the dispute, but achieve a degree of healing that may be necessary to avoid a future conflict. In discussing and evaluating settlement options, the attorney and client should keep in mind that nothing is settled finally until it is settled justly.[62] Many controversies, particularly if between individuals that have an on-going relationship, tend to reoccur. A divorce settlement, for example, may result in an agreement that provides a blueprint for how the parties will function after the divorce. The agreement will resolve a dispute about the distribution of marital assets and liabilities or child custody, and provide for visitation for the non-custodial parent, and sometimes will require the payment of child support, alimony or both.

The agreement, however, does not always finally resolve the dispute. Sometimes the parties continue to be angry with one another and crave an additional fight, or are unhappy with the settlement and want to reopen it. Sometimes one of the parties will refuse or cease to be able to comply with the settlement. Moreover, situations change. One of the parties may lose his or her job or otherwise realize a significant change in economic situation. One of the former spouses may remarry, and perhaps move to another state. The child's needs may change. Disputes may erupt concerning the details of visitation or how best to meet the child's health or educational needs. In all of these contexts, the potential is great that the controversy will resurface, resulting in the possibility of litigation. How can the matrimonial lawyer representing a party in the original divorce proceedings craft a settlement agreement that will minimize the potential of future litigation?

In crafting the settlement, the attorney should consider whether it will succeed in diffusing the controversy and facilitate healing for both parties. What kind of dispute resolution mechanisms can produce greater satisfaction for the parties and increase the likelihood that they will comply with the resolution they have reached or that has been imposed upon them? What kinds of agreements can build in the flexibility necessary to deal with future changes in circumstance? What kinds of alternative dispute resolution approaches can be suggested for dealing with future disputes, and how can agreements be drafted that commit the parties to the use of such mechanisms in lieu of litigation? Can the parties agree in advance to mediate or arbitrate future disputes, or to employ a collaborative law model for dealing with them?[63]

Moreover, the recurrence of controversy is not limited to the matrimonial context. Landlord/tenant disputes frequently spawn recurrent controversy, as do disputes between suppliers and manufacturers and other business people engaged in an on-going course of conduct. Some employer/employee disputes are on-going, as are disputes between neighbors about barking dogs, alleged nuisances, common walls, and the like. In all of these contexts, lawyers should understand the potential for repeated conflict and try to minimize its potential by including provisions that commit the parties to the use of alternative dispute resolution mechanisms rather than litigation.

Another potential for recurrent controversy arises when it is anticipated that the client's adversary will not comply with the agreement at some point in the future. This problem frequently can be avoided by inclusion in the settlement agreement of a default provision. Such a provision governs what will happen in the event one of the parties fails to comply with a material portion of the agreement. For example, if the agreement requires the adversary to make installment payments or periodic alimony or support payments, the default clause could contain an acceleration provision, making the entire amount that is owed due and payable upon the non-payment of an installment for more than a certain number of days, perhaps after a period has passed following notice and a demand for payment. An even more stringent provision could call for the execution in advance of a cognovit note or a confession of judgment, which would become effective after a period of non-payment following notice and demand. The adversary may object to such a provision as too severe but can be reminded that a default clause only comes into play following a specified period of unremedied non-compliance with the obligations he or she is assuming by entering into the settlement agreement. A less stringent measure, of course, is a late fee that would be due if payment is late for more than a specified period. Provisions of this kind function to impress the adversary with the seriousness of the obligations he or she is assuming, and function as a deterrent to non-payment or late payment. As such, they constitute a preventive law device for avoiding future difficulties of non-compliance.

Compliance, either with a court order or the terms of the settlement agreement, can sometimes be a serious problem. The adversary may comply for a period, but later come to regret the settlement terms, and lingering feelings of anger and resentment may lead him to rationalize non-compliance or partial or late compliance. Such a response is more likely if the adversary felt coerced into accepting the settlement as a result of the threat of litigation or other pressure perceived to be unfair. In addition, it may occur if the party perceived the dispute resolution process that produced the settlement to be unfair or disrespectful, or to deny him a reasonable opportunity to voice his position or offer an explanation for his actions.

To minimize this risk, the attorney should be careful, in whatever dispute resolution process is used, not to be too heavy-handed with the adversary. In determining how to deal with the adversary, the lawyer should be aware of the literature on the psychology of procedural justice.[64] This literature shows that parties to litigation, arbitration proceedings, and other hearings feel more satisfied with the process involved if they are treated fairly, with dignity and respect, and in good faith; and also if they are given a sense of "voice" (the opportunity to tell their story) and "validation" (the feeling that what they had to say was taken seriously). Not only are litigants treated in this way likely to feel more satisfaction about the process—they also are likely to comply more willingly with the outcome, even if unfavorable to them.[65] By extension, the attorney should be careful, in whatever dispute resolution process is used, to treat the adversary in ways that will satisfy these elements of procedural justice.

In a negotiation, mediation, or arbitration, it is important that the adversary feel that he is being treated with dignity and respect. The attorney should make sure that the adversary is given the full opportunity to voice his side of the story and to offer whatever explanations for his conduct that he might wish to make. Even if these explanations do not justify his actions, allowing him to voice them and listening attentively to what he has to say will likely increase his satisfaction with the settlement process and increase the likelihood that he will comply with the terms of whatever agreement is reached.

Conclusion

If a lawyer in a civil dispute can settle the case in a way that the client finds acceptable, the lawyer will save the client considerable cost, delay, and embarrassment, and will avoid the ethical dilemmas and anti-therapeutic consequences that litigation can produce. In settling the case, the lawyer can function as a peacemaker and healer. Therapeutic jurisprudence has much to offer the lawyer in this context. It calls for an increased psychological sensitivity in the attorney/client relationship, and awareness of some basic principles and techniques of psychology, enhanced interpersonal skills, well developed interviewing and counseling skills, and approaches for identifying and dealing with the variety of emotional issues and responses that the dispute is likely to produce.[66]

Settlement is often a difficult role for counsel, but an extremely important one. The settlement lawyer, as well as litigation lawyers generally, must master the various techniques of alternative dispute resolution and be able to effectively discuss them with the client. Matching the appropriate technique to the client and the circumstances constitutes a difficult professional challenge. Discussing these issues with the client, dealing with the psychological barriers to settlement that frequently arise, and helping the client to resolve the dispute in a way that will prevent recurring conflict call for a high level of interviewing, counseling, and interpersonal skills. Being a peacemaker is one of the law's most noble callings. Being a skilled settlement lawyer can provide the opportunity to help the client through one of life's most difficult challenges, and can bring great professional and personal satisfaction.

As lawyers, we should heed the advice of Abraham Lincoln: "Discourage litigation. Persuade your neighbors to compromise whenever you can. Point out to them how the nominal winner is often a real loser—in fees, expenses, and waste of time. As a peacemaker the lawyer has a superior opportunity of being a good man. There will still be business enough."[67]

References

Bandura, Albert. *Social Foundations of Thought and Action: A Social Cognitive Theory.* Englewood Cliffs, N.J.: Prentice-Hall, 1986.

Bastress, Robert M. and Joseph D. Harbaugh. *Interviewing, Counseling, and Negotiating Skills for Effective Representation.* Boston: Little, Brown, 1990.

Beck, Aaron T., Arthur Freeman, Denise D. Davis et al. *Cognitive Therapy of Personality Disorders.* 2d ed. New York: Guilford Press, 2004.

Beck, Aaron T., A.J. Rush, B.F. Shaw, and G. Emery. *Cognitive Therapy of Depression.* New York: Guilford, 1979.

Bellow, Gary and Bea Moulton. *The Lawyering Process: Materials for Clinical Instruction in Advocacy.* Mineola, N.Y.: Foundation Press, 1978.

Binder, David A., Paul Bergman, and Susan C. Price. *Lawyers as Counselors: A Client Centered Approach.* 2d ed. St. Paul, MN: Thomson/West, 2004.

Birgden, Astrid. "Dealing with the Resistant Criminal Client: A Psychologically-minded Strategy for More Effective Legal Counseling." 38 *Crim. L. Bull.* 225 (2002).

Brooks, Susan L. and Robert G. Madden, ed. *Relationship-Centered Lawyering: Social Science Theory for Transforming Legal Practice.* Durham, NC: Carolina Academic Press, 2010.

Bryan, Penelope E. *Constructive Divorce: Procedural Justice and Sociolegal Reform.* Washington, DC: American Psychological Association, 2005.

Burton, Robert. "Anatomy of Melancholy: Democritus to the Reader (1621)." In *2,000 Classical Legal Quotations,* edited by M. Frances McNamara, 408. Rochester, NY: Lawyers Cooperative, 1992.

Bush, Robert A. Baruch and Joseph P. Folger. *The Promise of Mediation: The Transformative Approach to Conflict.* Rev. Ed. San Francisco: Jossey-Bass, 2005.

Bush, Robert A. Baruch. "Substituting Mediation for Arbitration: The Growing Market for Evaluative Mediation and What it Means for the ADR Field." 3 *Pepperdine Disp. Resol. L. J.* 111 (2002).

Bush, Robert A. Baruch and Sally Ganong Pope. "Changing the Quality of Conflict Interaction: Principles and Practice of Transformative Mediation." 3 *Pepperdine Disp. Resol. L. J.* 67 (2002).

Cohen, Jonathan R. "The Culture of Legal Denial." 84 *Nebraska L. Rev.* 247 (2005).

Cohen, Jonathan R. "The Immorality of Denial." 79 *Tulane L. Rev.* 903 (2005).

Cohen, Jonathan R. "Legislating Apology: The Pros and Cons." 70 *U. Cin. L. Rev.* 819 (2002).

Cohen, Jonathan R. "Advising Clients to Apologize." 71 *S. Cal. L. Rev.* 1009 (1999).

Coyne, Jr., William F. "The Case for Settlement Counsel." 14 *Ohio St. J. on Disp. Resol.* 367 (1999).

Daicoff, Susan. "Afterword, The Role of Therapeutic Jurisprudence within the Comprehensive Law Movement." In *Practicing Therapeutic Jurisprudence: Law as a Helping Profession*, edited by Bruce J. Winick, David B. Wexler, and Dennis P. Stolle, 465–492. Durham, N.C.: Carolina Academic Press, 2000.

Dauer, Edward A. "Reflections on Therapeutic Jurisprudence, Creative Problem Solving, and Clinical Education in the Transactional Curriculum." 17 *St. Thomas L. Rev.* 483 (2005).

Dinerstein, Robert D. "Client-Centered Counseling: Reappraisal and Refinement." 32 *Ariz. L. Rev.* 501 (1990).

Dohrenwend, Barbara S., Askenasy, A. R., Krasnoff, L., and Dohrenwend, B. P. "Exemplification of a Method for Scaling Life Events: The PERI Life Events Scale." 19 J. Health & Soc. Behav. 205 (1978).

Fisher, Roger and William Ury. *Getting to Yes: Negotiating Agreement Without Giving In.* (2d ed.) New York, N.Y: Penguin Books, 1991.

Fiss, Owen M. "Against Settlement." 93 *Yale L. J.* 1073 (1984).

Folger, Joseph P. and Robert A. Baruch Bush. *Designing Mediation: Approaches to Training and Practice within a Transformative Framework.* New York: Institute for the Study of Conflict Transformation, 2001.

Galanter, Marc S. *The Day After the Litigation Explosion.* 46 Md. L. Rev. 3 (1986).

Goffman, Erving. *Relations in Public: Microstudies of the Public Order.* New York: Basic Books, 1971.

Goldberg, Steven B., Frank E.A. Sander, and Nancy H. Rogers. *Dispute Resolution: Negotiation, Mediation, and Other Processes.* (rev. 3d ed.) New York: Aspen Publishers, 2003.

Goleman, Daniel. *Emotional Intelligence.* New York: Bantam Books, 1995.

Goleman, Daniel. *Working with Emotional Intelligence.* New York: Bantam Books, 1998.

Hand, Learned. "The Deficiencies of Trials to Reach the Heart of the Matter—Address Delivered Before the Association of the Bar of the City of New York, Nov. 17, 1921," quoted in *Cases and Materials on Pleading and Procedure: State and Federal*, edited by David W. Louisell, Geoffrey C. Hazard, Jr., and Colin C. Tait. 6th ed. Westbury, N.Y.: Foundation Press, 1989.

Harman, Danna. "Lawyers Who Heal?" *Christian Science Monitor,* July 21, 2004. Accessed December 8, 2014. http://csmonitor.com/2004/0721/p17s01-lire.html.

Institute for the Study of Conflict Transformation, Inc. Accessed Dec. 9, 2014. http://www.transformativemediation.org/.

International Academy of Collaborative Professionals. Accessed December 9, 2014. http://www.collaborativepractice.com/.

Jones, Edward E. with Rita de S. French. *Social Stigma: The Psychology of Marked Relationships.* New York: W.H. Freeman, 1984.

Kovach, Kimberlee K. and Lela P. Love. "Evaluative Mediation is an Oxymoron." 14 *Alternatives to High Cost Litig.* 31 (1996).

Kovach, Kimberlee K. *Mediation: Principles and Practice.* St. Paul, Minn.: West Pub. Co., 1994.

Keeva, Steven. "Does Law Mean Never Having to Say You're Sorry?" 85-Dec A.B.A J. 64 (1999).

Lazare, Aaron. *On Apology.* New York: Oxford University Press, 2004.

Lewis, Jordana and Jerry Adler. "Forgive and Let Live." *Newsweek,* September 27, 2004.

Lincoln, Abraham. "Notes for a Law Lecture (July 1, 1850)." In *The Collected Works of Abraham Lincoln, Second Supplement: 1848–1865,* edited by Roy P. Basler and Christian O. Basler. New Brunswick: Rutgers University Press, 1990.

Lind, E. Allan, Ruth Kanfer, and P Christopher Earley. "Voice, Control, and Procedural Justice: Instrumental and Noninstrumental Concerns in Fairness Judgments." 59 *J. Personality & Soc. Psychol.* 952 (1990).

Lind, E. Allen and Tom R. Tyler. *The Social Psychology of Procedural Justice.* New York: Plenum Press, 1988.

MacCoun, Robert J, E. Allan Lind and Tom R. Tyler. "Alternative Dispute Resolution in Trial and Appellate Courts." In *Handbook of Psychology and Law,* edited by D.K. Kagehiro and W.S. Laufer, 95. New York: Springer-Verlag, 1992.

Margulies, Peter. "Representation of Domestic Violence Survivors as a New Paradigm of Poverty Law in Search of Access, Connection and Voice." 63 *Geo. Wash. L. Rev.* 1071 (1995).

McGraw, Phillip C. *Life Strategies: Doing What Works, Doing What Matters.* New York: Hyperion Books, 1999.

Meichenbaum, Donald. *Cognitive Behavior Modification: An Integrative Approach.* New York: Plenum Press, 1977.

Menkel-Meadow, Carrie J. "Narrowing the Gap by Narrowing the Field: What's Missing from the MacGrate Report—Of Skill, Human Science and Being a Human Being." 69 *Wash. L. Rev.* 593 (1994).

Menkel-Meadow, Carrie J. "Pursuing Settlement in an Adversary Culture: A Tale of Innovation Co-Opted or 'The Law of ADR.'" 19 *Fla. St. U. L. Rev.* 1 (1991).

Miller, William R. and Rollnick, Stephen. *Motivational Interviewing: Preparing People for Change.* 2d Ed. New York: Guilford Press, 2007.

Mills, Linda G. "Affective Lawyering: The Emotional Dimensions of the Lawyer-Client Relation." In *Practicing Therapeutic Jurisprudence: Law as a Helping Profession*, edited by Bruce J. Winick, David B. Wexler, and Dennis P. Stolle, 419–446. Durham, N.C.: Carolina Academic Press, 2000.

Mills, Linda G. "On the Other Side of Silence: Affective Lawyering for Intimate Abuse." 81 *Cornell L. Rev.* 1225 (1996).

Moffitt, Michael L. "Schmediation And The Dimensions Of Definition." 10 *Harv. Negot. L. Rev.* 69 (2005).

Noce, Dorothy Della, Robert A. Baruch Bush, and Joseph P. Folger. "Clarifying the Theoretical Underpinnings of Mediation: Implications for Practice and Policy." 3 *Pepperdine Disp. Resol. L. J.* 39 (2002).

Orenstein, Aviva. "Apology Excepted: Incorporating a Feminist Analysis into Evidence Policy Where You Would Least Expect It." 28 *Sw. U. L. Rev.* 221 (1999).

Persons, Jacqueline B. *Cognitive Therapy in Practice: A Case Formulation Approach.* New York: Norton, 1989.

Resnik Judith. "Many Doors? Closing Doors? Alternative Dispute Resolution and Adjudication." 10 *Ohio St. J. Disp. Resol.* 211 (1995).

Riskin, Leonard L. and James E. Westbrook. *Dispute Resolution and Lawyers.* (2d ed.) St. Paul, Minn.: West Pub. Co., 1997.

Riskin, Leonard. "*Understanding Mediators' Orientations, Strategies, and Techniques: A Grid for the Perplexed.*" 1 *Harv. Negotiation L. Rev.* 7 (1996).

Robbennolt, Jennifer K. "Apologies and Legal Settlement: An Empirical Examination." 102 *Mich. L. Rev.* 460 (2003).

Saccuzzo, Dennis P. "How Should the Police Respond to Domestic Violence: A Therapeutic Jurisprudence Analysis of Mandatory Arrest." 39 *Santa Clara L. Rev.* 765 (1999).

Scher, Steven J. and John M. Darley. "How Effective Are the Things People Say to Apologize? Effects of the Realization of the Apology Speech Act." 26 *J. Psycholinguistic Res.* 127 (1997).

Shuman, Daniel. "The Role of Apology in Tort Law." 83 *Judicature* 180 (2000).

Silver, Marjorie A., ed. *The Affective Assistance of Counsel: Practicing Law as a Healing Profession.* Durham, NC: Carolina Academic Press, 2007.

Silver, Marjorie A. "Love, Hate, and Other Emotional Interference in the Lawyer/Client Relationship." In *Practicing Therapeutic Jurisprudence: Law as a Helping Profession,* edited by Dennis P. Stolle, David B. Wexler and Bruce J. Winick, Chp. 13. Durham: Carolina Academic Press, 2000.

Silver, Marjorie A. "Emotional Intelligence and Legal Education." 5 *Psychol. Pub. Pol'y & L.* 1173 (1999).

Snyder, Mark. "On the Self-Perpetuating Nature of Social Stereotypes." In *Cognitive Processes in Stereotyping and Intergroup Behavior,* edited by David L. Hamilton, 183. Hillsdale, N.J.: L. Erlbaum Associates, 1981.

Tesler, Pauline H. *Collaborative Law: Achieving Effective Resolution in Divorce Without Litigation.* Chicago: Section of Family Law, American Bar Association, 2001.

Tesler, Pauline H. "Collaborative Law: What It Is and Why Lawyers Need to Know About It." 13 Am. J. Fam. L. 215 (1999). In *Practicing Therapeutic Jurisprudence: Law as a Helping Profession,* edited by Dennis P. Stolle, David B. Wexler and Bruce J. Winick, 187–205. Durham: Carolina Academic Press, 2000.

Tesler, Pauline H. "Collaborative Law: A New Paradigm for Divorce Lawyers." 5 *Psychol. Pub. Pol'y & L.* 967 (1999).

Tesler, Pauline H. "The Believing Game, The Doubting Game, and Collaborative Law: A Reply to Penelope Bryan." 5 *Psychol. Pub. Pol'y & L.* 1018 (1999).

Thibaut, John and Laurens Walker. "A Theory of Procedure." 66 *Calif. L. Rev.* 541 (1978). Accessed Dec. 3, 2014. Available at: http://scholarship.law.berkeley.edu/californialawreview/vol66/iss3/2.

Trubek, David M., David M. Trubek, Austin Sarat, William L.F. Felstiner, Herbert M. Kritzer, and Joel B. Grossman. "The Costs of Ordinary Litigation." 31 *UCLA L. Rev.* 72 (1983).

Tyler, Tom R. *Why People Obey the Law.* New Haven: Yale University Press, 1990.

Wagatsuma, Hiroshi and Arthur Rosett. "The Implications of Apology: Law and Culture in Japan and the United States." 20 *Law & Soc'y Rev.* 461 (1986).

Waldman, Ellen. "The Evaluative-Facilitative Debate in Mediation: Applying the Lens of Therapeutic Jurisprudence." 82 *Marquette L. Rev.* 155 (1998).

Wilcox, Ella Wheeler. "An Inspiration." In *Poems of Power.* Chicago: W. B. Conkey Company, 1902.

Williams, Gerald R. "Negotiation as a Healing Process." 1996 *J. Dis. Resol.* 1 (1996).

Winick, Bruce J. "Using Therapeutic Jurisprudence In Teaching Lawyering Skills: Meeting The Challenge Of The New Aba Standards." 17 *St. Thomas L. Rev.* 429 (2005).

Winick, Bruce J. and David B. Wexler. *Judging in a Therapeutic Key: Therapeutic Jurisprudence and the Courts.* Durham, N.C.: Carolina Academic Press, 2003.

Winick, Bruce J. "The Expanding Scope of Preventive Law." 3 *Fla. Coastal L. J.* 189 (2002).

Winick, Bruce J. "Therapeutic Jurisprudence and the Role of Counsel in Litigation." 37 *Cal. W. L. Rev.* 105 (2000).

Winick, Bruce J. "Applying the Law Therapeutically in Domestic Violence Cases." 69 *UMKC Law Review* 33 (1999).

Winick, Bruce J. "Redefining the Role of the Criminal Defense Lawyer at Plea Bargaining and Sentencing: A Therapeutic Jurisprudence/Preventive Law Model." 5 *Psychol. Pub. Pol'y & L.* 1034 (1999).

Winick, Bruce J. "Client Denial and Resistance in the Advance Directive Context: Reflections On How Attorneys Can Identify And Deal With A Psycholegal Soft Spot." 4 *Psychol. Pub. Pol'y & L.* 901 (1998).

Winick, Bruce J. *Therapeutic Jurisprudence Applied: Essays on Mental Health Law.* Durham, N.C.: Carolina Academic Press, 1997.

Winick, Bruce J. "Coercion and Mental Health Treatment." 74 *Denver U. L. Rev.* 1145 (1997).

Winick, Bruce J. "On Autonomy: Legal and Psychological Perspectives." 37 *Vill. L. Rev.* 1705 (1992).

28 U.S.C.A. Federal Rules of Civil Procedure, Rule 12(b)(6).

28 U.S.C.A. Federal Rules of Civil Procedure, Rule 16.

28 U.S.C.A. Federal Rules of Evidence, Rule 801(d)(2).

Notes

1. *See, e.g.,* David M. Trubek et al., *The Costs of Ordinary Litigation,* 31 UCLA L. REV. 72 (1983).

2. Marc Galanter, *The Day After the Litigation Explosion,* 46 MD. L. REV. 3, 8–11 (1986). As the following discussion shows, litigation ordinarily is anti-therapeutic for both parties. There are, of course, exceptions. Sometimes a lawsuit can be cathartic. In some instances, for example involving a victim of domestic violence, it can be empowering in ways that can be psychologically beneficial. Although sometimes these psychological benefits may outweigh the antitherapeutic effects of litigation described herein, other ways of achieving them—in counseling, for example—frequently will exist.

3. Barbara S. Dohrenwend, et al., *Exemplification of a Method for Scaling Life Events: The PERI Life Events Scale,* 19 J. HEALTH & SOC. BEHAV. 205 (1978).

4. Learned Hand, *The Deficiencies of Trials to Reach the Heart of the Matter,* address delivered before the association of the bar of the City of New York, Nov. 17, 1921, *quoted in* PLEADING AND PROCEDURE: STATE AND FEDERAL 36, 37 (David W. Louisell et al., eds. 6th

ed. 1989).

5. *See, e.g.,* ROBERT M. BASTRESS & JOSEPH D. HARBAUGH, INTERVIEWING, COUNSELING, & NEGOTIATING, SKILLS FOR EFFECTIVE REPRESENTATION 334–38 (1990); DAVID A. BINDER ET AL., LAWYERS AS COUNSELORS: A CLIENT CENTERED APPROACH, 2–13 (2d ed. 2004); Robert D. Dinerstein, *Client-Centered Counseling: Reappraisal and Refinement,* 32 ARIZ. L. REV. 501 (1990); Bruce J. Winick, *Redefining the Role of the Criminal Defense Lawyer at Plea Bargaining and Sentencing: A Therapeutic Jurisprudence/Preventive Law Model,* 5 PSYCHOL. PUB. POL'Y & L. 1034, 1067 (1999).

6. Robert Burton, *Anatomy of Melancholy: Democritus to the Reader* (1621) *in* M. FRANCES MCNAMARA, CLASSIC LEGAL QUOTATIONS 408 (1992).

7. One exception involves test cases or cases having great precedential value, such as civil rights cases. *See* Owen M. Fiss, *Against Settlement,* 93 YALE L. J. 1073 (1984).

8. *See* Danna Harman, *Lawyers Who Heal?,* CHRISTIAN SCI. MON., July 21, 2004, http://csmonitor.com/2004/0721/p17s01-lire.html (last accessed December 8, 2014) (describing client's satisfaction following advice of his attorney who had discouraged litigation).

9. *See generally* STEVEN GOLDBERG, ET AL., DISPUTE RESOLUTION (3d ed. 2000); KIMBERLEE K. KOVACH, MEDIATION: PRINCIPLES AND PRACTICE (1994); LEONARD L. RISKIN & JAMES E. WESTBROOK, DISPUTE RESOLUTION AND LAWYERS (2d ed. 1997); Carrie Menkel-Meadow, *Pursuing Settlement in an Adversary Culture: A Tale of Innovation Co-Opted or "The Law of ADR",* 19 FLA. ST. U. L. REV. 1 (1991); Judith Resnik, *Many Doors? Closing Doors? Alternative Dispute Resolution and Adjudication,* 10 OHIO ST. J. DISP. RESOL. 211 (1995); Leonard Riskin, *Understanding Mediators' Orientations, Strategies, and Techniques: A Grid for the Perplexed,* 1 HARV. NEGOTIATION L. REV. 7 (1996). For discussion of the relatively new dispute resolution model known as collaborative law, see *infra* note 21, and accompanying text.

10. *See* Gerald R. Williams, *Negotiation as a Healing Process,* 1996 J. DIS. RESOL. 1 (1996).

11. *See* ROGER FISHER & WILLIAM URY, GETTING TO YES: NEGOTIATING AGREEMENT WITHOUT GIVING IN 166 (2d ed. 1991); *see also generally* GARY BELLOW & BEA MOULTON, THE LAWYERING PROCESS 140–56 (1978).

12. *See* BRUCE J. WINICK, THERAPEUTIC JURISPRUDENCE APPLIED: ESSAYS ON MENTAL HEALTH LAW, 68–83 (1997); Bruce J. Winick, *On Autonomy: Legal and Psychological Perspectives,* 37 VILL. L. REV. 1705, 1755–68 (1992).

13. *See* FISHER & URY, *supra* note 11, at 166. In general, people feel better about making choices for themselves, and less well when others make choices for them that they experience as coercion. *See* Bruce J. Winick, *Coercion and Mental Health Treatment,* 74 DENVER U. L. REV. 1145, 1155–67 (1997) (discussing voluntariness and coercion in the context of civil commitment of those with mental illness); Winick, *supra* note 12, at 1755–68 (discussing the psychological value of choices in a wide variety of matters).

14. *See* PHILLIP C. MCGRAW, LIFE STRATEGIES: DOING WHAT WORKS, DOING WHAT MATTERS, 201 (1999).

15. FISHER & URY, *supra* note 11 (distinguishing interest from position-based negotiation).

16. Ellen Waldman, *The Evaluative-Facilitative Debate in Mediation: Applying the Lens of Therapeutic Jurisprudence,* 82 MARQUETTE L. REV. 155 (1998) (comparing evaluative and facilitative mediation and discussing the therapeutic effects of facilitative mediation).

17. *Id.* For criticism of evaluative mediation, see Kimberlee K. Kovach & Lela P. Love, *Evaluative Mediation is an Oxymoron,* 14 ALTERNATIVES TO HIGH COST LITIG. 31 (1996); Michael L. Moffitt, *Schmediation And The Dimensions Of Definition,* 10 HARV. NEGOT. L.

Rev. 69, 83–84 (2005).

18. Robert A. Baruch Bush & Joseph P. Folger, The Promise of Mediation: The Transformative Approach to Conflict (2005); Joseph P. Folger & Robert A. Baruch Bush, Designing Mediation: Approaches to Training and Practice within a Transformative Framework (2001); Dorothy Della Noce, Robert A. Baruch Bush, & Joseph P. Folger, *Clarifying the Theoretical Underpinnings of Mediation: Implications for Practice and Policy*, 3 Pepperdine Disp. Resol. L. J. 39 (2002); Robert A. Baruch Bush and Sally Ganong Pope, *Changing the Quality of Conflict Interaction: Principles and Practice of Transformative Mediation* 3 Pepperdine Disp. Resol. L. J. 67 (2002); Robert A. Baruch Bush, *Substituting Mediation for Arbitration: The Growing Market for Evaluative Mediation and What it Means for the ADR Field*, 3 Pepperdine Disp. Resol. L. J. 111 (2002); Susan Daicoff, *Afterword, The Role of Therapeutic Jurisprudence within the Comprehensive Law Movement* in Practicing Therapeutic Jurisprudence (2000) at 465, 479; Moffitt *supra* note 17, at 86–87. For more information on transformative mediation, see the web site of the Institute for the Study of Conflict Transformation, Inc., http://www.transformativemediation.org/ (last accessed Jan. 13, 2015).

19. *See* Penelope E. Bryan, Constructive Divorce : Procedural Justice and Sociolegal Reform (2005).

20. This practice, which seems particularly pervasive in the matrimonial bar, is unethical. The lawyer is a fiduciary, who never should place his or her own interests above those of the client.

21. For discussion of the collaborative law model in the divorce context, see Pauline H. Tesler, Collaborative Law: Achieving Effective Resolution in Divorce Without Litigation (2001); Pauline H. Tesler, *Collaborative Law: A New Paradigm for Divorce Lawyers*, 5 Psychol. Pub. Pol'y & L. 967 (1999); Pauline H. Tesler, *The Believing Game, The Doubting Game, and Collaborative Law: A Reply to Penelope Bryan*, 5 Psychol. Pub. Pol'y & L. 1018 (1999); Pauline H. Tesler, *Collaborative Law: What it is and Why Lawyers Need to Know About It*, 13 Am. J. Fam. L. 215 (1999), *reprinted in* Practicing Therapeutic Jurisprudence, *supra* note 18, at 187. The leading professional organization for collaborative family practice is the International Academy of Collaborative Professionals, which maintains a website at http://www.collaborativepractice.com/ (last accessed Jan. 6, 2015).

22. Edward A. Dauer, *Reflections on Therapeutic Jurisprudence, Creative Problem Solving, and Clinical Education in the Transactional Curriculum*, 17 St. Thomas L, Rev 483, 486–87 (2005).

23. *See generally*, Bastress & Harbaugh, *supra* note 5; Binder, et al., *supra* note 5.

24. *See, e.g.,* Edward E. Jones et al., Social Stigma: The Psychology of Marked Relationships 177–78 (1984); Mark Snyder, *On the Self-Perpetuating Nature of Social Stereotypes, in* Cognitive Processes in Stereotyping and Intergroup Behavior 183 (David L. Hamilton ed., 1981).

25. Albert Bandura, Social Foundations of Thought and Action: A Social Cognitive Theory 338, 363, 368, 412–13, 467, 469–72 (1986).

26. *See supra* note 18, and accompanying text.

27. *See, e.g.,* Fed. R. Civ. P. 12(b)(6).

28. Bruce J. Winick, *The Expanding Scope of Preventive Law*, 3 Fla. Coastal L. J. 189 (2002).

29. William F. Coyne Jr., *The Case For Settlement Counsel*, 14 Ohio St. J. on Disp. Resol.

367, 367 (1999).

30. Fed. R. Civ. P. 16; *see* Robert J. MacCoun et al., *Alternative Dispute Resolution in Trial and Appellate Courts, in* Handbook of Psychology and Law 95, 107 (D.K. Kagehiro & W.S. Laufer eds., 1992).

31. *See* Bruce J. Winick, *Client Denial and Resistance in the Advance Directive Context: Reflections On How Attorneys Can Identify And Deal With A Psycholegal Soft Spot,* 4 Psychol. Pub. Pol'y & L. 901 (1998).

32. Jordana Lewis & Jerry Adler, *Forgive and Let Live,* Newsweek, Sept. 27, 2004, at 52.

33. This process bears a relationship to the motivational interviewing technique developed by counselors in the area of substance abuse treatment, which psychologist Astrid Birgden has adapted for use in conversations with a criminal client who is unwilling to accept responsibility for his wrongdoing or is resistant to potential rehabilitation. *See* Astrid Birgden, *Dealing with the Resistant Criminal Client: A Psychologically-minded Strategy for More Effective Legal Counseling,* 38 Crim. L. Bull. 225 (2002).

34. *See e.g.,* Bandura, *supra* note 25; Aaron T. Beck, Cognitive Treatment of Depression (1992); Aaron T. Beck, et al., Cognitive Therapy of Personality Disorders (2003); Donald. Meichenbaum, Cognitive Behavior Modification: An Integrative Approach (1977).

35. For general discussions of interviewing and counseling skills, see sources cited in *supra* note 5.

36. *See,* Bruce J. Winick, *Applying the Law Therapeutically in Domestic Violence Cases* 69 UMKC L. Rev. 33, 77 (2000) ("Cognitive restructuring seeks to break down the [individual's] cognitive distortions and to replace them with more accurate, functional, adaptive, and effective thought patterns."); *see also* Jacqueline B. Persons, Cognitive Therapy in Practice: A Case Formulation Approach (1989); Dennis P. Saccuzzo, *How Should the Police Respond to Domestic Violence: A Therapeutic Jurisprudence Analysis of Mandatory Arrest,* 39 Santa Clara L. Rev. 765, 781 (1999).

37. *See* text prior to and accompanying note 23.

38. *See* Winick, *supra* note 31, at 904 (references omitted). *See also* the extensive discussion of denial in Chapter 6(2)(D), *infra.*

39. *See id.* at 908–17.

40. Jonathan R. Cohen, *The Culture of Legal Denial,* 84 Nebraska Law Review 247 (2005); Jonathan R. Cohen, *The Immorality of Denial,* 79 Tulane L. Rev. 903 (2005).

41. *See supra* note 5 and accompanying text.

42. Winick, *supra* note 31, at 906–17.

43. *See* Cohen, *The Culture of Legal Denial, supra* note 40, at 271–82 (making suggestions concerning how the lawyer can discuss responsibility-taking with the client, including techniques of building trust and confidence, listening, conveying empathy, and the differing styles of confrontation that the lawyer can use in raising the subject with the client—confrontation, indirection, and engagement).

44. *See* Winick, *supra* note 31, at 912–13.

45. *See* Daniel Goleman, Emotional Intelligence (1997); Daniel Goleman, Working with Emotional Intelligence 73 (1998); Marjorie A. Silver, *Emotional Intelligence and Legal Education,* 5 Psychol. Pub. Pol'y & L. 1173 (1999).

46. *See* Peter Margulies, *Representation of Domestic Violence Survivors as a New Paradigm of Poverty Law in Search of Access, Connection and Voice,* 63 Geo. Wash. L. Rev. 1071 (1995);

Carrie J. Menkel-Meadow, *Narrowing the Gap by Narrowing the Field: What's Missing from the MacGrate Report—Of Skill, Human Science and Being a Human Being*, 69 WASH. L. REV. 593 (1994); Linda G. Mills, *On the Other Side of Silence: Affective Lawyering for Intimate Abuse*, 81 CORNELL L. REV. 1225 (1996); Linda G. Mills, *Affective Lawyering: The Emotional Dimensions of the Lawyer-Client Relation, in* PRACTICING THERAPEUTIC JURISPRUDENCE, *supra* note 18, at 419.

47. See *supra* note 33, and accompanying text. For discussion of the techniques of motivational interviewing, see WILLIAM R. MILLER & STEPHEN ROLLNICK, MOTIVATIONAL INTERVIEWING: PREPARING PEOPLE TO CHANGE ADDICTIVE BEHAVIOR 33–51 (2d ed. 2002).

48. *See* Birgden, *supra* note 33.

49. MILLER & ROLLNICK, *supra* note 47, at 37.

50. *Id.*, at 38–39.

51. *Id.*, at 39–40.

52. FED R. EVID. 801 (d) (2) (party admissions exception to the hearsay rule).

53. Jennifer K. Robbennolt, *Apologies and Legal Settlement: An Empirical Examination*, 102 MICH. L. REV. 460, 461 (2003); *see also*, Hiroshi Wagatsuma & Arthur Rosett, *The Implications of Apology: Law and Culture in Japan and the United States*, 20 LAW & SOC'Y REV. 461 (1986) (comparing practices in Japan and the U.S.).

54. *See e.g.*, Jonathan R. Cohen, *Advising Clients to Apologize*, 71 S. CAL. L. REV. 1009 (1999); Steven Keeva, *Does Law Mean Never Having to Say You're Sorry?* A.B.A J., Dec. 1999, at 64; Aviva Orenstein, *Incorporating a Feminist Analysis into Evidence Policy Where You Would Least Expect It*, 28 SW. U. L. REV. 221 (1999); Robbennolt, *supra* note 53, at 461; Daniel Shuman, *The Role of Apology in Tort Law*, 83 JUDICATURE 180 (2000).

55. *See* Robbennolt, *supra* note 53, at 470–71; *id.* at 470 & n.44 (listing statutes); *see also* Jonathan R. Cohen, *Legislating Apology: The Pros and Cons*, 70 U. CIN. L. REV. 819 (2002).

56. Robbennolt, *supra* note 53, at 471.

57. ERVING GOFFMAN, RELATIONS IN PUBLIC: MICROSTUDIES OF THE PUBLIC ORDER 113 (1971); AARON LAZARE, ON APOLOGY 39 (2004); Robbennolt, *supra* note 53, at 477–80; Steven J. Scher & John M. Darley, *How Effective Are the Things People Say to Apologize? Effects of the Realization of the Apology Speech Act*, 26 J. PSYCHOLINGUISTIC RES. 127, 134–36 (1997); Wagatsuma & Rosett, *supra* note 53.

58. LAZARE, *supra* note 57, at 39.

59. LAZARE, *supra* note 57, at 44; Robbennolt, *supra* note 53, at 477–80.

60. LAZARE, *supra* note 57, at 228–50.

61. Robbennolt, *supra* note 53, at 471, 515–16.

62. Although I have heard this statement attributed to Abraham Lincoln, research has failed to discover this quote in Lincoln's writings. A closely related point is made by poet Ella Wheeler Wilcox, who wrote that "No question is ever settled, until it is settled right." Ella Wheeler Wilcox, *An Inspiration, in* ELLA WHEELER WILCOX, POEMS OF POWER 142–143 (1902, 2003). The entire poem is as follows:

> "*An Inspiration*
>
> However the battle is ended,
> Though proudly the victor comes
> With fluttering flags and prancing nags
> And echoing roll of drums,

Still truth proclaims this motto
In letters of living light,
No question is ever settled
Until it is settled right.

Though the heel of the strong oppressor
May grind the weak in the dust;
And the voices of fame with one acclaim
May call him great and just,
Let those who applaud take warning.
And keep this motto in sight,
No question is ever settled
Until it is settled right.

Let those who have failed take courage;
Though the enemy seems to have won,
Though his ranks are strong, if he be in the wrong
The battle is not yet done;
For, sure as the morning follows
The darkest hour of the night,
No question is ever settled
Until it is settled right.

O man bowed down with labour!
O woman young, yet old!
O heart oppressed in the toiler's breast
And crushed by the power of gold
Keep on with your weary battle
Against triumphant might;
No question is ever settled
Until it is settled right."

63. For discussion of the collaborative law model in the divorce context, see Tesler, *supra* note 21.

64. *See e.g.*, E. ALLEN LIND & TOM R. TYLER, THE SOCIAL PSYCHOLOGY OF PROCEDURAL JUSTICE (1988); TOM R. TYLER, WHY PEOPLE OBEY THE LAW (1990); E. Allan Lind *et al.*, *Voice, Control, and Procedural Justice: Instrumental and Noninstrumental Concerns in Fairness Judgments*, 59 J. PERSONALITY & SOC. PSYCHOL. 952 (1990); John Thibaut & Laurens Walker, *A Theory of Procedure*, 66 CALIF. L. REV. 541 (1978). The likelihood that the individual will experience feelings of coercion will be increased if they are not accorded procedural justice. *See* Bruce J. Winick, *Therapeutic Jurisprudence and the Role of Counsel in Litigation*, 37 CAL. W. L. REV. 105, 116–19 (2000) (reviewing research by the MacArthur Research Network on Law and Mental Health concerning the perception of coercion by patients in the civil commitment context).

65. *See* JUDGING IN A THERAPEUTIC KEY: THERAPEUTIC JURISPRUDENCE AND THE COURTS, ed. Bruce J. Winick et al., (Durham, N.C.: Carolina Academic Press, 2003), 129–64 (discussing how judges can increase court compliance through use of procedural justice); Winick, *supra* note 64, at 116–19 (discussing how attorneys can use procedural justice).

66. For a discussion of how these skills can be taught in law school, see Bruce J. Winick,

Using Therapeutic Jurisprudence in Teaching Lawyering Skills: Meeting the Challenge of the New ABA Standards, 17 St. Thomas L. Rev. 429 (2005).

67. Abraham Lincoln, *Notes for a Law Lecture (July 1, 1850), in* The Collected Works of Abraham Lincoln, 1848–1865: Supplement Two, (Roy P. Basler, ed. 1990).

Chapter 6

Lawyer as Healer

Introduction

Clients bring to the law office many of the worst problems encountered in life. They have been indicted for crime. They are facing the major surgery of divorce. They have suffered serious personal injury as a result of a tort committed by another. They are encountering increasing infirmities and diminished capacities as a result of aging or illness. They have been abused and betrayed by someone in whom they have placed their trust—an intimate partner, family member, a business partner, employer or employee, for example. They've encountered legal difficulties as a result of mental illness or substance abuse. They are suffering from an illness or disability that has or is likely to produce troubles in the workplace. They have suffered persecution in their homeland and are battling with a resistant immigration and customs enforcement bureaucracy to obtain political asylum.

In each of these situations, the individual seeks legal help to deal with or prevent a difficult legal problem. But the legal problem also often produces a variety of emotional reactions and difficulties. The concept of psycholegal soft spots and opportunity points is helpful in this connection. The legal involvement may produce predictable emotional reactions, such as anger, hard or hurt feelings, stress, sadness, anxiety, depression, and the like. The lawyer needs to recognize these emotional states, and apply strategies designed to minimize them. This is a task that calls upon the lawyer's creativity and the psychological insights that therapeutic jurisprudence brings to the lawyering process. In addition to dealing with the legal problem, the therapeutic jurisprudence/preventive lawyer must take these emotional problems into account and strive to minimize or avoid the adverse emotional difficulties that the legal problem has or is likely to produce. In this respect, the therapeutic jurisprudence/preventive lawyer functions in part as a healer.

Attorneys applying the model of lawyering set forth in this book must be sensitive to these emotional problems and develop ways of addressing them when they arise in the lawyer/client relationship. The lawyer must be alert to the signs and symptoms of these emotional difficulties and express empathy when they occur. Ignoring the overt expressions of these emotional difficulties is likely to cause the client to feel misunderstood and to regard the lawyer as callous and uncaring. The trust and confidence necessary for the lawyer/client relationship to work effectively may be eroded or destroyed. A lawyer who addresses only the client's legal rights and interests, but who is blind to the client's emotional difficulties, may be missing an important opportunity to help the client through a difficult time. The client is under great stress and experiencing emotional turmoil, and visiting a lawyer who seems oblivious to this aspect of his problems may make him feel even worse. A lawyer who is concerned with his client's emotional well-being and who sees ministering to these difficulties as part of his professional responsibilities will more likely increase client satisfaction and, if he can be helpful, his own feeling of professional satisfaction.

Many of the examples previously discussed in this book illustrate the opportunities that lawyers have for helping the client to achieve reconciliation and healing. The preventive lawyer assists his clients in accomplishing their goals while avoiding legal difficulties. By avoiding litigation, attorneys can prevent or minimize a wide assortment of emotional problems that could otherwise occur, helping their clients to repair relationships, and to restore their equilibrium. Therapeutic jurisprudence/preventive lawyers allow their clients to get past the dispute and to experience the pleasures in their business or personal lives that the cloud of litigation often makes difficult. The lawyer/peacemaker who settles disputes can increase the client's ability to move on with his life and maintain beneficial relationships that otherwise would be destroyed or compromised.

Meetings and interactions with the client thus serve a dual purpose. In addition to dealing with a present or future legal problem, they provide the opportunity to help the client let go of anger or other negative emotions that otherwise would diminish the quality of his life. Traditional lawyering ignores this opportunity. The lawyer who is psychologically-minded and who embraces an ethic of care, however, can provide invaluable assistance to the client in a great many ways. He can help the client to avoid repeating the types of mistakes that have gotten him into trouble in the past. He can help the client to leave behind the cognitive distortions that may have prevented successful functioning in his business or personal life. He can provide a measure of healing and reconciliation.

The lawyer, of course, is not a therapist, and shouldn't presume to take the place of a clinical psychologist or psychiatrist. But there are a range of emotional problems that are closely entwined with the legal issues the client faces that a psychologically-minded lawyer can help the client to deal with. The lawyer needs developed interpersonal skills and to be knowledgeable about the clinical resources that exist in the community. When other resources are needed by the client, he should be aware of relevant specialists in the community and how to have the sometimes sensitive conversation with the client concerning the advisability of such services. Many clients will be disinclined to see themselves in need of such services. But they bring their problems to the law office, and thereby provide the lawyer with an opportunity to be helpful. Rather than ignoring them, the lawyer can help to increase their recognition and understanding of their problems, and ways of dealing with them.

Discussions with the client about his emotional difficulties present problems that may be beyond the range of the lawyer's skills. This book seeks to acquaint the lawyer with at least some of these issues and to suggest that legal education's mission should be broadened to include interpersonal skills training.

The role of lawyer as healer can perhaps best be illustrated in the context of criminal law practice. As a result, this chapter develops this role of the lawyer by focusing mainly on the criminal context. It advances a therapeutic and preventive role for defense lawyers in the plea-bargaining and sentencing process, and then discusses many of the psychological skills that are needed to play this role well. The chapter then examines a criminal context in which the prosecutor can play a healing role for the victim of the crime. Finally, it contains a short description of several examples outside of the criminal arena to which these insights can easily be adapted.

1. The Criminal Defense Lawyer's Role in the Rehabilitation of the Client

Many criminal clients will have mental health or substance abuse problems or other emotional difficulties that contribute to their being charged with crime. Some will be falsely accused, of course, and they deserve the kind of vigorous lawyering that criminal defense lawyers specialize in. But many will be guilty of their offense, and likely to repeat such behavior, as a result of their emotional problems. Seeing this possibility, the lawyer can help the client to gain an awareness that a psychosocial problem might be at the root of his difficulties and to consider whether the time has come for him to deal with it. The therapeutic jurisprudence/preventive law practitioner in the criminal area therefore has many opportunities to assist in the client's rehabilitation and healing.

Several recent developments suggest the need for rethinking the role of the criminal defense lawyer at plea bargaining and sentencing. The defense attorney's traditional function at sentencing is to present arguments to mitigate a sentence, designed either to obtain a term of probation or (where imprisonment is likely) to minimize the term of imprisonment imposed. The traditional role of counsel at plea bargaining is to work out the best possible deal for the client in the circumstances, and it frequently involves making to the prosecutor similar arguments in mitigation of sentence. Rehabilitation has always been one of the important aims of criminal sentencing. Since the mid-1970s, however, the rehabilitative ideal has not been taken seriously. Scholarly work in the early 1970s on the efficacy of correctional rehabilitation seemed to conclude that nothing worked. This conclusion now seems to have been premature. Perhaps the most that could accurately have been said at that point is that we could not answer the question of what works in correctional rehabilitation and that we simply did not know. This was the analysis of a National Academy of Sciences panel that studied the issue of correctional rehabilitation and its alternatives in the late 1970s.

Recently, however, some studies have provided more optimistic evidence concerning the prospects for rehabilitation of criminal offenders. British psychologist James McGuire's edited book *What Works? Reducing Reoffending* provides a synthesis of the most successful rehabilitative approaches that have been reported in the current literature. McGuire trumpeted the promise of cognitive behavioral methods, including the reasoning and rehabilitative cognitive skills training package now widely in use. These programs involve a variety of techniques designed to make the individual aware of existing behavior patterns and of alternative problem-solving approaches. In particular, they involve relapse prevention models designed to develop in the offender an internal self-management system that allows the individual to identify those situations and events that often lead to criminal behavior and to develop and use strategies for avoiding high-risk situations or minimizing the likelihood that they trigger the individual's customary behavior patterns.

A related development has been the emergence over the past twenty years of what has become known as "problem-solving courts." These include Drug Treatment Court, Domestic Violence Court, Mental Health Court, and various hybrid models. Offenders may plead not guilty and face their charges. In the alternative, they may plead guilty pursuant to a plea bargain or submit to the sentencing discretion of the trial judge. Finally, if they recognize that they have a problem and wish to deal with it, they may elect to participate in a problem-solving court program. Defendants electing such participation enter into a type of behavioral contract with the court in which they undertake to participate in rehabilitative efforts, which are monitored by the court, and to report to court periodically. In Drug Treatment Court, for example, the defendant agrees to participate in drug treatment in the community and to submit to urinalysis drug testing to monitor his compliance. He reports to court every two weeks or so. If his urine is clean, the judge praises him and other drug court participants in the courtroom applaud his efforts. If his drug test is positive, the judge sanctions him and expresses displeasure. If the defendant succeeds in the program, which may last one to one-and-a-half years, charges are dismissed and there is a celebration that includes the defendant's family and friends and other program participants. At the ceremony, the arresting officer presents him with a diploma. Drug Treatment Court has succeeded in rehabilitating many substance abusers and in reducing recidivism. Based on the Drug Treatment Court model, other problem solving courts have been developed to deal with such problems as domestic violence and untreated mental illness.

These promising new models pose significant new opportunities for rehabilitating offenders that, particularly in this age of prison overcrowding, many judges and prosecutors will respond to with interest and even enthusiasm. These cognitive self-change and relapse prevention methods and the problem solving courts join a variety of promising models used by judges in fashioning creative community alternatives to incarceration that include counseling programs, home confinement and electronic monitoring, restitution, and community service. Criminal defense attorneys need to understand these emerging approaches and to use them to help fashion rehabilitative plans for their clients that can be urged as the basis for a more advantageous plea bargain, probation, or more lenient sentencing, or a problem-solving court diversion from the criminal process.

Several additional developments magnify the importance of criminal defense attorneys becoming acquainted with these new rehabilitative methodologies. Post-offense rehabilitation has traditionally served as a ground for mitigating sentences in both federal and state courts. At the federal level, until 2005, criminal sentencing had been dominated by approaches using sentencing guidelines that significantly limited the discretion of trial judges in the setting of criminal sentences. These approaches were designed to emphasize a "just desserts" approach to criminal punishment, to remedy what had been the growing problem of sentencing disparity (in which trial judges were generally perceived as sentencing similar defendants committing similar crimes to widely differing terms of imprisonment), and to increase sentences in part as a result of the perception that some judges were "soft on crime."

Tension remained, however, between the goal of avoiding sentencing disparity and that of accomplishing individualized justice. This lead many federal sentencing judges to seek to manipulate the sentencing guidelines by granting downward departures from the range of sentences contemplated when special circumstances justified such departures. Federal circuit and district courts increasingly recognized that post-offense rehabilitation itself may qualify as a ground for a downward departure. In 2005, the Supreme Court in *United States v. Booker* held that portions of the guidelines violated the Sixth Amendment right to jury trial. In fashioning a remedy the Court left the guidelines in place, but made them discretionary. Thereafter, sentencing judges largely followed the guidelines, but possessed considerably broader discretion to depart from them in the interest of fashioning a just sentence. Recent proposed amendments to the Federal Sentencing Guidelines specifically inform sentencing judges that downward departures are warranted where the offender's criminal activity is related to a treatment issue such as drug or alcohol abuse or significant mental illness. In such cases, the guidelines allow for alternative penalties such as home or community confinement or intermittent confinement. These developments provide an added reason for the criminal defense lawyer to explore with the client various rehabilitative options and to advocate for these in plea bargaining and sentencing.

Sentencing guideline approaches also are increasingly being used in the states. Almost half of the states have such guidelines, and the degree to which judges can depart from the specified range varies. Other states allow considerably more discretion in sentencing. As a result, criminal defense lawyers in state practice also should explore rehabilitative options and use them to diminish the client's sentence.

These developments place a premium on criminal defense attorneys understanding the new rehabilitative approaches, being able to persuade their clients of their value, and helping those who are interested to fashion rehabilitative and relapse prevention plans. They also need to develop creative ways of presenting the facts of their clients' rehabilitation more effectively to prosecutors in plea bargaining negotiations and probation officers who design presentence reports. In addition, in sentencing hearings they need to present these arguments to sentencing judges concerning the justifications for granting downward departures and for exercising their discretion in designing a rehabilitative rather than a punitive sentence.

The confluence of these recent developments call for a rethinking and broadening of the role of criminal defense attorneys in the plea bargaining and sentencing process. Not only do these attorneys need to develop new skills, but they need to think of themselves in new ways. They need to understand the vocabulary and techniques of these new rehabilitative approaches. They need to develop techniques for dealing with their clients about the issue of rehabilitation with a higher degree of psychological sensitivity. They need to understand whether they know it or not, they are functioning as therapeutic agents in their interactions with their clients, particularly in the plea and sentencing process. They need to recognize the opportunities that these new developments provide to offer new modes of assistance to their clients that can promote both their interests in maintaining their liberty and in achieving a higher degree of psychological well-being. They need to see themselves as healers. Moreover, they need to understand that playing these new roles can have important positive effects for their own mental health and personal and professional satisfaction. In short, they need to understand the insights of therapeutic jurisprudence and preventive law and to see themselves as therapeutic jurisprudence/preventive lawyers.

These recent developments thus provide a new opportunity for criminal defense lawyers to assist their clients to obtain post-offense rehabilitation. They allow defense lawyers to urge in plea bargaining discussions and at sentencing hearings that their clients' rehabilitative efforts should constitute grounds for a downward departure from the sentencing range they otherwise would have received under the Guidelines, or for probation or a lesser sentence in nonguideline jurisdictions. To effectively play this role, defense attorneys need to familiarize themselves with the full range of rehabilitative opportunities that might be available in their community, including the problem-solving courts, the conditions for eligibility for admission into these programs, and the mechanics of assisting their clients to gain entry into them. They need to consider at an early point in the professional relationship, preferably at the initial client interview, whether the client is a suitable candidate for rehabilitation and desires or can be persuaded to undertake rehabilitative efforts. They should advise their clients of the value of such rehabilitative efforts in the plea bargaining, sentencing, or diversion process. They should assist willing clients to enter such programs or otherwise obtain needed rehabilitative or therapeutic services at an early point. In appropriate cases, they should assist the client to design a rehabilitative program tailored to the client's needs and interests. They should monitor their clients' progress in these programs, periodically reminding them of the value they may provide both in obtaining more favorable sentencing and in adjusting to post-sentence life.

When clients have successfully completed such rehabilitative efforts or are making encouraging progress in them, defense attorneys should bring this to the attention of prosecutors in the plea bargaining process, urging such rehabilitative efforts as a ground for a plea bargained sentence lower than that otherwise authorized under the Guidelines or a lowered sentence recommendation on the part of the prosecutor. They should inform the court's probation department about such rehabilitative efforts, because the department often prepares a presentence report for the court, and its recommendation concerning the range of sentences authorized under the Guidelines and the appropriate sentence in the particular case is frequently given great weight. In cases in which a plea bargain does not specify a particular sentence, defense attorneys should focus on such rehabilitative efforts at their presentation at the sentencing hearing, urging them as a basis for a downward departure. Even in the case of clients who had been convicted following trial, any post-offense rehabilitative efforts that have occurred may similarly be urged at the sentencing hearing as a basis for a reduced sentence. In addition, there may be opportunities to raise rehabilitation as a basis for a post-sentencing motion to reduce a sentence. For example, many states' codes of criminal procedure allow the court to use "shock probation" or "shock sentencing." In these situations, the sentencing judge retains plenary jurisdiction over the case for a certain period of time after the defendant has been incarcerated. At any time during this jurisdictional period, the court can conduct a hearing to determine whether the defendant should be subjected to further incarceration. Furthermore, for defendants who have been sentenced to a term of imprisonment, their participation in rehabilitative efforts within the correctional setting can be urged as a basis for favorable resentencing should appellate review of their conviction or sentence result in a resentencing proceeding. Even when resentencing does not occur, these prison rehabilitative efforts can favorably impress the parole board when the defendant becomes eligible for parole consideration.

In all of these circumstances, attorneys can assert, when appropriate, the rehabilitative efforts of their clients as grounds for a sentence of probation rather than of imprisonment. In these times of overcrowded prisons, sentencing judges are especially interested in rehabilitative alternatives to incarceration. Prisons, particularly those that are overcrowded and underfunded and can offer little in the way of rehabilitation, may be criminogenic, schooling inmates in the ways of crime and breeding anger and resentment that are not conducive to rehabilitation. Allowing offenders to continue to remain in the community, particularly if residing with their family or other support group, permits them to engage or continue to engage in productive employment, helping to earn funds to make restitution to the victim or pay fines or court-imposed costs. Probation can also allow offenders to remain in a rehabilitative, treatment, or educational program in which they already are engaged, and continuation in such a program can be made a condition of probation.

In all of these contexts, defense arguments based on client rehabilitation may be met by a degree of cynicism. Prosecutors in plea bargaining, judges engaged in sentencing, and probation officers making recommendations to the courts may be skeptical concerning the genuineness of the defendant's asserted rehabilitation. What can defense counsel do to meet this skepticism? Clients themselves can be placed on the stand and their personal testimony can reveal the genuineness of their rehabilitation. A heart-felt apology can be made to the victim and to the court. Moreover, letters from program staff, family members, and even victims can be introduced, where appropriate, to help demonstrate the genuineness of rehabilitative efforts and of apology. In addition, where the question is raised as to whether participation in rehabilitation or the making of an apology has not been genuine, defense counsel may consider the use of an expert witness on malingering. In recent years, psychiatrists and psychologists have developed increased ability to detect deception and malingering and a variety of psychometric instruments for this purpose. In adducing expert testimony that the defendant's rehabilitative efforts or apology are genuine, defense counsel should use an expert who is independent of the treatment process. A clinician involved in the defendant's treatment may not be placed in the role of validating the genuineness of efforts consistent with the requirements of professional ethics.

The redefined role for counsel proposed in this chapter may not be an altogether new role for some criminal defense attorneys, but it is for many. Moreover, the broader opportunities made possible by case law authorizing a downward departure for rehabilitative efforts make it imperative that all criminal defense attorneys master the role of lawyer as healer. Playing this role and playing it well can not only significantly reduce the sentence a client might otherwise receive, but it can provide the attorney an opportunity to assist clients to turn their lives around in ways that safeguard both their future liberty and their future health and happiness. Moreover, making such a contribution can bring a measure of personal and professional satisfaction that many criminal defense lawyers rarely experience. These are the dividends of being a therapeutic jurisprudence/preventive lawyer.

When an offender desires to (or can be persuaded to) engage in rehabilitative efforts but there is insufficient time between the offense and the commence-ment of plea discussions or the occurrence of sentencing, defense counsel may have little more than the client's good intentions to use in support of arguments to mitigate a sentence on rehabilitative grounds. Good intentions alone will not suffice, however. Unless a period of meaningful engagement in rehabilitation has occurred in which the defendant has had the opportunity to demonstrate a significant degree of rehabilitative progress, prosecutors and judges rarely are willing to take such efforts into account in a material way in their plea bargaining and sentencing decisions. In addition, absent such progress, sentencing judges will be unlikely to find that post-offense rehabilitation is present to the degree necessary to justify a downward departure or a reduced sentence on this basis.

What can the defense attorney do in these circumstances? Brief postponements of the sentencing hearing can usually be obtained, but time usually runs out before serious rehabilitative efforts can occur or bear fruit. The solution to this dilemma may be to seek a deferred sentencing to enable the defendant to achieve what at that point may seem only a potential for successful rehabilitation.

The deferred sentencing option was the subject of a significant and highly creative opinion by one of the nation's most well-regarded federal judges, Federal District Judge Jack B. Weinstein. In *United States v. Flowers*, the court faced the question of first impression of whether, under the Federal Sentencing Guidelines, a court may defer sentencing to assure itself that the defendant has been rehabilitated. The defendant, a 21-year-old single mother of a 4-year-old child, lived in a two-room apartment in Brooklyn. Her father, an alcoholic, had abandoned the family when she was two. She worked at many short-term, low-paying positions without chance for advancement. The sole support of her minor child, she succumbed to a suggestion made by a friend of a friend that she act as a drug courier for money. The defendant was arrested at the airport when she returned from Barbados with 3.77 kilograms of cocaine secreted in her luggage. She pled guilty to one count of conspiracy to import, distribute, and possess cocaine. In the courtroom, the defendant appeared to be contrite, nervous, soft-spoken, and "somewhat naive, a person open to suggestion." Because of the amount of drugs involved, even after a downward departure for acceptance of responsibility and minimal participation, she faced a prison sentence of between 37 and 46 months, which would separate her from her child during some of the most important years of the child's life.

The court found that rehabilitation "seems to be well under way" but that further time would be necessary to determine its extent before deciding on whether a downward departure to a lesser term of imprisonment or to probation with conditions was appropriate. The court granted a deferral of sentencing, noting that deferring final adjudication to allow a defendant time needed to improve her circumstances was not new to the law. Reasonable delay, the court found, "may help insure that the sentence fit both the crime and the circumstances of the defendant and her family."

In a lengthy, scholarly opinion, Judge Weinstein reviewed the history of innovative alternative sentencing designed to achieve rehabilitation and to protect
the public by effectively preventing crime. These have included probation,
house arrest and electronic monitoring used in lieu of incarceration,
community service orders, "shock" sentencing to a short term of military-style
boot camp, and pretrial diversion or deferred prosecution. These differing
models of providing alternatives to incarceration have allowed judges to fashion
creative conditions that must be complied with by the offender, including the
payment of restitution, the maintenance of employment, attendance at alcohol
and other drug treatment or other counseling programs, and the performance
of community service. These creative approaches have allowed countless offenders, particularly first offenders, to avoid the harsh consequences of imprisonment and to achieve rehabilitation in the community.

In his opinion in *Flowers*, Judge Weinstein rejected the contention that the
Federal Sentencing Guidelines were designed to give rehabilitation a subsidiary
role in sentencing. Noting the increasing recognition of post-offense rehabilitation as a ground for a downward departure under the Guidelines, the court
then considered whether a deferral of sentencing to enable an offender to
demonstrate sufficient rehabilitative efforts to qualify for a downward
departure on this basis would be permissible under the Federal Rules of Criminal Procedure.

The Federal Rules of Criminal Procedure do not explicitly authorize a delay
in sentencing at the request of the defendant. However, as the *Flowers* court
reasoned, the text and history of *Fed.R.Crim.P. 32* contemplate an exercise of
discretion by the trial judge in determining when sentencing shall occur. The
original version of *Rule 32(a)* called for imposition of sentence "without unreasonable delay," necessitating a degree of discretion by the trial judge in determining what was reasonable in the circumstances. The 1987 amendments
to the Federal Rules changed the language to provide that sentencing shall occur
"without unnecessary delay, but the court may, upon motion that is jointly
filed by the defendant and the attorney for the government and that asserts a
factor important to the sentencing determination is not capable of being resolved at that time, postpone the imposition of sentence for a reasonable time
until the factor is capable of being resolved." In 1989, the *Rule* was again mod-
ified, this time eliminating the requirement that both parties request and agree
on a delay in sentencing. The legislative history of this amendment demonstrated that it was intended to dispel any implication that a motion for a delay
made by one party only might be considered unreasonable. It explicitly noted
the intention to provide the sentencing judge with "desirable discretion to
assure that relevant factors are considered and accurately resolved." This amend-

ment restored the district judge's previous discretion and stressed the importance of leaving such discretion in the hands of the judge in order to allow full consideration of all factors that might be relevant to the sentencing task made more complicated by the Guidelines.

The *Rule* was revised once again in 1994. The current version retained the sentencing judge's power to postpone sentencing, but it substituted a "good cause" standard governing such discretion. None of the reasons motivating the 1994 amendment purport to limit the trial judge's discretion in setting a sentencing date. Moreover, what constitutes "just cause" to authorize a delay must be considered in light of the greater complexity of the sentencing hearing necessitated by the Guidelines regime, and this has been recognized by a variety of courts. In addition, the post-Guideline amendments to *Rule 35 of the Federal Rules of Criminal Procedure* substantially restricted the previous ability of the trial judge to correct a sentence already imposed, therefore making it "imperative that judges have the full picture at the time of sentencing."

Judge Weinstein therefore concluded that federal judges possess a wide discretion to postpone sentencing to enable full consideration of all issues that might be relevant concerning sentencing under the Guidelines. When the defendant seeks such a postponement, whatever limitations imposed on this discretion by the defendant's constitutional right to speedy trial are absent. Noting that presentence rehabilitation is an important consideration for the sentencing judge to take into account, Judge Weinstein granted a 1-year postponement of sentencing to allow the defendant to demonstrate her entitlement to a downward departure on this basis. It is the duty of sentencing judges to consider every possible ground for a departure from the sentencing range set forth in the Guidelines, he noted, and the facts of this case made it appropriate to provide the defendant an opportunity to engage in rehabilitative efforts that seemed likely to succeed and therefore to constitute a basis for a possible downward departure.

Judge Weinstein's pioneering decision in *Flowers* thus provides sentencing judges with wide discretion to postpone sentencing in appropriate cases to allow defendants to engage in rehabilitative efforts that seem likely to provide an ultimate basis for a downward departure. In so doing, Judge Weinstein recognized the importance of the therapeutic role that sentencing judges can play. During the period of sentence postponement to enable rehabilitation to occur, the incentives for the defendant to succeed are maximized. Success in rehabilitative efforts is likely to be rewarded by a reduced sentence; failure to participate meaningfully in such efforts will likely not bring such a reduction.

This ability to seek a postponement of sentencing to allow rehabilitative efforts to bear fruit constitutes an important new tool for the criminal defense lawyer. It provides defense attorneys a broader opportunity to develop rehabilitative plans in conjunction with their clients that can provide significant therapeutic and legal value to them. This tool enables a significant expansion of the role of the criminal defense lawyer at sentencing, permitting such attorneys to realize the advantages, for both their clients and themselves, of becoming therapeutic jurisprudence/preventive lawyers.

2. Attorney/Client Conversations about Rehabilitation: Applying Insights from Psychology

Criminal defense lawyers who apply a therapeutic jurisprudence/preventive law model in the plea bargaining and sentencing process therefore have much to offer their clients. As the previous section indicates, there are many advantages to counseling appropriate clients about the benefits of rehabilitative programs and of presenting such rehabilitative options to prosecutors, probation officers, and sentencing judges as bases for plea bargains and reduced sentencing. Talking to clients about their own rehabilitation, however, can be a delicate matter requiring a high degree of sensitivity and skill on the part of the attorney. The following subsections draw from the field of psychology to provide a variety of psychological insights, techniques, and strategies that can be used by the therapeutic jurisprudence/preventive lawyer to successfully engage clients in meaningful dialogue about their rehabilitative options.

A. "Psycholegal Soft Spots" in the Attorney/Client Dialogue

Holding conversations with clients about the value of rehabilitative efforts can trigger negative emotional reactions on the part of the client if not performed with sensitivity. Many clients resist having such conversations or are uncomfortable and experience psychological distress during them. Therapeutic jurisprudence/preventive lawyers recognize these conversations as "psycholegal soft spots," situations in which the legal involvement or attorney/client relationship will likely produce predictable emotional reactions on the part of the client. The lawyer needs to be alert to recognize these psycholegal soft spots and to develop strategies to deal with the emotional aspects of the attorney/ client conversation. What insights does psychology have for the conduct of these sensitive conversations? How far should the attorney go in counseling the client in the direction of seeking rehabilitation, and how should such counseling occur?

In a variety of criminal cases, it may be fairly clear to the attorney that the client has a psychological problem that relates to his or her criminality. Perhaps the client is a substance abuser who commits theft offenses in order to support a drug habit. Perhaps the client is an alcoholic whose drinking contributes to repetitive acts of domestic violence, impaired driving, or assault. Perhaps the client's pedophilia coupled with cognitive distortions and denial about his culpability or the pain that his conduct causes his child victims contributes to his repetitive acts of sexual violence directed at children. Perhaps the client suffers from pyromania which contributes to crimes of arson, kleptomania which contributes to repetitive shoplifting, or compulsive gambling which contributes to illegal gambling and crimes of theft or embezzlement designed to obtain funds needed for such activity. Perhaps the client suffers from schizophrenia or other mental illness, and the client's refusal to take needed medication contributes to the repetitive commission of various nuisance offenses such as trespassing, loitering, or urinating in public. Although the attorney may correctly analyze the client's repetitive criminality as a product of psychological or behavioral problems that could successfully respond to a variety of rehabilitative efforts, attorney/client conversations about these issues are bound to be highly sensitive and to touch a number of emotional issues that are the subject of client denial, suppression, or repression. These are conversations that must be engaged in with a high degree of psychological sensitivity.

B. Avoiding Paternalism and Coercion

At the outset, attorneys must be careful to avoid being paternalistic with their clients in such counseling sessions. These are contexts in which it is easy for the attorney to respond paternalistically. The attorney may be strongly convinced, often correctly, that the client suffers from an emotional problem that produces repetitive criminality and that could respond effectively to available rehabilitative programs. The attorney, therefore, may think that if only the client could see the light (i.e., could understand matters in the way that the attorney does), the client would agree to obtain needed help. Paternalism, however, particularly on the part of those who are not close family members or friends (and sometimes even then), is often experienced as offensive by its recipients. Moreover, because people often resent being the subject of paternalism, a paternalistic approach on the part of the attorney may backfire, producing a psychological reactance to the advice offered that might in fact be counterproductive. In addition, many offenders in these circumstances are in denial about their alcoholism and other drug abuse or other psychological or behavioral problems that contribute to their repetitive offending. Paternalism on the part of the attorney is unlikely to succeed in allowing clients to deal with such denial and may instead provoke anxiety and other psychological distress that simply drives them out of the attorney's office.

How can attorneys avoid the specter of paternalism in their conversations with clients about the desirability of engaging in rehabilitative efforts? Rather than being committed to a traditional legal counseling model that assumes that clients are passive and implicitly delegate decision-making authority to their lawyers, therapeutic jurisprudence/preventive lawyers are committed to the model of client-centered counseling. Under this model, the attorney is the agent of the client, and the client, rather than the lawyer, makes the critical decisions. This model is based on deference to client autonomy and is designed to foster client decision-making. It seeks to provide opportunities for client self-determination, allowing clients to make decisions for themselves rather than to have them made by others, such as the attorney. Under this approach to the attorney/client relationship, the lawyer's role is to engage the client in an exploration of possible alternatives and the advantages and disadvantages of each. Together, the attorney and client identify and evaluate the legal, social, economic, and psychological consequences of available alternative courses of action. The lawyer is the agent of the client, helping the client to reach the best decision in the circumstances. The attorney guides the client through the decision-making process but allows the client to make the ultimate decision. This conception of the role of the attorney parallels that of the clinician applying what psychologist Carl Rogers called "client-centered therapy." The Rogerian approach to therapy and the client-centered approach to lawyering are both based on the premise that individuals can achieve their full potential for self-actualization when facilitated by a relationship with a helping person who is genuine, empathic, and nonjudgmental.

Even when the attorney has what he or she is convinced is a superior understanding of the situation, the attorney must be careful to cede choice to clients. Rather than dictating a course of action in a way that seems to clients to be an exercise in power subordination, the attorney should state that the ultimate decision is up to them. This approach can be empowering to clients who often feel powerless and helpless, fostering the value of individual autonomy and helping to achieve the goal of preventive law.

The function of the criminal defense attorney attempting to suggest to the client the value of obtaining rehabilitation is properly regarded as one of persuasion, not coercion. In this context, lawyers should be aware of the psychological value of choice. Attorneys counseling clients in the criminal justice context need to understand that client self-determination is an essential aspect of psychological health and that people who make their own choices (if perceived by them as noncoerced) function more effectively and with greater satisfaction. They need to realize that people who feel coerced, by contrast, may respond with a negative psychological reactance and may experience a variety of other psychological difficulties. Attorneys therefore need to communicate to their clients their views concerning the client's best interests, but to do so in a way that makes clear that this is solely the attorney's view and that the decision is up to the client. Moreover, the psychological value of choice should be considered in the design of a rehabilitative plan. There typically may be many options available in fashioning the plan, including variations in rehabilitative techniques and service providers. The attorney can lay the options out for the client, who then can exercise choice. Perhaps even better, the attorney can allow the client to fashion his own rehabilitative plan, and offer mild counterarguments that a judge or a prosecutor might raise. The client then can be asked what his response might be. This process of allowing the client to participate in fashioning the rehabilitative plan is more likely to ensure that the client will make the plan his own, rather than following it because his attorney said to do so. The individual's choice concerning the various issues that arise in the design of the plan can itself influence the likelihood of success.

The line between coercion and choice can be a narrow one. The therapeutic jurisprudence/preventive lawyer counseling clients in the criminal sentencing context concerning the advantages of rehabilitative efforts must therefore understand what makes people feel coerced and what makes them feel that they have acted voluntarily. They should understand the implications of recent research on coercion conducted under the auspices of the MacArthur Network on Mental Health and the Law. This research studied the causes and correlates of what makes people feel coerced and determined that, even when people are subjected to legal coercion, such as involuntary civil commitment, they feel noncoerced when they are treated with dignity and respect by people who they perceive as acting with genuine benevolence and who accord them a sense of voice, the ability to have their say, and validation, the impression that what they say is taken seriously. In the attorney/client dialogue concerning rehabilitation, attorneys should always respect the dignity and autonomy of their clients. They should remind their clients that, as attorneys, they are agents whose professional responsibility is to safeguard their clients' best interests, and that the attorney's advice is given in furtherance of their fiduciary duty to their clients and not based on other considerations, such as the interests of the state, the community, or the victim. The attorney's task is to communicate to the client that counsel's professional advice is based on the attorney's perceptions of what would be best for the client legally (and when relevant, economically, socially, and psychologically), but that the ultimate decision is that of the client. The attorney should give the client ample opportunity to express his or her views (voice) and should take those views seriously (validation).

If handled properly by counsel, conversations about rehabilitation can be an opportunity for empowering the client in ways that can have positive psychological value. During the attorney's initial interview with a client, the attorney typically seeks to ascertain whether the client is guilty of the crime. When the client admits guilt to counsel, counsel can point out that the one part of the criminal justice system in which the client can be powerful and proactive and create favorable evidence is the sentencing process. With regard to the guilt or innocence issue, the client lacks the ability to change the evidence as it existed at the time of the offense. The fingerprint, bloodstain, DNA sample, eyewitness, and smoking gun are what they are. Defense counsel and the client cannot ethically manufacture new evidence to change much of anything about this phase of the case. By entering rehabilitation programs and successfully completing them, the client thereby can create facts, documents, testifying expert witnesses, testifying fact witnesses, and a positive theme for his case through his or her own efforts. Clients often are excited and energized by the sense of power and control that is produced when counsel points out this aspect of what they can do for themselves.

C. Techniques of Persuasion and Motivation

Criminal defense attorneys engaged in these attorney/client conversations should also have an awareness of the social psychology of persuasion. This body of psychological research identifies three elements of the persuasion process as critical—source, message, and receiver. The likelihood of persuasion is significantly influenced by both the content of the message and the way it is delivered. Persuasion theory has postulated an "elaboration likelihood" model. Under this model, certain persuasive elements are seen as being influenced by the extent to which the receiver of information is actively involved in the processing of the information presented. The literature on the psychology of persuasion distinguishes between two differing routes to persuasion—central and peripheral. Central route persuasion focuses on the content of the message and postulates that the potential for persuasion is maximized when the receivers of the information have a high likelihood of elaboration, that is, when they engage in issue-relevant thinking about the content of the message itself. The potential for persuasion is heightened if the message has personal relevance to the recipients and the recipients have prior knowledge about the issue. It can be assumed that clients facing criminal sentencing wish to minimize their risk of imprisonment and value strategies that achieve this result. Thus, attorneys can explain to their clients how the Guidelines work, how they would apply to the client's situation, the range of possible sentences authorized by the Guidelines in the client's case, and the possibility of obtaining a downward departure from this authorized range based on post-offense rehabilitation. Attorneys can also explain the option of seeking deferred sentencing to allow rehabilitative efforts to commence so as to develop a basis for such a downward departure. In addition, when representing corporations or other organizations, attorneys can explain the special provisions contained in the Guidelines that allow a reduction in sentence because of the existence of organizational compliance programs designed to avoid unlawful conduct and to prevent its repetition. Lawyers also can explain to their clients the various diversion options that exist in their jurisdiction, including participation in Drug Treatment court, Domestic Violence court, or Mental Health court. Clients understanding these considerations can then be left free to engage in instrumental thinking concerning the value to themselves of making rehabilitative efforts. After explaining these possible avenues to a reduction of sentence, attorneys can ask their clients whether they think that any of these options might be available in their cases, allowing the clients to engage in their own processing of the information conveyed to them and apply their own preferences to the decision of whether to pursue these options.

Allowing clients to think through for themselves the value to them of undertaking rehabilitative efforts after supplying them with several of the factual and legal premises necessary to a consideration of the issue is fully consistent with principles of client-centered counseling and can be an effective means of persuading clients to accept rehabilitation. Indeed, it can be more effective than pressuring the client to seek rehabilitation or presenting arguments that spell out in detail why the attorney thinks this course would be preferable. Moreover, allowing clients to come to such decisions for themselves can permit them more effectively to internalize the rehabilitative goal and can increase their intrinsic motivation to achieve it. Thus, effective use of the "elaboration likelihood" model in this manner not only can persuade the client to seek rehabilitation, but can do so in a way that is more likely to be successful. Particularly for cognitive behavioral approaches, those that are seen as most likely to be effective in offender rehabilitation, the motivation and commitment to succeed of the individual are crucial to success. Thus, allowing clients to come to the decision to engage in rehabilitation for themselves would be more effective than pressuring them to do so. Moreover, allowing clients to develop their own rehabilitative and relapse prevention plans rather than having the attorney do it for them can also increase the likelihood of positive results. It would also increase the willingness of sentencing judges to view the offender's rehabilitative efforts as genuine and to take them into account favorably in their sentencing decisions.

Criminal lawyers can also use a standard preventive law technique with their clients, the rewind technique. The client can be asked to engage in a thought experiment in which the scene prior to the occurrence of the violation is imagined and the client is asked what could have been done differently to have prevented the result that occurred. This technique can help the client to understand the need for a relapse prevention plan and to design one more effectively. Moreover, it can increase the effectiveness of such a plan and the potential that sentencing courts would be willing to rely on it in granting probation, reduced sentence, downward departure, or deferral of sentencing.

Attorneys should be aware that there are peripheral routes to persuasion that can supplement the "elaboration likelihood" technique discussed above. When clients seem uninterested in the content of the message the attorneys seek to communicate relating to the advantages of rehabilitation, the likelihood of central route persuasion occurring is significantly diminished. In such cases, the client may simply wish to defer to the attorney in the same way that patients frequently defer to the judgment of their physicians. In these instances, the client's decision-making process may be influenced largely by some heuristic principle unrelated to the content of the message. Two common heuristic principles are applied by most people—the credibility heuristic and the liking heuristic. The former is grounded in the assumption that a message delivered by a credible source can be trusted; the latter, by the assumption that a message delivered by a liked source is agreeable. Attorneys intuitively understand these insights of psychology. In accordance with these insights, attorneys should attempt to be both credible and likeable in their conversations with clients concerning the advisability of engaging in rehabilitative efforts. They should dress appropriately and professionally and should act in ways calculated to increase client confidence and trust. They should communicate clearly, cogently, and authoritatively. They should be warm, gracious, and friendly. They should create for their clients an image of competence and expertise, thereby enhancing their perceived credibility. They should appear knowledgeable and trustworthy and give the impression that they are presenting information accurately and without distortion. In their conversations with clients, attorneys should avoid lack of fluency in speech, including repetition, inarticulateness, and misstatement, all of which may tend to decrease perceived competence. Attorneys should be prepared to back up their factual and legal assertions with credible sources of information, thereby increasing their credibility and ultimate persuasiveness. To the extent that the attorney shares a common background, outlook, or set of values with the client, at least on some matters, these commonalties should be demonstrated to the client, thereby increasing the attorney's likeability and consequent persuasiveness. For example, if the attorney has recovered from alcoholism or other drug abuse, he or she can share these experiences with the client, and such sharing can help to forge an emotional connection that can increase attorney persuasiveness. These suggestions for increasing persuasiveness are common sense to most attorneys, but they are useful reminders of how to act in the professional relationship when discussing sensitive subjects.

The therapeutic jurisprudence/preventive lawyer also should master the techniques of motivational interviewing. In conversations with the client, the defense attorney should avoid being paternalistic and attempt to spark the client's intrinsic motivation to deal with his problem and participate in the program. In many ways, the task is like that faced by addiction counselors in motivating their patients to deal with their problems of substance abuse. People suffering from alcoholism or drug addiction often lack insight into their problems. They frequently deny that they have a problem with alcohol or drugs, and as a result, don't see the need for treatment. Various techniques have been developed for motivating people to deal with their addiction problems, and it therefore may be helpful for defense lawyers dealing with their clients to understand the techniques that are widely used in the addiction context. Particularly helpful would seem to be the technique of motivational interviewing, a way to help people recognize and do something about their present or potential problems that has been shown to be useful for people who are reluctant to change or ambivalent about it.

Four basic principles underlie motivational interviewing. First, the interviewer needs to express empathy by trying to understand the individual's feelings and perspectives (through careful and respectful listening to the individual) without judging, criticizing, or blaming. Reflective listening and acceptance are essential to this process. It is often the case that the individual is reluctant and ambivalent in the beginning. Those traits should not be considered pathological, but rather treated as an ordinary aspect of human behavior. Second, the interviewer, in a non-confrontational way, should seek to identify discrepancies between the individual's present behavior and important personal goals. The interviewer thus must elicit the individual's underlying goals and objectives, and through interviewing techniques, including open-ended questioning, reflective listening, the provision of frequent statements of affirmation and support, and the elicitation of self-motivational statements, should attempt to enable the individual to recognize the existence of a problem. It is important that the interviewer point the individual in the right direction, but it must be left to the individual to express the intention to change and the feeling he can do so on his own. For example, if the individual wishes to obtain and keep a particular job, the interviewer should ask questions designed to probe the relationship between his not taking medication and poor performance in previous employment that may have resulted in dismissal. Only when people perceive the discrepancy between how they are behaving and the achievement of their personal goals will motivation for change be created.

Third, when resistance is encountered, the interviewer must attempt to roll with the resistance rather than become confrontational. This requires listening with empathy and providing feedback to what the individual is saying by introducing new information, thereby allowing the individual to remain in control, to make his own decisions, and to create solutions to his problems. The interviewer should avoid arguing with the individual, which can be counterproductive and create defensiveness.

Fourth, it is important for the interviewer to foster self-efficacy in the individual. Unless the individual feels that he can reach a goal, overcome barriers and obstacles to its achievement, and succeed in effecting change, no change will be attempted. Most individuals will possess strength or capabilities in certain areas of their functioning, even though lacking them in some others. The interviewer should help the individual to identify the existence of his strengths and attempt to build upon them. By reminding the individual of his strengths, the interviewer can help to build self-esteem and a sense of self-efficacy, which may be necessary for the individual to undertake the often difficult task of dealing with his problems. The interviewer should stress the importance of personal responsibility—only the individual himself can make the change. The interviewer may also share the success stories of others and emphasize the number of different methods available to the individual to effect change. These examples can boost his hope and expectancy that he also can succeed, as have many others in similar circumstances.

In their conversations with their clients about rehabilitative alternatives, defense attorneys should learn and apply these techniques of motivational interviewing. Psychologist Astrid Birgden adapts this approach for use by criminal defense lawyers dealing with clients with recurring problems who are in denial about their problems and resistant to change. In addition, Amador and Johanson describe use of a form of motivational interviewing for dealing with treatment resistant mental patients who lack insight about their illness and the need for treatment. The use of motivational interviewing and related psychological strategies for sparking and maintaining motivation to accept needed treatment can greatly increase the potential that the client will confront his problems and attempt to deal with them.

The literature on motivational interviewing dovetails with a separate literature on stages of change. This literature identifies five separate stages relevant to the individual's undertaking to change his behavior. The first is the pre-contemplation stage, in which the individual has no intention to change in the near future and may be unaware of any problems. In this stage, the individual may be resistant to recognizing or modifying the problem behavior, or if he wishes to change, may not seriously consider it in the near future. He is likely to be unaware of the consequences of his behavior. The second stage is the contemplation stage. The individual is aware of the existence of his problem and is seriously considering facing it, but has not yet committed to action. He probably is ambivalent about how to balance the costs and benefits of his behavior. He often will remain stuck in this stage for a long period.

The third stage is preparation. At this stage, the individual has made a decision to deal with his problem, and may have taken small steps in that direction. He has not, however, fully abstained from his problem behavior. The fourth stage is action. The individual has undertaken overt behavior change, modifying his conduct or the environment that reinforces it. He has succeeded in abstaining from the problem behavior. Action, however, should not prematurely be equated with real change. Vigilance against relapse is critical. The fifth stage is maintenance. Here, the individual consciously works to avoid relapse, and to consolidate existing gains. His confidence that change can occur and sense of self-efficacy in accomplishing it have been heightened. Maintenance of these patterns may be required for a lifetime.

Therapeutic jurisprudence/preventive lawyers seeking to motivate their clients to change their problematic behaviors need to understand these stages and to develop differing strategies for dealing with them. They need to match the appropriate motivational interviewing technique with the individual's stage of change. Only if the individual is ready for change, or is open to considering it, can he be motivated to confront his problem. The criminal charge may function as a catalyst for change, jolting the individual into a state where he at least is ready to contemplate its possibility. His substance abuse or psychological problem is responsible for his being charged criminally, and the attorney can guide him to see this connection and point out that unless he deals with the problem, the risk is great that this criminal behavior will reoccur and that he will face even stiffer penalties.

Thus, the attorney can help to bring the client out of the pre-contemplation stage and into the contemplation, preparation and action stages of change.

D. Improving Interviewing, Counseling, and Interpersonal Skills

A special sensitivity to the client's pain, shame, sadness, and anxiety in coming to terms with the existence of psychological or behavioral problems that have produced criminality and the victimization of others is called for in determining what to say to the client and how to say it. This is an example of a psycholegal soft spot. Attorneys must be alert to identify these triggers to strong emotional reactions and to develop strategies to deal with them.

Criminal defense attorneys performing this function need to improve their interviewing, counseling, and interpersonal skills. Even though attorneys at times may strongly disapprove of the conduct of the client, they must strive in the attorney/client dialogue to be supportive, empathic, warm, and good listeners. These are highly sensitive conversations, and clients are disinclined to engage in them with attorneys they perceive to be cold, insensitive, or judgmental.

Some clients will be in denial about their wrongdoing or the fact that they suffer from substance abuse or other psychological problems that have contributed to the offense. As a result, they may misinterpret the reason that they stand accused criminally, and psychologically seek to avoid responsibility. For example, it may be apparent to the lawyer that a client charged with a second or a third driving under the influence offense probably has an alcohol or substance abuse problem. The client, however, may not be ready to admit this, either to himself or his attorney. He claims that he is merely a social drinker and doesn't have a drinking problem. Or he may attribute his arrest to bad luck, or think that the arresting officer was out to get him. He is in denial about his wrongdoing and the contribution that his addiction has made to it, or minimizes or rationalizes the problem. Unless the lawyer can help the client to understand the reality of the situation, the client is unlikely to learn a lesson from his arrest and may be doomed to repeating his criminal conduct, with increasingly more severe consequences.

An excellent technique for doing this is motivational interviewing, discussed in the preceding section of this chapter. In a non-confrontational and non-judgmental way, the attorney can gently probe the client's resistance. "You deny that you have a drinking problem," the attorney might say, "but do you think your friends and family agree?" "Have you ever lost a job or gotten in trouble with your boss when drinking was involved?" "How do you think a jury will react to your account that the policeman was out to get you?" "In view of the evidence, don't you think it is likely that they will convict?" "I'm not telling you what you should do in connection with drinking and driving, or that you should plead guilty if you consider yourself to be not guilty. I'm just trying to help you understand how the judge and jury might view the evidence, and to assist you in understanding the likely consequences of your plea options." "Your prior record of drunk driving offenses might be considered by the judge as ground for a harsh sentence, whereas should you plead guilty, acknowledge a drinking problem, and agree to accept treatment, this may help with your sentence." Applying the techniques of motivational interviewing, the lawyer, functioning as Socratic teacher and coach, can attempt to help to bring the client out of the precontemplation stage and into the contemplation, preparation and action stages of change.

In applying these motivational techniques, the lawyer will need to understand denial and other forms of psychological resistance. Denial is a defense mechanism that operates unconsciously. It functions as a means to avoid inner conflicts and anxiety through the disavowal of thoughts, wishes, needs, or external reality factors that would be consciously intolerable. Denial involves more than simply pretending that something is not as it truly is. In denial, unacceptable facts are vanished from awareness entirely, and the individual has no access to them. Although usually defined as an unconscious process, denial sometimes involves conscious mechanisms. It thus can be broadly understood as the conscious or unconscious repudiation of the meaning, or even occurrence, of an event to avoid anxiety or other unpleasant effects.

The concept of denial is derived from the work of Sigmund Freud, who viewed denial as a protective personality mechanism that, by reducing anxiety, allows the individual to function. Under the classic psychoanalytic paradigm, denial is an unconscious process designed to protect and preserve the individual's functioning. Freud posited that the unpleasant feelings that create anxiety cause the ego to respond in a defensive manner. Denial is thus an unconscious defense mechanism resulting from the ego's need to remove or rescue itself from actual or perceived danger. The term is also sometimes used to describe the conscious process by which an individual protects himself from a crisis and threat by consciously limiting the amount of information taken in.

Denial can be a healthy coping mechanism by which an individual limits anxiety and maintains self-esteem and a sense of control. For example, denial can frequently be a healthy defense mechanism early in the course of a terminal illness, allowing an individual to act on unrealistic plans and, thereby, function during a time when functioning is still possible. Denial can serve as a buffer to shield an individual from unexpected, shocking news, such as the diagnosis of a terminal illness. It can allow a person "to collect himself" and, with time, mobilize other, less radical defenses. Denial can be an effective strategy for reducing or alleviating stress that can otherwise be debilitating. Although it is generally best for an individual to face a problem and deal with it, there is increasing recognition that defensive mechanisms like denial may be extremely useful. Denial of some deficits associated with old age, for example, may be less problematic for an individual than dwelling on the deficits, particularly if nothing can be done. Everyone experiences denial concerning some aspects of their life and in some circumstances it can be a healthy, functional means of coping with certain stressors, maintaining equilibrium, and going on with life.

On the other hand, denial can be unhealthy and harmful. It is inevitably distorting. It can prevent the individual from understanding reality and from dealing with it effectively. Denial may prevent seeking treatment that is needed, such as when a woman ignores the growing lump in her breast for many months, thereby reducing the effectiveness of any therapy undertaken. It can create a serious hazard for an individual and for others, as when an elderly person ignores serious visual or reflex deficits and continues to drive an automobile when it is no longer safe to do so.

Denial bears certain similarities to other defense mechanisms like repression and suppression (which is technically not a defense mechanism). Like denial, repression operates unconsciously. This defense mechanism vanishes unacceptable ideas, fantasies, affects, or impulses from consciousness. Suppression, on the other hand, is the conscious effort to control and conceal unacceptable impulses, thoughts, feelings, or acts. Repression, the fundamental defense mechanism that underlies all others, is like forgetting. Thoughts, memories, and feelings are forced by the conscious mind into the unconscious and actively kept out of awareness. According to Anna Freud, denial functions as a precursor to repression. An individual learns how to defend against distressing internal feelings that are triggered by external experiences by denying those external experiences. Denial of the external stimuli facilitates the repression of these internal feelings. Repression prevents the recognition of thoughts and feelings; denial prevents the recognition of external reality. So strong is the need to avoid inner pain or anxiety that an individual disbelieves a fact of external reality. To avoid these distressing feelings, an individual in effect lies to himself. As a result, denial may produce grossly distorted thinking and behavior. For example, people are frequently in denial about the existence of a serious physical illness and may, as a result, delay consulting a physician about ominous symptoms until it is too late. Similarly, a criminal defendant may be in denial about the existence of a substance abuse or psychological problem that contributes to his repeated criminality. It is not surprising that people suffering from such problems are in denial concerning them and the need for rehabilitation. How should a defense attorney deal with such client denial and resistance?

A word of caution is appropriate at the outset: What appears to be denial may actually be something else. Perhaps the client has good reason not to confront what appears to the attorney to be a psychosocial problem. Perhaps the client has thought about the matter and would prefer to deal with his criminal charges instead of his problem. He may be innocent, or think that he is, and wish to raise a defense. He may wish to seek suppression of key evidence in the hope that, without it, the prosecutor will be unable to prove his guilt. These may be rational responses to his predicament.

It may be offensive to such clients to suggest that although they think they have good reasons for preferring the status quo, in truth, they are in denial about the real reasons for their unwillingness to take the lawyer's advice. Here, the lawyer, if satisfied that the client has fully considered the question, should accept the client's decision. It may be appropriate to determine whether the client has considered certain issues that the attorney thinks may have been overlooked or misunderstood, but if this is not the case, the attorney should not assume that denial is the reason for the client's refusal to follow counsel's advice. The Freudian concept of denial assumes an objective reality that the individual fails to see or distorts for psychological reasons. Yet the client's reality may differ from the attorney's perception. Seeing something differently or evaluating it differently does not necessarily indicate denial on the part of the client. Attorneys need to be careful to eliminate other possible explanations for the client's disinclination to accept counsel's advice before jumping to the conclusion that denial is the culprit.

Denial should be suspected when the client, without any apparent good reason, is unwilling to engage in a discussion of the issue of whether he suffers from substance abuse or a psychological problem that has contributed to his criminality. The attorney should observe the client carefully for signs of stress and anxiety. Only when a gentle probing of the client's unwillingness suggests that the client's stated reasons for not wishing to consider the matter are pretextual and, thus, grounded in the psychological distress presented by the issue should the attorney conclude that the client's resistance is psychologically based.

If this inquiry leads the attorney to conclude that the client's resistance is psychological, what should counsel do? It may be helpful for attorneys to consider how mental health clinicians deal with denial on the part of their patients. There are basically two schools of thought in dealing with denial. One method is to approach patients subtly, allowing them to deal with their feelings slowly, confronting such individuals but also giving them time to deal with feelings that were uncovered, like taking baby steps. This is a gradual approach in which the therapist is consistent, but it allows patients the time to pace themselves. The other leading approach is more direct and confrontational. This latter approach is based on an intervention model, in which everything is brought out at once and is dealt with accordingly. Clinicians have the professional ability to deal with the ramifications of this dramatic technique. However, lawyers (or at least those who have not had clinical training) do not possess the appropriate professional skills, and thus should avoid being so confrontational. Another reason for avoiding such a dramatic approach is that it will drive many clients from the lawyer's office and have the effect of ending the professional relationship rather than allowing them to see the benefits of admitting their problems and attempting to deal with them.

An attorney must be sensitive to the client's anxiety level. When acute anxiety is unleashed, a physician can prescribe medication, but a lawyer cannot. The attorney should observe the client carefully during the lawyer/client conversation for signs of agitation, anger, and distress. The attorney should proceed gently. This conversation is not a closing argument to a jury; it is a difficult discussion about an intimate and sensitive subject. The attorney should watch the client closely for such obvious signs of distress as teary eyes, fidgeting, and a shaky voice. If the attorney detects any of these warning signals or if the client seems to be behaving inappropriately, the attorney should consider a shift in tone or strategy. "Can we continue discussing this?" the attorney might say. "I can see that you're uncomfortable. Many people are uncomfortable discussing this subject. Can we continue?" the attorney might ask in a gentle voice. Or, perhaps, "I think it's worthwhile to continue even if you're uncomfortable, but what do you think? If it becomes too uncomfortable, let me know and we will stop. If so, you can think about what I said, and we'll talk about it another day."

In the context of denial concerning the ability of the client to identify that he suffers from a substance abuse or other psychological problem, and his need to deal with it, the source of denial will ordinarily be fairly obvious. Raising and dealing with the issue when it arises in the attorney/client relationship should only rarely require clinical training and experience. When it does, of course, attorneys should consult with clinicians or refer their clients to them. Such referral discussions should be handled with great sensitivity, as many clients will be offended at the suggestion that they need therapy. It might be helpful for the attorney to recount prior experiences with other clients in which counseling proved helpful in dealing with issues arising in the attorney's representation, such as divorce counseling or counseling for depression accompanying loss of a job. The attorney can then gently suggest the possibility of a referral to a known and trusted psychologist or social worker to help the individual deal with the rehabilitative need identified by the attorney. Although such referrals may occasionally be desirable, other than in unusual circumstances, attorneys can and should attempt to deal with these issues themselves and should develop and improve the skills needed to do so.

There is a growing awareness of the need for lawyers to be sensitive to their clients' emotional needs and the psychological dimensions of the attorney/client interaction. These attorneys develop an expertise in the interpersonal aspects of the attorney/client relationship and a sensitivity to the emotional needs of the client. They are psychologically minded and sensitive to the emotional climate of the professional relationship. They attempt to use their interpersonal skills to enhance the emotional well-being of their clients. They are relational lawyers, affective lawyers, and therapeutic jurisprudence/preventive lawyers.

Empathy is an important skill these lawyers need to develop. The client's willingness to deal with the strong feelings that coming to terms with his criminality may produce requires an environment in which the client feels safe and comfortable. Perhaps the most important way in which the attorney can create such an environment is through the conveyance of empathy. Empathy involves the ability to enter another person's feelings and to see the world through that other person's eyes.

Just as empathy has been recognized to be an important ingredient in the professional relationship of physicians, psychologists, social workers, and nurses with their patients and clients, the psychologically minded therapeutic jurisprudence lawyer understands the centrality of empathy in the attorney/client relationship. Because a central feature of the various techniques used by clinicians in dealing with denial on the part of their clients is empathy, this concept is especially significant to the lawyer confronting client denial and resistance. In addition to seeing the world through another's eyes, empathy involves the ability to perceive the meanings of another person and to communicate that feeling back to the other person. The word *empathy* is derived from the Greek *empatheia*, which implies an act of appreciation of another person's feeling experience. Empathy has both cognitive and affective components. It involves both an intellectual response to the person, conveying the sense that the listener thinks the same way as the speaker, and an emotional response, conveying the sense that the listener feels the way the speaker does. The empathic listener should strive to convey a perception and understanding of the experiences of the other and communicate a quality of felt awareness of his or her experiences.

Psychotherapist Carl Rogers has had a major impact on our thinking about empathy in professional relationships. In his client-centered therapy, Rogers emphasized facilitating the growth and development of human personality toward its maximum potential. Rogers posited that the ability of one individual to help another is dependent on the creation of a relationship fostering warmth, genuineness, sensitivity, and empathy. Empathy involves the capacity to perceive others as having goals, interests, and emotions similar to one's own; to imagine the situation of another; and to respond in ways calculated to ease the other person's pain. It involves exuding a feeling of caring and sincerely trying to understand the other in a nonjudgmental and helping way. To be effective at expressing empathy, attorneys must learn to project themselves into the feelings and situations of their clients, expressing the warmth and understanding that create a comfortable space within which clients can express their own emotions. Empathy involves an openness to suffering that is most pronounced in people who themselves have experienced suffering, particularly in matters of separation and attachment. Although lawyers who have experienced their own suffering may be better able to communicate empathy to their clients, the social science literature suggests that empathy can be taught.

Attorneys need to be able to develop techniques for putting the client at ease so that he or she can feel comfortable in expressing emotion. When the client holds on to strong feelings and does not express them, as will be the case when those feelings are repressed or denied, decision-making is inevitably distorted. Being able to express one's emotions has the salutary effect of freeing the individual to think more clearly. Forging a connection with the client, an emotional bond that can be palpable, and experiencing an emotional and energetic exchange with the client can thus enable clients to touch their own fear and anxiety concerning facing their psychological or substance abuse problems and dealing effectively with them. In this respect, the attorney can be an effective vehicle for the client's opening up, enabling the expression of feelings that can then allow the client to deal more straightforwardly and rationally in facing his or her problems.

A number of approaches by the attorney may be helpful in facilitating the client's willingness to express emotions to the attorney. Lawyers need to learn how to be good listeners. To do so, attorneys need to understand that a lawyer/ client counseling session is a dialogue, not a speech. To have a true dialogue, attorneys need to stop speaking at some point and allow the room to become silent, thereby encouraging the client to speak. Attorneys need to devote time exclusively to the client and eliminate distractions by conducting the counseling session in a quiet room, holding incoming telephone calls, and directing secretaries or other lawyers in the office not to disturb the conversation. Attorneys need to convey to their clients that they genuinely wish to listen to them and that they are eager to hear and understand their problems. In listening to their clients, attorneys need to be attentive, nonjudgmental, and sympathetic. The attorney should validate the feelings expressed by the client, making appropriate verbal and nonverbal responses that express interest, caring, warmth, and sympathy.

Empathy requires the ability to become adept at reading another person's nonverbal communications and interpreting another's underlying feelings. Such feelings, of course, are not always expressed verbally. Indeed, many clients will not be in touch with their own feelings and will have difficulty talking about them. Human communication is a complex process that involves considerably more than verbal utterances. It involves many subconscious messages that are exchanged nonverbally. Nonverbal cues, such as the tone of voice and facial expression and body language of the speaker, are important ingredients in what is communicated. Also important is the context in which the communication is delivered, like the setting and expectation of the listener. Attorneys need to learn how to listen with their "third ear" to such meta-messages. Though some attorneys may be instinctively sensitive to these subtle aspects of communication, many are not. These are skills that can and should be taught in law school and in continuing legal education.

Several specific listening techniques for dealing with denial may be especially helpful. These techniques include the active listening response and the passive listening response. In what is known as passive listening, the lawyer allows periods of silence to punctuate the lawyer/client dialogue, thereby communicating to the client that the lawyer is listening and that the client is free to go ahead at his own speed. The lawyer also responds periodically with brief comments, indicating acknowledgment of the client's statements or feelings. These are noncommittal responses because they do not reveal how the lawyer feels about what the client has said but acknowledge that the attorney is listening. Open-ended questions, another technique of passive listening, encourage the client to tell his or her story in a narrative fashion without specific direction. These passive listening devices—silence, noncommittal acknowledgments, and open-ended questions—function to give the client space in the interview to truly express thoughts and feelings.

Active listening, developed by Carl Rogers, is the process of picking up what the client has stated and sending it back in a reflective statement that mirrors the content of what the client has said. By mirroring what has been said, the lawyer demonstrates that he or she has been listening intently and understands what the client has expressed. Moreover, this technique does not judge what has been said but merely accepts it and therefore constitutes an entirely empathic response. The lawyer's active listening response can be a particularly effective way of getting at the client's feelings, many of which may be withheld or only ambiguously stated. The lawyer's precise reflection of what he understands to be the feeling conveyed helps the client to better understand his own emotional reactions. For example, "Our discussion about substance abuse may make you feel angry ... Did it?" "It may have made you feel anxious." Identifying the client's feelings when they are unstated or only ambiguously stated may be difficult, but an experienced lawyer, skilled at interpersonal relations, will be able to form hypotheses based in part on what is said and in part on the client's visual and auditory (i.e., nonverbal) cues. These techniques can be effective ways of expressing empathy and rapport and providing the client with a comfortable space in which to express his or her emotions.

Another potential problem to effective attorney/client communication occurs when the lawyer and the client are of different cultural, racial, ethnic, social class, or other categories of difference. Lawyers need to be sensitive to such areas of difference and to acquire cross-cultural competence. They need to become aware of their perhaps unexamined and unconscious assumptions that the client shares their world view. They need to identify cultural differences and commonalities. They need to put themselves in the client's shoes, exercising cultural imagination to understand things from the client's perspective. They need to spot signs of communication problems and develop ways of communicating more effectively across cultures. They need to discard any inappropriate assumptions, biases, and stereotypes about the client's group membership. Developing such cross-cultural competence will enable the lawyer to analyze the client's problem more accurately, to counsel him more effectively, to provide empathy, and to create a climate of comfort in which the client can develop needed trust and confidence and open up to the lawyer.

By way of recap, to improve their interpersonal skills lawyers and law students should be made aware of some basic insights of psychology. These include techniques of persuasion, motivation, interviewing, and counseling. They should learn about potential psychological obstacles to applying these approaches, including denial and resistance. An additional psychological concept they need to understand is transference.

Transference, a psychoanalytic concept, occurs when the patient transfers or projects feelings onto the therapist that originated in prior relationships with others, notably parents and siblings. Similarly, in the attorney/client relationship, clients may often transfer onto the attorney feelings relating to prior relationships. These are relational images that we all carry and impose on new relationships. Negative transference occurs when a past experience produced negative emotions that are transferred onto the new relationship. When feelings that arose in the old relationship were positive and are transferred to the new relationship, it is considered positive transference. By being empathic, warm, and caring, the attorney can inspire positive transference, invoking feelings on the part of the client that may have been associated with a trusted grandparent, parent, friend, or teacher. These traits may also be the best defense against negative transference toward the attorney that some clients may have developed as a result of prior unpleasant experiences with other lawyers or negative associations with lawyers, generally stemming from negative portrayals of attorneys in the media and popular entertainment. "I'm not one of those aggressive Rambo litigators that you see on TV or in the movies, or one of those greedy lawyers that is the subject of the lawyer jokes you may have heard," the attorney can assure the client. "I see myself as a member of a helping profession, and I hope that is why you have sought my services."

In conducting the professional dialogue, an attorney must also be aware of the potential dangers of countertransference. Countertransference arises when the therapist (or lawyer) transfers feelings from a prior relationship of his or her own onto the patient (or client). An attorney should be sensitive to the possibility that his or her reaction to the client might be heavily colored by feelings engendered in a prior personal relationship, either positive or negative. Countertransference, occurring when the client reminds the lawyer of someone else and evokes in the lawyer feelings associated with that other person, may inhibit the attorney's ability to express empathy and to develop rapport with the client.

In discussing rehabilitation with their clients, attorneys should communicate a sense of caring, sympathy, genuineness, and understanding. Only then can they hope to create a comfortable space in which clients can feel free to express their emotions and deal effectively with them. Improving their interviewing, listening, communication, and counseling skills, as well as the ability to convey empathy and deal with psychological defense mechanisms arising in the attorney/client relationship are thus essential for successfully having conversations with the client about rehabilitation. To do so requires a degree of psychological sensitivity to the client that is the hallmark of the therapeutic jurisprudence/ preventive lawyer.

3. The Prosecutor's Role in the Rehabilitation of the Victim

This discussion of the psychological techniques that therapeutic jurisprudence/preventive lawyers can use in holding sensitive conversations about rehabilitation with their criminal clients applies as well in other contexts where lawyers can function as healers. For example, although prosecutors regard the general public as their clients, they have multiple interactions with the victim of the crime. In their interactions, they should be aware that they function as therapeutic agents. Their conduct can either diminish or improve the psychological well-being of the victim. Sometimes, their conduct can help the victim to avoid future victimization. In this respect, they too can be seen as therapeutic jurisprudence/preventive lawyers.

A good example is presented by the context of domestic violence. Domestic violence is a growing problem. It is estimated that one million women are the victims of domestic violence each year. Moreover, it is estimated that only one in ten incidents of domestic violence is reported to law enforcement officials. It is further estimated that from 20 to 50% of all female patients seen in hospital emergency rooms are battered women.

How can prosecutors help to turn domestic violence victims into survivors? The prosecutor's interactions with the victim should be animated in important part by a concern for her needs. The victim has been subjected to what often is a regime of violence occurring over an extended period. She has been terrorized, isolated, and made the subject of subordination through force and threat of force. She experiences shame, depression, and a reduced sense of self-esteem and self-efficacy. She often has had to live a secret and a lie, mandating reduced and shallow social interactions. Because her abuser has been an intimate—a spouse, boyfriend or girlfriend, parent or child—the experience has shattered her sense of trust and willingness to have intimate relations in the future.

What does the victim of intimate violence need and want? First and foremost, she needs an end to the reign of terror to which she has been subjected. She needs a sense of security. She needs to get in touch with the strong feelings she has denied, suppressed, or repressed. She needs to understand what has happened and the impact it has had on her and on those around her. She needs sympathy and understanding, not blame. She needs to reframe her experience. She needs to reassert a sense of control over her life. She needs to have the opportunity to tell her story to listeners who will be sympathetic and nonjudgmental. If she will continue her relationship with the perpetrator of the violence, she may need a genuine apology from him and reasonable assurances that the abuse will stop.

In the healing process, most wounds do well with a healthy dose of fresh air and sunlight. At the point at which the victim of intimate violence has brought her case to the attention of the judicial process, her problems have moved from the closet of secrecy to the public spotlight of police and court processes. How can these processes help her to move out of the shadows, to move forward to a new life?

Some victims of domestic or other types of intimate violence develop a form of learned helplessness, a syndrome that limits effective performance in a variety of areas, inhibits motivation, and produces feelings of helplessness, hopelessness, and emotional reactions that mirror clinical depression. Some victims acquire a form of post-traumatic stress disorder. Prosecutors need to understand these conditions and act in ways designed to facilitate their amelioration rather than their exacerbation.

People treated in ways that produce a form of learned helplessness feel a sense of lack of control over important issues in their lives, particularly if they experience this lack of control as a result of personal shortcomings, as reflecting a global rather than a limited deficiency on their part, and as permanent rather than changeable. Prosecutorial procedures and practices should attempt, whenever possible, to empower the victim rather than perpetuate her sense of not being in control. They need to show her that she does not bear responsibility for her victimization. They need to teach her ways of helping to prevent future violence and how to take charge of her life.

Domestic violence victims have been disempowered in ways that often diminish their self-esteem and self-confidence. In his interactions with the victim, the prosecutor can do much to provide healing. The prosecutor's role is not merely to prosecute cases; it is to help people. In interviewing the victim, the prosecutor should be aware of the lessons of the psychology of procedural justice.

Extensive studies in this field show that when litigants are treated in ways that accord them a sense of participation and dignity, and are given the feeling that court actors have good intentions, they respond with higher satisfaction to judicial proceedings and the results of such proceedings, even if unfavorable. Victims need to be accorded a sense of "voice," the ability to tell their side of the story, and "validation," the sense that what they have to say is taken seriously. They should be treated with dignity and respect by prosecutors who convey to them a sense that the proceedings are in their best interests and done with good rather than bad intentions. Treating people in this way also diminishes the extent to which they feel coerced and gives them a sense of voluntary choice even in inherently coercive contexts. People given choice rather than made to feel coerced respond better, with greater satisfaction and with more motivation and effective performance. Indeed, experiencing choice and a sense of self-determination is often vital to an individual's sense of her own locus of control and may be essential to emotional well-being. Prosecutors need to be given training in these techniques.

To the extent that victims suffer from a form of post-traumatic stress disorder, prosecutors should encourage them to "open up" about their experiences and how they feel about them. This could be accomplished by designing intake and other processing forms to enable victims to write out a description of what occurred to them and what feelings they experienced. At a minimum, victims should be encouraged to do this on a voluntary basis and told that such descriptions will be helpful for improving police and judicial proceedings in these cases, for public understanding of these problems, and for helping other victims. Such written descriptions should be shared with other victims and the public on an anonymous basis, and the victim should be assured of privacy in this respect. Psychologist James Pennebaker, in his book *Opening Up*, has shown that people suffering a variety of traumas including war trauma, natural disasters, or being victims of crime or accidental injury gain significant psychological benefits from telling their stories to others, particularly if in writing. Legal proceedings in the domestic violence context should thus encourage such opening up by the victim whenever possible. For example, when police, prosecutors, and court officials interview a victim who seems reluctant to tell her full story and ambivalent about her abuser, getting her to describe how she feels about him may assist her to begin the process of detaching from him or of reflecting critically on the relationship. In addition, even testifying at a deposition or in court about her story may have a healing effect for the victim. When it can be demonstrated that the perpetrator confronting the victim in court or at a deposition will bring a special measure of psychological pain and distress to the victim, alternative approaches such as the use of videotaped testimony should be considered, and under the authority of *Maryland v. Craig*, may not violate the Sixth Amendment confrontation rights of the defendant.

Domestic violence victims often experience denial, rationalization, and minimization concerning their victimization. The victim might suffer from the maladaptive belief that if she doesn't remain in her present relationship, she never again will be in another one. She may also feel that it is better to be in an abusive relationship than in none at all. She also may harbor feelings of guilt that make her place responsibility for the abuse on herself rather than on her abuser. These cognitive distortions may prevent her from taking steps to change her situation. They may distort her judgment in ways that make her ignore signs of danger or fail to take appropriate action to protect herself. The arrest of her batterer can have the tendency to make her challenge these cognitive distortions and replace them with more realistic and rational cognitive models. The arrest of the batterer and the prosecutor's interview with her may cause her to challenge her feelings of helplessness, conveying to her feelings that she is not alone and that she has more resources than she had thought. Although she may be ambivalent about the reasons for arresting the batterer, the prosecutor can help her to understand that arrest can be empowering.

For prosecutors to effectively help victims of domestic violence to survive their ordeals thus requires that their actions always take account of the likely impact on the victim, including the children of the victim, who themselves often are secondary victims of domestic violence. There needs to be special training programs for prosecutors to sensitize them to the needs of domestic violence victims and to teach them techniques for effectively dealing with them. These prosecutors need to learn how to be good listeners, to convey sympathy and empathy, and in general to recognize their role as either therapeutic or anti-therapeutic agents in this context.

4. Other Opportunities for Lawyers as Healers

Virtually every other area of legal practice will present a client in need of healing whom the therapeutic/preventive lawyer can help using the techniques and approaches described above. For example, many clients who come to the law office have suffered trauma and pain related to their legal involvement. They may be feeling guilt and shame over marital failure, and may be anxious about child custody arrangements, property division, alimony, and child support obligations. They are attempting to immigrate to a new country and are anxious about what is permitted and whether they will be able to stay or be deported, sometimes to face persecution. They may have been in an accident and face permanent injuries. In many of these instances, the legal case is often a symptom of an underlying need for healing. Although the lawyer's principal role is to protect and promote the client's legal rights and interests, the therapeutic jurisprudence/preventive lawyer should regard the client holistically and take this healing dimension into account in his interviewing and counseling of the client.

By focusing on the client's physical, emotional, financial, moral and spiritual needs, the lawyer can guide the client to make decisions regarding his legal problem that will provide him with the greatest level of satisfaction. A lawyer who sees this therapeutic role as part of his professional responsibility will recognize that litigation may not be the best course of action.

Rick Halpert, a therapeutic jurisprudence/preventive lawyer specializing in traumatic personal injury cases provides two examples from his practice. One case involved a sexual assault on a disabled girl in a nursing home. The facility was forthright in disclosing the incident, and the family was reluctant to sue. Through empathetic listening, and the help of the family's clergyman, the lawyer was able to understand the family's reluctance to bringing suit and helped them to think through the issues presented. The family's religious beliefs opposed litigation and the family also thought the child was receiving good care at the facility and wished to have her remain there. Other lawyers might have litigated the issue. Halpert, however, realized that the moral arguments over the litigation were threatening to tear the family apart and settled for an apology and the implementation of appropriate precautions to prevent reoccurrence of the incident.

In the second example drawn from Halpert's practice, a policeman was involved in a motor vehicle accident that rendered him paraplegic. In that one moment, his identity changed. After leading a life in which his masculinity and physical assertiveness were important elements in his work, he experienced a significant degree of lowered self-esteem and feared that his wife would leave him. In addition to bringing a lawsuit against the at-fault driver, Halpert counseled his client to obtain appropriate psychological help, which succeeded in avoiding his potential suicide.

Opportunities for healing frequently present themselves in the context of immigration practice. Those seeking asylum in the United States are likely to be experiencing continued trauma as a result of persecution in their homelands. Indeed, they may have developed post-traumatic stress disorder, making it difficult to recollect the details of their persecution. Moreover, a language and cultural barrier between the client and his lawyer typically will exist. Successfully interviewing and counseling such a client presents a difficult challenge to the immigration lawyer. The client's inherent suspiciousness and probable lack of familiarity with the role of the lawyer underscores the central need to establish trust and confidence. Many of the psychological techniques described above can be adapted to this context. In particular, the lawyer needs to be a good listener and provide the client with procedural justice—treating him with dignity and respect and providing him with voice and validation. Rapid-fire questioning should be replaced with an open narrative in which the client has the time to open up and tell his story.

Conclusion

As the examples in this chapter show, the therapeutic jurisprudence/ preventive lawyer should view himself as a healer. Many clients will be in need of healing as a result of the legal incident that brings them to the office, and many will be in need of clinical services and rehabilitation. Rather than ignoring this aspect of the lawyer's function, the therapeutic jurisprudence/ preventive lawyer will see this as an opportunity to serve the client in a multidimensional way. The therapeutic jurisprudence/preventive lawyer practices with an ethic of care and sees his role as a member of a helping profession. He views the client's well-being, and especially his emotional well-being, as almost inevitable aspects of the legal relationship. He is psychologically minded and has developed refined interviewing and counseling techniques and relational skills. Lawyers playing this healing role can significantly increase their client's satisfaction with the professional relationship and achieve a special type of personal gratification. They can come home at the end of the day, and tell their families "I really helped someone today."

References

Amador, Xavier and Anna-Lisa Johanson. *I Am Not Sick, I Don't Need Help! Helping the Seriously Mentally Ill Accept Treatment: A Practical Guide for Families and Therapists.* New York: Vida Press, 2000.

Binder, David, Paul Bergman, and Susan Price. *Lawyers As Counselors: A Client-Centered Approach.* St. Paul: West Pub. Co., 1991.

Birgden, Astrid. "Dealing with the Resistant Criminal Client: A Psychologically-minded Strategy for More Effective Legal Counseling." 38 *Crim. L. Bull.* 225 (2002).

Freud, Sigmund. "*The Ego And The Id.*" Edited and translated by J. Strachey. In Vol. 19 of *The Standard Edition of the Complete Psychological Works of Sigmund Freud,* 3–66. London: Hogarth Press, 1961. (Originally published in 1923).

Freud, Sigmund. *The Problem Of Anxiety.* New York: W. W. Norton, 1936.

Halpert, Richard L. "More Than One Kind of Recovery." 89 *A.B.A. J.* 58–59 (May 2003).

Lind, E. Allan and Tom R. Tyler. *The Social Psychology of Procedural Justice.* New York: Plenum Press, 1988.

Maryland v. Craig, 497 U.S. 836 (1990).

McGuire, James. *What Works? Reducing Reoffending.* New York: Wiley, 1995.

Miller, William R. and Stephen Rollnick. *Motivational Interviewing: Preparing People for Change.* 2d Ed. New York: Guilford Press, 2007.

National Research Council. *The Rehabilitation of Criminal Offenders: Problems and Prospects.* Washington, DC: The National Academies Press, 1979. https://doi.org/10.17226/19848.

Pennebaker, James W. *Opening Up: The Healing Power of Confiding in Others.* New York: W. Morrow, 1990.

Prochaska, James O., Carlo DiClemente and John C. Norcross. "In Search of How People Change: Applications to Addictive Behaviors." *47 Am. Psychol. 1102* (1992). [Ed. The "stages of change" model is sometimes erroneously referred to as having a sixth stage sometimes labeled "termination" or "relapse." While "termination" and "relapse" are important concepts describing how individuals progress or regress through the five stages of change, they do not form an additional stage according to the authors of the stages of change model. See Connors, Gerard J., Carlo C. DiClemente, Mary M. Velasquez, Dennis M. Donovan. *Substance Abuse Treatment and the Stages of Change: Selecting and Planning Interventions.* 2nd Ed, 6–15. New York, Guilford Press, 2013.]

Prochaska, James O. and John C. Norcross. *Systems Of Psychotherapy: A Transtheoretical Analysis.* 3rd Ed. Pacific Grove, Calif.: Brooks/Cole Pub. Co., 1994.

Rogers, Carl R. *Client-Centered Therapy.* Boston: Houghton Mifflin, 1951.

Sandler, Joseph and Anna Freud. *The Analysis of Defense: The Ego and the Mechanisms of Defense Revisited.* New York: International Universities Press, 1985.

Tyler, Tom R. *Why People Obey the Law.* New Haven: Yale University Press, 1990.

Wexler, David B. "Therapeutic Jurisprudence and the Rehabilitative Role of the Criminal Defense Lawyer." 17 *St. Thomas L. Rev.* 743 (2005).

Winick, Bruce J. "Redefining the Role of the Criminal Defense Lawyer at Plea Bargaining and Sentencing: A Therapeutic Jurisprudence/Preventive Law Model." 5 *Psychol. Pub. Pol'y & L.* 1034 (1999). [Ed. Chapter 6 is a reworked and streamlined version of this longer article, with some important additions and updates to the material.]

Winick, Bruce J. "Applying the Law Therapeutically in Domestic Violence Cases." 69 *UMKC Law Review* 33 (1999).

Winick, Bruce J. "Client Denial and Resistance in the Advance Directive Context: Reflections On How Attorneys Can Identify And Deal With A Psycholegal Soft Spot, 4 *Psychol. Pub. Pol'y L.* 901–23 (1998).

United States Sentencing Guidelines § 5C1.1, 18 U.S.C.A. (Imposition of a Term of Imprisonment).

U.S. Sentencing Guidelines Manual § 5C1.1, cmt. n.6 and Amendment 738 (2013).

United States v. Booker, 543 U.S. 220 (2005).

United States v. Flowers, 983 F. Supp. 159 (E.D. N.Y. 1997). [Ed. In cases where sentences are appealed, defense lawyers may now also rely on *post-sentence* rehabilitation evidence in seeking downward departures during resentencing. See *Pepper v. United States,* 131 S. Ct. 1229, (2011).]

18 U.S.C.A. Federal Rules of Criminal Procedure, Rule 32.

18 U.S.C.A. Federal Rules of Criminal Procedure, Rule 35.

Index

In re Fla. Bd. of Bar Exam'r, xxiin4
Inspiration, An (Wilcox), 109n62
Integrative Law Movement, xxi,
xxvn67. *See also* Comprehensive
Law Movement
Interdisciplinary, 19, 20, 23. *See also*
Therapeutic jurisprudence
Interests, legal v. other, 114, 128–129,
148–149. *See also* Best-interests;
Legal issue, underlying; Non-
legal interests
International Academy of Law and
Mental Health, xxiin13
Interpersonal skills. *See* Lawyering
skills
Interruptions, xiii, 32, 35. *See also*
Attorney/client interview;
Lawyering skills
Interviewing, counseling, and inter-
personal skills. *See* under Attor-
ney/client interview; Lawyering
skills.
Involuntary civil commitment, viii,
xxiin6, 128. *See also* Kansas v.
Hendricks

J

Johanson, Anna-Lisa, 133
Judges: procedural justice, 110n65;
sentencing, 117–125 passim, 131;
therapeutic role, xvii, 124. *See
also* Procedural justice;
Sentencing
Judgmental, 41–42, 127, 141. *See also*
Attorney/client interview
Jury trial, rights, 118. *See* Sixth
Amendment, U.S. Constitution
Justice, value of, 11, 13, 19, 36. *See
also* Legal education; Therapeutic
jurisprudence: definition

Juvenile rights, viii, xxiin7, xxiin8,
xxvin71, 19. *See also* Shackling,
youth

K

Kansas v. Hendricks, xxiin6
Kill a Mockingbird, To (Lee), 40
Krieger, Lawrence ("Larry"), S., 5, 12

L

Law and Emotion, scholarship, xxi,
xxvin70
Law and Society Association, 23
Law in a Therapeutic Key (Wexler,
Winick), xxiin9, 19
Law reform, viii, xxi, xxiin10, 19. *See
also* Therapeutic jurisprudence
Law school. *See* Legal education
Lawyer-client relationship. *See* Attor-
ney/client relationship
Lawyer dissatisfaction, x–xi, 3–4, 5.
See also Adversarialism; Depression rates; Emotions: v. rationality; Justice, value of; Lawyer
distress; Legal education; Meaningful; Moral hazard; Professionalism; Professional responsibility;
Socratic method; Substance
abuse
Lawyer distress, x, xviii, 4–16; and
coping mechanisms, x, 6, 7, 15,
136, 137; factors contributing to,
8–13; and personality traits, 13–
15 (*see* Personality). *See also*
Lawyer dissatisfaction
Lawyering models, xx–xxi: business,
xx, xxvn62, 7–8; intersection of,
xx, xxvn64, xxvn65; public interest, xx; zealous advocate,
xxvn61, 9. *See also* TJ/preventive

ing Guidelines; Organizational clients

Overstepping, professional boundaries, xvi, xviii, xxivn37, 138–139. *See also* TJ/preventive model

Overworking, x, 4, 6, 7, 8, 15. *See also* Lawyer dissatisfaction; Lawyer distress

P

Parole, 120. *See also* Rehabilitation

Passive listening. *See* Listening skills

Paternalism, xii, xv–xvi, xvii, xxivn37, 21, 30, 42, 93, 126–128. *See also* Coercion

Peacemaker, lawyer as, xv, 16, 99, 71–111. *See also* TJ/preventive model; Dispute resolution

Pennebaker, James, xxviii, xxivn42, 147

People v. Fitzpatrick, xxin1

Personal injury, 113, 148, 149

Personality traits, lawyer, 13–15. *See also* Lawyer dissatisfaction; Lawyer distress

Persuasion, 34, 67, 126–128; techniques, 129–134; theory, 129, 131–132. *See also* Coercion; Paternalism

Philippe Pinel Award, xxiin13

Physician/patient dialogue. *See* Doctor/patient relationship

Plea-bargaining and sentencing, 38, 106n5, 116–122. *See also* Dispute resolution; Sentencing; Rehabilitation

Political asylum, 113, 149. *See also* Immigration

Post-traumatic stress disorder, xviii, xxivn42, 146, 149. *See also* Opening up; Political asylum; Victims, domestic violence

Power of attorney, 58. *See also* Elder law; Guardianship

Premature probate, 58. *See also* Elder law; Guardianship

Presentence reports, 118, 120. *See also* Plea bargaining and sentencing

"Presumptive arrest," xxvn50. *See also* Mandatory arrest; Prosecutors; Victims, domestic violence

Preventive law, xi, xxvn66, 20, 21; and corporate law, 62–67 (*see also* In-house counsel); definition, 22, 45; educating about, 47; integration with therapeutic jurisprudence, 22, 45; and planning, 45–46; and preventive medicine, 45. *See also* Therapeutic jurisprudence; TJ/preventive model

Prisons, overcrowding, 117; criminogenic, 120. *See also* Incarceration, alternatives to; Diversion

Probation, 118–122 passim. *See also* Plea bargaining and sentencing

Problem-avoider, lawyer as, 16, 24–25, 45–68. *See also* TJ/preventive model; Preventive law

Problem-solver, lawyer as, xv, 21, 23, 67, 81. *See also* TJ/preventive model

Problem-Solving, in legal education, x, 9, 25 (*see also* Legal education); and rehabilitation, 116 (*see* Rehabilitation)

Problem-solving courts, xvii, xxvn66, 20, 116–117, 118. *See also* Domestic violence courts; Drug treatment courts; Mental health courts

Procedural justice, xiii, xvi, xxiiin24, xxivn33, xxivn34, xxvn66, 32–33, 110n64; and compliance, 98, 110n65; dignity and respect, xiii, xvi, 32–33, 94, 98, 128; and dispute resolution, 98–99, 110n64; and domestic violence victims, 146; and lasting settlements, 98, 110n64; validation and voice: xiii, xvi, xviii–xix, 33, 98 (definition), 128, 129. *See also* Compliance; Dispute resolution; Settlement; Victims, domestic violence

Professional ethics. *See* Professional responsibility

Professionalism, x, xix, xxiiin23, xxivn33, xxvn56, xxvn59, 6, 7, 8. *See also* Lawyer dissatisfaction; Lawyer distress

Professional responsibility, xii, xxvn61, 6, 9, 128, 148; moral non-accountability, 9 (*see also* Moral hazard); zealous advocacy, xii, xix, xxiiin21; therapist, 121. *See also* Professionalism; Professional satisfaction

Professional satisfaction, 121, 149–150. *See also* Lawyer dissatisfaction; Lawyer distress; Meaningful; Professionalism

Prosecutors: discretion of, xviii; and domestic violence victims, xviii, xxivnn44–45, 145–148; role of, xvii–xviii, 144–148; training, 148. *See also* Victims, domestic violence

Psychoanalytic, 136, 143. *See also* Defense mechanisms; Freud, Sigmund; Transference

Psycholegal soft spots, definition, 23–24, 26, 41; examples, 50, 51, 55, 68, 113, 125–126, 135. *See also* Attorney/client dialogue

Psychological, harm or damage, xx (*see also* Impact, anti-therapeutic); orientation of lawyers, xvi, 21, 115, 139

Psychology, unlicensed practice of, xvi, 115, 139. *See also* Overstepping, professional boundaries; Psychological: orientation of lawyers

Public interest: drift away from, 14; model of lawyering, xx–xxi, xxvn63. *See also* Values: extrinsic v. intrinsic

Putnam, Samuel, M., 36

Q
Questioning, forms of: open-ended, xiii–xiv, 33, 34, 35, 93, 142, 149; Socratic (*see* Socratic method). *See also* Attorney/client interview; Lawyering skills; Listening skills: active; Motivational interviewing

R
Rambo, litigator, 7, 9, 80, 144. *See also* Lawyer dissatisfaction; Lawyer distress

Rapport, xiii, 36, 40–41, 114, 143, 149; with doctors, 39, 40; trust, xiv, xv, xviii, 8, 36; confidence, xv, 36. *See also* Attorney/client interview; Lawyering skills

Rationality. *See* Emotions: v. rationality

Recidivism, 117. *See also* Drug treatment court